"You are drawn into the story right from the beginning. Lisa's knowledge of the historical and cultural attitudes of 19th-century Germany really add credibility to the story, making this another book you won't be able to put down until the end!"

—Gail Kreek, London, Ontario

"A phenomenal book! It shows the trials of womanhood are not much different today as they were 150 years ago. The author's great-grandmother true life story—abandoned as a baby, forced into a marriage as a teen, raising children alone, surviving two world wars—a must-read for today's generation. I highly recommend it."

—E. Robinson, retired history teacher, Toronto

"The author has captured a difficult period in history, bringing it alive and personalizing it through the story of her great-grandmother, a remarkable human being. Bertha lived and persevered through extreme hardships and heartache. She embodied the strength a woman can find to face insurmountable odds in order to protect her family and survive. I laughed, cried, and often held my breath; it was impossible to put this book down."

—Carol Burton, Tiny, Ontario

"Lisa's writing has such a natural flow and her stories pull the reader in so that the pages just keep turning. The immediacy of her style enables the reader to inhabit the lives of the characters. I kept wondering throughout both *Iron Annie* and *Bertha* what my choices would have been had I lived in the circumstances of those two women."

—Sherri Bennewies, Library Technician

"*Bertha* is a fascinating historical romance that I couldn't put down. Lisa's descriptive writing moves the reader to lose oneself in the emotions and circumstances of the characters. I feel like I lived through the ghastly treatment of women in the early 1900s and survived triumphantly. Wonderful book!"

—Diane Lyoness, author of *The 13th Configuration*

"*Bertha*—An awe-inspiring chronicle of family ancestry. Through war, peace, and turbulent times, how families gathered strength through Faith, Hope and Love. But the greatest of these is Love."

—Marj A., School Administrator

"Lisa, you have done it again! Even though I have known you all my life, I never truly realized the struggles your family has had in their lives. First the incredible account of your parents lives in *Iron Annie and a Long Journey* and now the inspiring life story of your great-grandmother Bertha. And what a life that was! Beautifully told, a book to get lost in. I highly recommend it."

—M. G. B., Counsellor

"*Bertha*, a treat for lovers of historical romance. A tale of love told from the perspective of a German family who lived through gut-wrenching trials and tribulations that will keep you captivated. A mesmerizing, eye-opening story of pre- and post-war-torn Germany, with the power of family, love, and endurance shining through."

—Cheryl Hunt, Corporate Lead Volunteer Services, Huron Perth Healthcare Alliance

BERTHA

BERTHA

Shine like the Dawn

Lisa M. Hutchison

ISBN: 978-1-4866-1803-3

Word Alive Press
119 De Baets Street Winnipeg, MB R2J 3R9
www.wordalivepress.ca

WORD ALIVE
—PRESS—

Cataloguing in Publication information may be obtained through Library and Archives Canada.

PREFACE

My beloved spoke and said to me, "Arise, my darling, my beautiful one, come with me. See! The winter is past; the rains are over and gone. Flowers appear on the earth; the season of singing has come, the cooing of doves is heard in our land. The fig tree forms its early fruit; the blossoming vines spread their fragrance. Arise, come, my darling; my beautiful one, come with me." (Song of Songs 2:10–13, NIV)

BOOK ONE
EMILIA

Chapter One: 1863

Hamburg's coastline was slowly disappearing in the damp November fog as the S.S. Germania picked up speed on its way to New York. A forlorn figure stood at the railing staring across the slightly roiling sea, hoping to catch a final glimpse of Germany's coast. She was the last person still standing on the upper deck while most people had already busied themselves settling in for the three-weeks-long sea voyage.

Clad in a dark coat and pulling a woollen scarf around her while hunching her shoulders against the damp cold, she wiped a tear from her cold face. She felt the ship picking up speed and the planks under her feet quivered. Sailors shouted commands to each other, equipment was moved about, and the icy cold wind made her shrink even more into the big coat. Instinctively, she put her arms around her belly, swollen with child.

"Whatever possessed me to leave home and my two little girls?" she asked herself.

Just then, a man appeared and put his arms around her. "There you are. I have been looking all over for you. Come inside, it is far too cold out here."

She turned to him, a tiny smile on her face. "Yes, Wilhelm, is it?"

"Please, call me William, my real name," he gently interrupted.

"Yes, of course, Wilhelm—I mean William. Sorry, I keep forgetting."

He nodded with a slight frown. "While we are talking names, from now on, you are Emily, not Emilia."

"But I like my name just the way it is!" she protested.

"We are going to America, my home, and you will have an American name," William insisted. "Our child will be American, not German, and it, too, will have an American name," he stated firmly while steering her by the arm towards the door.

Emilia, now Emily, broke out in tears. *"Am I to lose everything to this man?"* she wondered fearfully. *"First my daughters, and now my own name?"*

She cried even harder. William sighed loudly. "Come, my darling, you are understandably emotional; a little rest and a hot cup of tea will do you good." And with that, he pulled her inside the warm lounge area of the ship.

With some reluctance, she allowed herself to be led to a chair. The lounge felt hot and thick with the smell of unwashed bodies; it was noisy with children screaming, women scolding them with loud voices and men rushing back and forth collecting baggage and trunks to stow away.

Emilia felt her stomach lurching and was afraid she might embarrass herself by throwing up. "You look pretty pale, young lady," one of the women nudged her. "Maybe you want the slop bucket?"

"No, no, I don't think so," Emilia quickly replied. "It's the baby—it is moving and making me uncomfortable."

The woman nodded. "My name is Maria Stumpf; my four children and I are joining my husband in America." She offered Emilia a handshake.

"Very nice to make your acquaintance; my name is Emilia Holtzmann" she responded without thought, then suddenly shook her head. "What's wrong with me? It is not Holtzmann anymore, but Hunt—actually, Emily Hunt. My husband, William, an American from Boston, and I just got married. I'm having a difficult time adjusting to my new name," she smiled nervously at Maria.

She just laughed. "No problem, my dear—you will get used to it. And that new baby of yours will be an American right away, no?"

Emilia nodded. "That's why William wanted us to go before it was born. He said it was easier that way, although I'm not so sure how I will make out the next three weeks. I am quite frightened."

"Oh, it won't be so bad," Maria tried to assure her. "It would be a lot worse if you were housed in steerage—a hundred people or more crammed into one big room with no fresh air and bad sanitary conditions. "I'm glad my husband paid for a cabin for the children and me."

Emilia shuddered at the thought of being stuffed like sardines into one of the many bunkbeds, and was grateful for William purchasing better accommodations for them.

Just then, William appeared, balancing a steaming mug of tea along with a plate of sandwiches on a tray. "Here you are, darling, this will make you feel better." He placed the tray on her lap. "I will now collect our luggage and stow it in our cabin. I'll be back in a little while to get you." And with that, he left.

"A caring husband, that one," Maria smiled wistfully, while eying the sandwiches hungrily.

Emilia nodded. "Yes, he's a good man," she agreed while sipping on the hot tea. "Would you like some sandwiches?" she offered Maria. "I don't feel hungry at all."

Greedily, Maria stuffed the sandwiches in her mouth. "I should really save some for the kids," she mumbled with her mouth stuffed, "but I am so hungry I could eat a horse!" She grinned and with that she rose to find her children among the throng of people. "We will see you around!" she called out as Emilia let herself lean back in the chair, trying to anticipate what lay ahead and what brought her to this point.

"*I don't have a good feeling about this,*" she thought. "*I should not have Wilhelm—er, William—talk me into this. I should have had the baby back home and then made the crossing.*"

But then, what was back home for her?

CHAPTER TWO: 1853

"EMILIA, EMILIA, WHERE IN GOD'S NAME ARE YOU HIDING AGAIN?" Emilia heard her mother, Anna Sehnke, calling from the back of the house. "Come in immediately! I told you to be ready by three o'clock."

Meanwhile, Emilia was crouched in a corner of the horse stable, admiring the tiny newborn kittens. "Oh Molly, you have beautiful children," she crooned, gently stroking the mother cat's fur. "Five new babies and one prettier than the next! Can I hold them?" The cat looked at her through sleepy eyes and made no move to keep Emilia from picking up the tiny balls of fur. She held them next to her face and breathed in the new kitten smell. "So sweet," she murmured, as she picked up one after the other.

She heard her mother calling once more. This time, she sent for Emilia's brother. "Ludwig, please find your sister and tell her to get home at once. She knows we are hosting the Holtzmanns for coffee and I expect her to be presentable when they arrive."

Ludwig just nodded and scampered off; he knew where his sister was hiding. "You heard Mama," he told Emilia. "You better get in before she gets really angry!"

Reluctantly, Emilia put the kittens back and stretched out her lean body. "She just wants to marry me off to Ferdinand Holtzmann," she griped while strolling alongside her older brother. "I'm only seventeen; I don't want to get married yet!" Ludwig just shrugged; he was nineteen and had just entered the officer's academy in Berlin. Marriage was a long way off for him yet.

By three o'clock, the family gathered in the sitting room with their guests, the Holtzmanns. Under her mother's stern gaze, Emilia refrained from stuffing a second piece of torte into her mouth and tried to stifle a yawn. She looked at her mother, still very slim, despite having had five children; her father, quite handsome in his suit; her brothers Ludwig, then fifteen-year-old August, twelve-year-old Werner, and the "baby," six-year-old Ludmilla.

She thought the Holtzmanns looked a little uncomfortable and secretly glanced at Ferdinand, their eldest son of two. He was tall, with dark hair and eyes and a moustache; she guessed him to be about twenty-five. Frau Holtzmann was rather short and somewhat plump and had a harsh look about her. She appeared to rule the roost. Emilia thought of her as a prospective mother-in-law and pulled an inner face. Rumours were that she had inherited the well flourishing factory and even though her husband ran it, the final decisions were up to her. There was a younger son, Waldemar, who, just like Ludwig, began his military career in Berlin.

While the men discussed business, Emilia and Ferdinand exchanged shy glances. Both did not know each other well and were unsure what to make of this obvious marital plot of their parents. Emilia's parents owned a medium-sized estate, mainly raising horses along with some farming. The Holtzmanns owned a good-sized factory producing handcrafted Christmas decorations—mostly wooden nutcrackers and carved advent pyramids. They were looking to expand into the very lucrative American market.

"We are searching for glassblowers now," Herr Holtzmann mentioned. "It seems the Americans are crazy for glass ornaments for their Christmas trees."

Ferdinand nodded vigorously. "I will be running that part!" he motioned more to Emilia than anyone else.

"It looks like you are well on your way to becoming rich!" Emilia's father teased, and some eager conversation followed.

The younger children became bored and were quickly excused. Ludwig and Waldemar took off to look at horses, leaving Emilia and Ferdinand a bit awkward and somewhat at a loss for words with each other.

"Why don't you two take a walk?" Emilia's mother suggested.

Emilia brightened up. "Yes, come along, I'll show you our new kittens!" She excitedly jumped up, pulling Ferdinand with her.

"Phew, I'm glad to be out of that house!" she exclaimed once they were outside. Ferdinand had to agree with her. Slowly, they made their way to see the kittens and Emilia was touched at how gentle Ferdinand was with them. *That's a good sign,"* she thought.

Later in the day, Emilia's mother casually asked how she had liked Ferdinand.

"Oh, Mama, I only just met him for a short time. Why are you asking anyway?"

"It is time for us to look for a suitable husband for you; soon you will turn eighteen and it would be prudent to introduce you along with your fiancé at your coming-of-age ball."

"And you want me to marry Ferdinand?" Emilia stared at her mother incredulously. "I did not think you seriously wanted to get rid of me so soon!"

"It is not a matter of getting rid of you," her mother spoke sternly. "And I forbid you to speak to me in this disrespectful manner!"

Emilia shook her head, and mumbled, "Sorry, Mama."

"The Holtzmanns are a wealthy family!" Emilia's mother continued. "You will be well taken care of, we cannot afford a large dowry for you, the boys' education will take a lot of money, and then there is still Ludmilla to think of!"

"So, you want me to be the family sacrificial lamb?!" Emilia retorted. "I don't want to marry at all—and you can't make me!" She stomped her feet.

Her mother stared in disbelief at her defiant daughter. "Your behaviour is totally out of line!" she scolded her. "Now go to your room—no supper for you today, and you can join us again once you've apologised. Now go!"

A very sullen Emilia stomped off to her room and angrily threw herself on her bed, punching her pillow furiously. *"Maybe I should just marry Ferdinand and get out of this house!"* she thought angrily.

She lay back and stared at the ceiling, trying to imagine married life. *"Maybe it won't be so bad. Ferdinand is a good-looking man, financially well-off; we could afford all kinds of help in a home of our own. Of course, there would be the physical part…"*

Emilia decided not to think about that and focus on the more fun things. A big wedding, the envy of her friends being the first one to get married, travelling with her handsome husband—suddenly, all of that started to appeal to her, and she decided to apologise to her mother and agree to have Ferdinand court her.

CHAPTER THREE: 1863

"EMILY, EMILY DARLING, WAKE UP!" EMILIA WAS SUDDENLY JOSTLED AWAKE BY William's light touch on her shoulder. She was still holding the now-cold tea cup in her hands.

"Oh my, I must have fallen asleep," she mumbled, a little confused.

William, grinning slightly, offered her his arm. "Come, I will show you our cabin; it's not very big, but it will do for the voyage. At least we are on our own; after that, it's suppertime."

Somewhat clumsily, Emilia rose from her chair and leaned heavily on William's arm. The ship was rolling from side to side and she had a hard time staying upright. Slowly they made their way to the cabin. It was indeed small, but it had at least a washbasin. Two bunkbeds, a small closet, and a chair completed the furnishings. Next to the basin was a slop bucket with a lid. Emilia wrinkled her nose when she saw that. She hoped they would not need it, but rather use the public lavatory down the hall. Their trunks and suitcases were stacked in another corner, leaving very little space to even turn around.

"You can sleep in the bottom bunk," William offered. "It is easier for me to climb the ladder."

"Can I lie down a while, William?"

"Not now, my dearest; it is almost time for dinner, and we need to get out of our travel attire and put on some fresh clothes."

Emilia felt sick to her stomach. The constant vibration, the noise all around her, the smell of fumes, and the rocking of the ship made her dizzy. "I don't think I can eat anything, William" she moaned.

William firmly shook his head. "You will feel much better once you have eaten," he declared. "It is fairly common to feel somewhat nauseated the first day or two, but you will soon get used to it. And in the company of others, you will not think about it; now come along and get ready, we don't want to be late!"

Swallowing the acrid taste in her mouth, Emilia changed and, once again clinging to her husband's arm, made her way to the dining area. The smell of greasy food hit her so hard she doubled over and ran outside to join others leaning over the railing, vomiting.

Quickly William was by her side. "Oh, my darling!" He held on to her while the ship pitched back and forth. Emilia retched until she thought she would pass out.

"My stomach hurts," she whimpered faintly.

"Come, we will go back to the cabin and you can lie down," William said softly. "You need to think of the baby." Once again, they slid along the narrow hallway, and then William helped her to bed. "Try to sleep. I will go and get something to eat. I'll bring you back some tea to settle your stomach."

Emilia immediately fell into a deep sleep. She dreamt of dry land and warm sunshine.

Suddenly jolted awake, she sat up, hitting her head on the upper bunk. Listening to the sounds around her, the creaks and groans of the ship, the gentle snoring of her husband on the upper bunk, feeling the never-ending vibrations and swaying, she felt panic rising in her throat. She also felt an urgent need to empty her bladder.

She slipped out of her bunk and with a feeling of disgust, pulled the slop bucket close to her, hoping William would not wake and see her in this most shameful position. It was stuffy and hot in the cabin and she could feel her stomach revolting once again.

"I need to get out and get some fresh air," she thought frantically, fumbling with the door latch. Trying to match her steps with the swaying of the ship, she finally made her way to the upper deck. Cold air and ocean spray almost took her breath away. Several people had gathered on the deck and either sat on blankets or stood leaning on railings trying to pass their first night at sea. She watched a couple embracing behind a pillar; some men were playing cards, and a woman was nursing her little one while another slept next to her.

A little farther away, she heard the bittersweet sounds of a violin. Nobody paid any attention to her as she made her way to a pile of coiled-up ropes to sit down. Shivering, she pulled her coat close around her and stared across the water. The sea looked relatively calm and a bright moon shimmered across the barely moving waves. The movement of the ship created ripples and frothy foam sprayed into the air. Emilia reflected on her surroundings and the forces of nature and once again mused about her life and the events that brought her to a ship on its way to America.

Chapter Four: 1854

On Emilia's eighteenth birthday, Ferdinand requested her hand in marriage. He looked so sombre and serious in his dark suit and a bouquet of flowers in his hand that Emilia broke out in nervous giggles.

"Yes, of course I will marry you!" she finally answered, and he gave her a quick kiss on the cheek.

Their engagement was celebrated with close family members only, and the wedding date was set September 23, 1854. And what a big wedding it was! Relatives from near and far arrived daily a few days prior to the big day. It took all of Emilia's family, as well as the Holtzmann family, to accommodate so many people.

The church was packed on a hot, sunny day when the radiant young bride and her handsome groom made their way to the altar. It was to be the absolute highlight in Emilia's life.

After the official ceremony was over, the less formal part of the day began. Several pigs were roasting on spits, servants ran back and forth with plates full of food, and drinks flowed freely.

Ferdinand and Emilia opened the dance on an outdoor platform built a few days prior.

"Are you happy my love?" Ferdinand whispered in her ear as they held each other closely while gently swaying to the music.

"Extremely so!" she replied with a smile, as she nestled closer into his arms.

The festivities went on for most of the night, but at some time, the young couple managed to slip away to begin their post-wedding trip. They had decided to visit Berlin and some family there who had been unable to attend the wedding. Their wedding night was spent dazed and half-asleep on the train.

Once they arrived at their hotel, and before unpacking, Ferdinand stretched out on the bed, fully dressed, and fell asleep in seconds. Emilia, nervously chewing on her thumb, looked around and wondered what to do next. The room was bright, the sun shining with full force, beckoning her to leave the hotel and explore Berlin. Slowly and quietly Emilia unpacked their luggage, hanging up clothes, stowing shoes and hats, and finally pulling out a lacy *negligée*.

Holding the lacy piece of tulle up and looking at her still-sleeping young husband, she suddenly had the overwhelming desire to run out into the sunshine.

"If this is marriage, it's very boring already!" She sat on the edge of the bed and wondered when *that part* of marriage would happen, the part her mother vaguely called the "duties of a wife." With three brothers, she was naturally familiar with the anatomy of a boy, as well as the pairing of the animals on her parents' estate but was still unsure when or how this "duty" was to happen.

Eventually, Ferdinand woke, apologising profusely to his young wife and rushing around to make amends. They had a lovely dinner, walked around the city, sat in a park, took a boat ride on the Spree, and generally enjoyed themselves.

Finally, it was time to return to their room and they shyly regarded each other. "I'll go downstairs while you get ready for bed," Ferdinand offered.

Grateful, Emilia undressed, carefully hung up her clothes, washed up, put on the lacy *negligée*, and hid under the bed covers. After a while, Ferdinand entered the room, smelling faintly of cognac, and quickly made his way to the bathroom to change. He re-emerged in striped pyjamas, buttoned up to the chin, and slid in bed next to her.

Both lay very still for some time when Ferdinand finally turned to her and whispered in her ear, "Did your mother tell you what happens between married couples?"

"Not really," Emilia whispered back shyly. "She talked about the duties of a wife, but that's about all."

Ferdinand broke out laughing and with that, they both laughed, and all awkwardness faded away. "I will show you how to enjoy the duties of a wife," Ferdinand smirked, while nibbling on her ear and still chuckling. Emilia soon responded to his kisses and caresses. He was a gentle and thoughtful lover and she started to look forward to these "duties."

Before their first anniversary, their firstborn child, Ella, was conceived. She was born on Easter morning in 1856 and two years later, their second daughter, little Bertha, was welcomed into the family.

At Bertha's baptism, her father-in-law made it a point to tell Emilia, "I hope the next one will be a boy; the factory needs an heir."

Emilia tried to laugh it off but felt hurt by that comment. "But you have Waldemar as the next in line," she pointed out, "and we love our girls dearly."

"Yes, yes, of course we all love the little girls," Herr Holtzmann tried to brush off his own comments, "but Waldemar is not suitable for the factory, having just married some floozy from Berlin!" he scoffed.

Ferdinand overheard that last comment "Annette is no floozy, father—she is a very nice girl and Waldemar is very fond of her."

Grumbling, Herr Holtzmann walked off.

Still absorbed in her memories of the early years of her marriage, Emilia attempted to shift into a more bearable position on the ship.

"I wonder what he thinks of Annette now," Emilia thought to herself while trying to keep some sort of balance on the uncomfortable coiled-up ropes. *"At least they produced the long-awaited heir!"* Suddenly, she could hardly keep herself from crying at the memories that now engulfed her.

Little Bertha had just been three months old when Ferdinand complained of a severe headache; a few hours later, he developed a high fever along with convulsions. The family quickly summoned the doctor, who diagnosed him with encephalitis, a potentially deadly illness. He told the family to prepare for the worst and in the meantime, to keep him comfortable and try to bring down the fever. Most of all, he advised to keep the children away from him. Emilia sat by his bedside night and day, wetting his dry lips, putting cold compresses on his head, but nothing worked.

Within a week, Ferdinand had passed away and Emilia was left a widow and single parent at just twenty-two.

Dry sobs now shook Emilia's body as she recalled the horrible events that followed the next months and few years. The long and draining funeral when she was too stunned to shed any tears. Two-year-old Ella constantly asking for her father and Emilia no longer being able to nurse Bertha since her milk had dried up almost overnight. One of the servants who just had a baby was feeding Bertha instead.

"Oh, how I miss my girls!" Emilia now sobbed out loud. A few close-by passengers looked over with curiosity, but thankfully left her alone.

Emilia continued in her thoughts of what had happened. Ferdinand had left no will; in reality, he owned nothing, as his parents were still alive and never considered an early death for their son. Emilia, Ella, and Bertha were now dependent on the mercy and goodwill of the Holtzmanns. Of course, she could have returned to her parents, but saw no advantage in that. Her parents had offered, but also let it be known that there was little room and even fewer extras for her and the children. So, Emilia's mother had encouraged her to stay with her in-laws since she and the girls were now Holtzmanns. They stayed, and over time, she developed a real knack for decorating glass ornaments destined for the American Christmas market.

Waldemar had been ordered back home to take over the glass blowing factory. Legal counsel was sought out and all assets transferred to Waldemar. His present son, Simon, and all subsequent sons, were co-heirs. Annette, any future daughters they might have, as well as Emilia and her two daughters, were given lifelong residence rights, along with a small annual bequest.

Emilia, never quite feeling at home with the family, spent many hours in the factory workshop, creating, painting, and designing shapes, colours, and seasonal scenes for the glass bulbs. Begrudgingly, her father-in-law began to praise her work and commend her obvious talents.

One day, Herr Holtzmann arrived in the shop with another man. Tall, quite blond, approximately thirty years old, very fashionably dressed, and speaking a heavily accented German, he was introduced as Mr. Wilhelm Hunt from America.

"Emilia, this is Mr. Hunt from Boston," her father-in-law introduced. "He is a buyer for a large American department store, and he would like to see your work. He has been here previously for large shipments of nutcrackers but now is very interested in our Christmas tree ornaments."

Emilia showed him the large collection carefully wrapped in wood shavings; one by one he looked them over, letting out an appreciative whistle every so often.

"You painted all these?" he asked Emilia incredulously. "They are beautiful— no, magnificent is more like it! We will take as many as you can possibly get done in the next few months."

Emilia was surprised and pleased by his enthusiasm.

Eventually, crate after crate filled with glass ornaments, nutcrackers, and angel pyramids were shipped to America. And Wilhelm Hunt stayed behind; as a matter of fact, he was still there a year later.

In the meantime, Wilhelm and Emilia had started to get to know each other better and Emilia sensed that he was developing romantic feelings for her. She was unsure how to react. She liked his company, his attention—something she really craved. She was still young and half-expected to remarry one day—but not an American! She would never leave her home.

One beautiful late spring evening, Wilhelm invited Emilia out for dinner at a little out-of-the-way restaurant. They sat on the patio, enjoying the warm breeze. The scent of lilacs in bloom and the heady smell of the many Linden trees in the nearby park filled the air. Sipping on some wine, they quickly fell into lighthearted conversation.

For the first time in years, Emilia felt like a woman again—not just a mother or a worker—and she went along with and even embraced Wilhelm's flirtatious banter. The night was soft as velvet, with a bright yellow moon rising over the treetops; it was a perfect night for lovers.

But when the romantic summer was over, Emilia had to tell Wilhelm that she was expecting a child.

He was overjoyed; Emilia not so. "What am I going to tell the Holtzmanns?" she panicked. "They will kick me out with the shame of it all, with me widowed only two years and now pregnant with another man's child. I am ruined!" she wailed.

Wilhelm quietly and patiently listened to her for some time. Finally, he spoke. "What is the problem my dear? We will get married and you will come with me to America; I can book passage for the late fall."

Emilia was surprised at his sudden solution. "But what about my girls, Wilhelm, what will happen to them?"

Wilhelm thought for a moment. "Hmm, yes, of course, your girls," he paused. "Honestly, I have not thought about them much, since they are hardly ever with us. But we can have them come a little later, once the two of us are established. What do you think of that?" he peered at Emilia expectantly.

Emilia protested. "No, they must come with us!"

He nodded, as he had expected that response, but deep down he did not want them along; however, of course he could not say that to her.

Soon that decision was taken out of his hands. Once Emilia told her in-laws about her pregnancy and Wilhelm's willingness to marry her, they were more than happy to let her go.

"You are *worse* than a floozy!" her mother-in-law spat out, angrily. "Sleeping with a foreigner? I never want to see you again! Our poor Ferdinand; he will turn in his grave because of what has become of his wife!"

"I am not a wife anymore; I am a widow!" Emilia shouted back. "I am twenty-three years old and I still deserve a life!"

"Yes, of course, do what you like," Herr Holtzmann interjected, "but don't expect to take your little girls; they stay here since we are their official guardians."

Emilia's mouth dropped. "You are *what*?"

A rather smug Herr Holtzmann explained. "We had our legal counsel draw up the necessary papers in case something were to happen to you; indeed, something did happen to you!" With that, he leaned back in his chair, puffing on a cigar.

"Nothing happened to me; I am still alive," Emilia could barely muster a weak whisper.

"Nobody would give the children to you to take them to an unknown future in an unknown country," Herr Holtzmann snapped at her. "You are an unfit mother who's pregnant by a foreign lover, so be grateful that your children have a home!"

Confiding in her parents did not fare any better. Her mother, Anna, was almost harsher than her father.

"Do you have any idea what shame you have brought on us, your brothers, and your sister?" Frau Sehnke exclaimed, outraged. "What honourable family will even consider marriage to any one of them?

"You best marry that scoundrel and leave the country with your bastard child before anybody even guesses the reasons of your marriage!" she continued angrily.

"Mama, can you not at least take little Ella and Bertha until we send for them?" Emilia sobbed, pleading.

"You know the Holtzmanns are their legal guardians, Emilia," her father interjected. "We can only hope to see them once in a while. You truly created an awful mess, my dear daughter."

Herr Sehnke shook his head sadly. "I can only hope and pray that you will become happy with this American. We will have to see what the future holds. I don't expect we will see each other again—America is so far away."

With that, he gave his eldest daughter a quick hug and slowly left the room.

Emilia was stunned. *"Is my family really abandoning me like this?"* she wondered anxiously.

"Mama, can *you* at least forgive me?" Emilia whimpered with tears rolling down her cheeks.

"Perhaps in time," her mother answered coldly and dispassionately. "For now, please leave!" Anna stormed out of the room, leaving a forlorn and wailing Emilia behind.

CHAPTER FIVE: 1863

DEEP DOWN, EMILIA ANTICIPATED HER DILEMMA; HER FATE AS AN UNWED MOTHER of a foreigner's child would be hell. Either way, she would be condemned, and she was better off with Wilhelm, so she relented in the hope that the situation would change in the future. First, she needed to get married.

Wilhelm (William) Hunt and Emilia (Emily) Holtzmann were married, October 12, 1863, and shipped out to America on November 2.

This is what led up to Emily now sitting outside on a hard roll of coiled-up rope on a constantly swaying ship on its way to America. She reflected on her situation. *"I must make the most of this, and be a good wife to William and a good mother to the new little one,"* she resolved to herself as she got up and quietly returned to the cabin.

The next few days went by in an endless rhythm of daily chores and nothing but a vast ocean and sky to look at. William and Emily worked at learning about and discovering each other and spent hours talking about their future lives together. William was praising life in America while Emily was missing her little girls.

Soon the attention turned to the expected child, with William hoping for a boy and Emily disinterested.

"I think we will call him Richard William," he suggested.

"Why not?" Emily shrugged. "Richard is good in German, as well."

As to a girl's name, they were undecided. No matter what, Emily just wished to have solid ground under her feet again. She felt a growing sense of unease at the little pangs of pain in her belly as well as some spotting in her underwear. "Hang on there, little one," she whispered. "Soon we will be in America and you can be born then."

Seven days at sea and a storm struck with unexpected fury. Suddenly, the sky had turned pitch black, the seas bucked up like a young horse, bucking, pitching, rolling, black, and cold.

The officers and crew rushed around ordering all passengers back inside and latching all doors shut. Frightened passengers huddled together as the storm seemed to increase in intensity. The ship pitched forward, raised up and slammed back down onto the water. People began to cry and wail. Some became violently seasick, others prayed loudly.

William held on to his wife as she, too, started vomiting. The stench became unbearable. "Let's go back to the cabin," William suggested, pulling Emily to her feet and half-carrying her back to the cabin.

The storm lasted two full days before finally letting up and the lower decks could be cleaned, and fresh air allowed back in. For two days, Emily vomited and retched almost nonstop and when the waters finally calmed, she went into labour. Screaming and writhing in agony, Emily squirmed around the narrow cot, reeling from the pain and felt the blood running between her legs. Her high-pitched screeches could be heard along the hallway and to the upper deck.

William had rushed to find the ship doctor and between the two of them, they laid Emily on the floor of the cabin. The doctor examined her as best he could. "I don't think I can save the babe!" he exclaimed. "We have to stop the bleeding, though—fast!"

William watched in shock as Emily drifted into a deep faint, and for a moment, he was grateful her painful screams had quieted.

Taking advantage of Emily's loss of consciousness, the doctor gently pulled the baby out, a gush of blood following. He shook his head, holding the tiny, lifeless bundle of bloody humanity in his hands, "It's a boy," he choked back his emotions. "I'm so sorry, but your wife will not survive this either." With that, he laid the bundle on Emily's stomach and left the cabin. William stared in disbelief at his dying wife and his tiny dead son. Slowly, he knelt down and stroked her pale, cold face as she took a last stuttering breath.

Dry sobs wracked William's body, as he rocked back and forth in grief.

Some women among the passengers came and cleaned up the baby and Emily. The ship's carpenter nailed a rough, wooden coffin together. The bottom half was filled with sand to make it heavier, holes were drilled into the side to increase the flow of water, again to make it easier for the coffin to sink.

Gently Emily was laid on top of the sand. The captain baptised the baby "Germain" as it was customary to name a stillborn child after the ship—the

Germania—on which it had passed. He laid the baby, wrapped in a blanket, in Emily's arm and covered them both with a rough blanket.

The coffin was nailed shut and after a short reading from the Bible and a prayer, several sailors grabbed the casket, and with a loud "Heave-ho!" they tossed it over the railing into the sea.

William, as well as most passengers standing on deck, watched the wooden box bobbing up and down, twisting and swirling and moving slowly away from the ship. Gradually, it took on water and then, it was gone.

BOOK TWO
YOUNG BERTHA

CHAPTER ONE: 1865

"Opi, Opi!" seven-year-old Ella came running through the door. "I have something for you!" and with that she waved a letter in her hand.

Heinrich Holtzmann looked up from his paper, watching his eldest grandchild sliding on the highly polished wooden floor. "Easy now, young lady, don't run like that," he admonished her good naturedly.

"But Opi, it's a letter with a strange-looking stamp; I have never seen a stamp like that."

"Well, bring it here, and we'll see where it is from." Herr Holtzmann was rather curious himself. When he saw the return address as William Hunt, Boston, America, he was a little thrown off guard. It was the first time any communication had come from his ex-daughter-in-law, Emilia—Ella and Bertha's mother—and her second husband, William. He was hesitant to open it.

"Who is it from?" asked Ella, always the curious one, pestered her grandfather. "Hmm, just somebody from America who used to order our Christmas decorations," replied. *No use getting the child all riled up about her mother,* he thought. "Now run along and let me read what the letter says."

With a pout Ella slowly made her way to the door.

"Oh wait," Heinrich stopped her quickly. "Here, you can have the stamp to keep."

"Oh, thank you, Opi!" A now-smiling Ella trotted out to show her younger sister the stamp.

In the meantime, Herr Holtzmann unfolded the one sheet of thin paper and was shocked at what he read:

Dear Herr and Frau Holtzmann,

I am sorry it took so long to write to you, and I am also very sorry to tell you that Emilia and our son Richard died two weeks into our voyage to America.

Emilia suffered greatly giving birth to a dead baby boy. We had decided to call him Richard William; however, the captain of the ship baptised and documented him as Germain Hunt. Both were buried at sea. I know this must come as a great shock to you and I would be obliged if you were to tell Emilia's parents as I do not have their address.

You do not need to concern yourself with me; I have remarried, and my wife is expecting a child. I wish you all the best and I apologise once more to be the bearer of bad news.

Sincerely,
William Hunt

"Grete!" Heinrich shouted for his wife. "Can you please come here immediately?" The gout in his left foot made it hard for him to walk.

Grete came as fast as she could. "What is it?"

"Look at this letter!"

"Yes, yes, I saw the envelope."

"Emilia and her baby are dead—have been for two years already!" Heinrich could hardly say it, he was so stunned.

"Two years?" Grete quickly grabbed a chair and sat down. "Let me read the letter." For a while, they both just sat in silence.

"It took him long enough to tell us, and already married again, what a cad!" Grete finally spoke, grumbling. "Do we tell the girls?"

Heinrich shook his head slowly. "What for? They don't even know their mother, especially Bertha; it would make no difference to them. But please tell Waldemar to bring this letter to the Sehnkes, she is their daughter and they need to know."

Thankfully, he had written the letter in German.

Grete nodded. "I'll tell him to take all the children along; he can take Simon and little Hans-Heinrich, as well, it will be a nice outing for all of them."

The following day, the horse-drawn carriage was filled with giggling and laughing little children for the two-hour ride to the Sehnkes' small estate.

Predictably, Emilia's parents were deeply saddened by the news of their daughter's untimely death. "Two years ago, already!" Anna was stunned. "I was wondering why we have never heard from her."

"I always thought she might come back to get the girls," Hermann Sehnke added as they all looked out the window where three of the little ones were playing tag while the baby was sleeping on a blanket under an apple tree, resplendent with pink and white blossoms. For a while, the three adults sat quietly, deeply preoccupied within their individual thoughts. "Now Ella and Bertha are orphans," Hermann murmured.

"I guess we will never find out any more particulars," Waldemar added. "There is no return address on the envelope, and we have had nobody coming from America to the factory the past couple of years—just written orders."

With a deep sigh, Anna rose to pour some coffee for the men and take some lemonade to the children, hot and excited from playing.

"Oma," Bertha shyly tugged at Anna's apron. "Can I stay with you and Opa for a little while?"

"And why would that be?" asked a slightly perplexed Anna.

"Ella is in school all day and Simon and Hans-Heinrich are too small to play with!"

Anna looked at her granddaughter. *"She looks so much like Emilia, with her thick dark hair and rosy cheeks,"* she thought as a wave of grief came over her. She had to turn away, so the child would not see her tears.

Finally getting a grip on herself, she answered Bertha. "You can come for a lengthy visit another time, dear; there is nobody to play with here either. Ludmilla is also in school and the boys are far too old to play with little girls. As well, you have no change of clothing with you and we must let your grandparents Holtzmann know. I will write a note for your Uncle Waldemar to take along and we can arrange something soon."

She suddenly bent down and hugged the little girl tightly to her, surprising Bertha with this rare gesture of affection.

Anna turned to go inside, picking the mewling baby up as she left. "Time for a change in diapers," she murmured into his little ear. *"I really need to spend more time with our granddaughters,"* she thought. *"They grow up so fast and they only have grandparents now."*

Waldemar and Hermann were deep in discussion—tensions between Prussia and Austria were mounting and the prospects of yet another war loomed over them.

"Can they never get along?" Hermann grumbled. "They just signed the Treaty of Vienna a few months ago; I have two sons in the army with the third one ready to join."

Waldemar, looking at his two sons, was concerned for himself. "I have a factory to run, a family to support, Annette is expecting again, she has an ailing father; I really can't be called up again." He rose with a deep breath. "Children, come along now, time to go home!" And he bid his farewell to the Sehnkes.

Waving goodbye, the children piled into the wagon once again and off they went.

Chapter Two: 1865

A LISTLESS ELLA CAME HOME FROM SCHOOL. "OPI, MY THROAT HURTS," SHE complained.

"Come and sit on my lap," Heinrich took a closer look at Ella and felt her forehead. *"She is burning up with a fever!"* he thought. "I'll call Omi, and she can put some cold clothes on your face." He tried to soothe the quietly sobbing child. Grete put the child to bed, sponging the small hot body with cool water to which she had added some vinegar.

"I don't like the looks of this," she remarked later to her husband. "I think I will send for the doctor."

Just then, Waldemar's wife Annette came running downstairs carrying a sick Simon in her arms. "He has trouble breathing!" she cried. Quickly Grete assessed the situation. "We'll put Simon together with Ella; they are both ill and we will wait for the doctor. In the meantime, keep Hans-Heinrich away from them while I keep Bertha in the kitchen."

"Diphtheria," the doctor later diagnosed both children.

"I was afraid of that," Grete whispered fearfully.

"It's spreading like wildfire through the community," the doctor added. He looked pale, tired, with deep dark circles under his eyes. "I don't have to tell you that this is a very serious disease, often with dire outcomes. I will send a nurse for the children; please keep the other children as far away as possible."

Ella and Simon struggled for breath, burning up with high fevers, and after seven long days, both children succumbed to the illness. Nobody else in the house had become ill. Annette and Waldemar had kept far away from their son, lest they infect Hans-Heinrich and the yet-unborn baby. Both were inconsolable at the death of their firstborn.

Five-year-old Bertha had snuck into Ella's bed each night when the nurse took a break, trying to cheer her ill sister up. On Ella's last night she had fallen asleep with her arms around her and was awakened by the shrill screams of the nurse.

"Child, have all senses left you?!" she cried. "Is it not enough with two children sick already? For sure you will get ill as well now," and with that, she ran off to alert Grete.

To everyone's surprise, Bertha did not come down with diphtheria. A later explanation revealed that her wet nurse had diphtheria as a child and most likely passed her antibodies on through her milk.

So now little Bertha had lost both her parents and her older sister; she was all alone at age five.

Many children in the area had lost their young lives in that year and many small graves were dug in the little cemetery. Bertha watched the two small caskets being lowered into the ground as the adults around her were crying. She did not understand why Ella and Simon had to be put into a box into this deep hole when they had trouble breathing anyway.

"Maybe there is a room down there that makes them better," she wondered, biting on her lower lip in thought. But when the men shovelled soil on top of the boxes, she began to protest. "Stop that! They won't be able to get out again!" She tried to take the shovel away from her uncle, who helplessly looked at her, not knowing what to say.

Quickly her grandmother, Anna, picked her up. "*Liebling*, Ella and Simon have gone to heaven, they are not down there anymore."

Bertha paused and stopped crying. "Gone to heaven?" she snivelled. "When did that happen? I never saw that, and why did they go there?"

Anna hugged her closer, "I will tell you sometime later, *ja*? It is hard to understand."

Bertha nodded solemnly. *"If it's hard to understand for Oma, well, it must be very hard for me."*

Slowly the cemetery emptied, and Bertha returned to her Holtzmann grandparents. It had become a very quiet house. Sometimes, eleven-year-old Ludmilla came for a few days during school vacation to play with her. Little Hans-Heinrich began walking on sturdy little legs. And soon enough, a new little one was born. Annette and Waldemar welcomed another little boy, baptised Erwin.

Opa Holtzmann (Opi) hobbled around with his cane and spent time with young Bertha, reading stories and helping her with her writing on her slate tablet once she started school.

Bertha was in third grade when her grandfather, Hermann Sehnke died. It was a blistering hot midsummer's day when Hermann was laid to rest. The church was filled to the rafters with sweating mourners dressed in their Sunday's clothes. Bertha's dress was hot and scratchy.

Never having had much of a connection with her Sehnke grandparents, she watched with interest the many flies buzzing around the sanctuary. Letting out a big yawn earned her a cuff from her grandmother, Grete Holtzmann. "Shh, a little more respect please," she hissed, pulling her ear for good measure. Bertha bit her lip and wished she was one of the flies. Once again, she watched a coffin disappear in the ground and was told, "Opa is in heaven"—she began to doubt this story.

"How do they get up to heaven?" she whispered to her cousins. "I never see anybody up there; do they sit on a cloud? What do they eat? Can they come down again?" August and Ludmilla barely shrugged and didn't bother to answer, too caught up in the grief of the death of their father.

Ludwig, Emilia's brother, turned to the minister. "This one will be hard on you in confirmation classes," he gave a little chuckle. The minister glanced at Bertha before turning back to Ludwig, looking smart in his uniform.

"We'll take care of it when the time comes," he said, giving Bertha a stern look. "But please, I only want to know!" Bertha begged before being pulled away by an enraged grandmother Holtzmann.

"You do *not* talk back to the pastor; you are a rude and naughty child, headstrong just like your mother was!" With that, she yanked Bertha away as quickly as she could.

This incident at the funeral became a turning point in Bertha's young life and her relationship with her Holtzmann grandparents. Secretly, she imagined her mother and how she would have liked to be with her. She resented these constant critical comparisons with a mother who was not even known to her.

Being an inquisitive child, she began to ask a lot of questions about her parents, so much so that she was told to stop this. She still did not stop, received very few answers, and was punished many times for her continued insistence.

Chapter Three: 1872

"It's time you earn your keep!" Grete Holtzmann announced one day when Bertha was about twelve years old.

"What do you mean, Oma?" Bertha looked at her grandmother's pinched face.

"You do realise we did not *need* to take you in once your mother abandoned you and your sister!" Frau Holtzmann snapped.

Bertha flinched at that comment. "But—you are my grandparents!"

Grete glared at her insolent granddaughter. "Oh, no, my dear, we could have put you into an orphanage; dreadful places they are!" she continued in a snarky tone. "Nevertheless, it is time you make yourself useful. Next week, you will start in the factory, apprenticing under Annette; she is expecting another child and will soon have to take a leave."

"What about school?" Bertha exclaimed.

"School is finished for you at Easter!" And with that, Grete turned and walked out of the room.

Bertha retreated to her favourite hiding place behind the woodshed, shivering slightly in the cool spring breeze. *"I don't even know what Annette does,"* she thought, a bit worried. Leaving school was not too upsetting to her; girls never spent too much time in school, as they were expected to marry, bear children, and keep house. Not much schooling was needed for that. Bertha would be able to complete sixth grade by Easter.

Later that day, Annette, looking worn out from yet another pregnancy, managed a smile when she heard her niece would start working with her. "We can sure use your nimble little fingers," she said. "The nutcrackers, angels, and glass ornaments have to be painted and decorated, cotton wool beards cut and glued on the nutcrackers' faces, a lot of finicky things. I hope you have the patience for that!" she warned Bertha, who shifted restlessly on her chair.

"I will try very hard, Tante Annette," she whispered in response.

At that, the conversation shifted to the state of the factory, the orders, and the shipments.

"A large order was lost at sea," Waldemar brought up. "That is the second time this year, and our agent in America is not happy with that."

"Well, neither are we!" Herr Holtzmann growled angrily. "Now we have to work twice as hard to send off another shipment at a great loss."

"It's been taken care of Papa," Waldemar replied while moving the food around his plate, not interested in eating. "We are splitting the costs and hope the shipping company will reimburse us." Then he stood up abruptly. "I have more work to do, so please excuse me."

"That boy has become so moody lately," Frau Holtzmann remarked after he left.

"That 'boy' is a husband and father!" Annette reminded her mother-in-law as she also rose to leave.

A disapproving Grete turned to her husband. "What is going on with those two?"

But before answering, Herr Holtzmann quickly turned to Bertha, who had been listening with interest. "You are excused, as well—and close the door on the way out," he sternly instructed.

Outside the room, Bertha closed the door just enough to leave a small crack open as she crouched behind a large floor vase to listen in on the rest of their conversation.

"Waldemar's heart is not in the factory," she heard her grandfather say. "It is such a shame that Ferdinand had to die so young; he loved all that here. Who will carry on our life's work?"

Before Bertha heard any answer, she was quickly discovered and shooed away by her uncle. "Bertha," Uncle Waldemar quietly scolded, "one does not listen secretly. You should know that. Now go and help Annette in the kitchen with the dishes." Waldemar shook his head as he walked away.

A few days after Easter, Bertha was finished with school and started working in the factory. Her job was pulling large cotton battens apart and form various sized beards and moustaches for the nutcrackers. Once these wooden dolls had been painted and decorated, the cotton beards were carefully glued in place, having been shaped to fit the different-sized nutcrackers, neither too full nor too skimpy.

Bertha struggled with her small fingers, sticky with glue, to position them just right. It was frustratingly slow work and by each day's end, she was literally covered with glue and tiny pieces of cotton. "You look like a half-plucked chicken," Annette would giggle. Oma Holtzmann was becoming frustrated at all the extra laundry.

Bertha improved over time, and when Annette gave birth to her first little girl, Klara, she was left all by herself and worked many nights to fill the orders. It was mind-numbing, dull work and she wondered if she would have to do this for the rest of her life.

By the time she was confirmed at church two years later, she had cut, shaped, and glued thousands of little beards on to thousands of little nutcrackers.

CHAPTER FOUR: 1876

BERTHA HAD BLOSSOMED INTO A PRETTY YOUNG WOMAN OF SIXTEEN WITH LARGE gray eyes and dark, slightly curly, thick hair. She presented with poise and self-confidence, far more advanced than her peers. Kind and quick-witted, she was well-liked and respected by the workers in the factory.

With Bertha's grandfather, Herr Holtzmann, ailing, Annette fully engaged in childcare and housework, and Waldemar becoming more and more sullen, the workers turned to Bertha for any problems. She was just beginning to enjoy her position and envisioned a rewarding and fulfilled life, when disaster struck.

"Fire! Fire! Fire!" a high-pitched voice pierced through the house one night in July.

A dazed and half-asleep Holtzmann family jumped out of their beds and ran outside as fast as they could to see flames shooting from the factory building.

"Oh, dear Father in heaven!" Annette started sobbing.

Waldemar ran inside to get the children out of the house and collect as many buckets as he could find. In the distance, they heard the tinny wail of the fire brigade, as well the urgent tolling of the church bells to indicate an emergency, rousing the whole village into action.

Quickly a bucket brigade was formed, and water filled buckets were handed down along one side and empty ones up the other. Hour after hour the buckets were passed on, weary people with blistered hands continued the task of containing the fire, fuelled by paints, glue, lacquers, wood, and cotton. It was a hopeless task.

By morning, the extent of the still-smouldering fire was shockingly visible. The factory was burnt completely to the ground and it was a miracle that the family home was still mostly intact.

Stunned townspeople stood and stared at the charred ruins, many of them now without jobs.

Waldemar was tending to his father, who had collapsed in front of the house. Grete sat on a chair, rocking back and forth in stunned anguish, and Annette herded her wailing and crying children back into the house. The smell of smoke was everywhere, making breathing difficult.

Bertha walked up and down the line of people, shaking their hands and thanking them for their service, as they slowly made their way to their homes. "All employees please come to the house tomorrow and pick up your wages," she told them with a sad, hoarse voice, earning her an angry look from Waldemar.

"And what makes you say that?" he croaked. "We have just lost everything, and you want us to spend *more* money?"

Standing tall, Bertha answered him with confidence. "Uncle Waldemar, these people already earned their money; payday would have been in two days, and they have no further income," she stated. "We have not lost everything; we can start again. The employees will get paid what is coming to them tomorrow."

Waldemar stared at his niece, wondering when she had taken charge at this young age, but finally relenting, he gave a slight nod before turning his attention back to his father. The old man, now sitting in his wheelchair, whispered to his son, "You better watch out, son," he warned seriously. "She is strong! With the resilience of her father and the charm of her mother, she will go places— you are too weak, Waldemar. I don't think you can build the factory up again." Completely exhausted, Herr Holtzmann sunk back into his chair.

Waldemar slowly walked away from his father, still stung by the harsh words, but deep down knowing full well that Heinrich was right. He had no interest in the nutcracker and Christmas ornaments factory. *"Maybe this is a sign for me to take my family, return to Leipzig, and go back to work as an electrical engineer,"* he pondered.

With a heavy sigh, he returned to the house to check on Annette and the children. By evening, everybody was coughing and wheezing from the overpowering smoke. Herr Holtzmann had to be rushed to hospital, where he succumbed to pneumonia several days later. Another funeral had to be arranged, and Grete Holtzmann was next to useless in her grief over the loss of her husband and the factory.

She suffered another blow when her son told her of his impending move to Leipzig and his disinterest in the factory. Bertha, still at just sixteen years, remained the stalwart in the house, making whatever arrangements needed to be made, inspected the ruins of the factory, salvaged a few items, and finally sat down with her grandmother to decide what to do next and where to start.

"Sit down, Bertha," Frau Holtzmann pointed to a chair in the sitting room. Bertha removed the sheet from the chair—still covered to protect it from the soot and smoke—and sat cautiously on the edge. "What are your plans now, child?" Frau Holtzmann asked her pointedly.

Bertha gave her a confused look. "My plans, Oma?" she asked. "I will help Waldemar with rebuilding the factory, and try to fill as many outstanding orders as possible."

"Waldemar is not rebuilding," Frau Holtzmann told her. "He is moving his family to Leipzig."

Bertha stared at her grandmother, stunned. "Leaving? The factory?"

Frau Holtzmann nodded while dabbing her eyes with a lacy handkerchief. "Yes. He really never wanted to be here, and now he can return to his former job."

Bertha fell back into her chair in stunned silence while her grandmother continued. "I can't run the factory—no, hear me out!" she held up her hand when Bertha tried to interrupt. "I can't run the factory, much less rebuild it. Waldemar will try to find a buyer for the property, and I will move to Berlin to my sister. I really never wanted to be here in this one-horse town anyway." She stopped to catch her breath before carrying on. "I think it will be best for you to move in with your maternal grandmother or find a man and get married."

"Get married?" Bertha was too bewildered to take it all in. "Oma, I'm only sixteen!" she managed to blurt out.

"You are seventeen in two months; plenty of girls get married at that age. I did." Frau Holtzmann replied.

"But Oma, I don't even know anybody to marry."

"We'll just have to find a young man. I will ask Waldemar if any of his friends are looking for a wife."

Bertha stared at her grandmother, open-mouthed. "No, I will not marry just to be taken care of!" she shook her head vigorously.

Grete shrugged. "Then do it your way. I will leave for Berlin in two weeks and Waldemar shortly after he gets things wrapped up here."

The conversation was over, and Bertha left the room in total turmoil.

She walked over to her uncle's part of the house to talk to him. Annette was busy sorting out things to pack and put chalk marks on furniture for the movers to take. Bertha took the crying baby from the crib and rocked her back and forth, while asking Annette if she perhaps could go with them to Leipzig.

"I don't think so," Annette responded slowly and a bit sadly. "I don't know how big the place is where we will move to, and what would you do there?"

"I could learn a trade, like dressmaking, or working in a factory."

"Do you have any idea what those factories are even like?" Annette asked her niece. "Here, you were the respected granddaughter of the owner. There, you are just one of the expendable women. Jobs are hard to get these days, and one could never live on the few pennies you make. We are fortunate—Waldemar can return to his former position and will make a decent life for us."

Annette stopped and took a long look at her niece. "You are a very nice-looking girl," she observed. "You should find yourself a husband. I will check with Waldemar."

"You, too?" Bertha bitterly responded. "Oma had the same solution! You all want to be rid of me and think I should find some man from somewhere, just for a roof over my head? Well, I will *not* do that!" She put the baby back and rushed out of the room, slamming the door behind her.

Back in her room, Bertha broke out in tears. *"What am I to do? I have no income, there's no inheritance for me. I will have to go begging to my Oma Sehnke."*

And begging she went. Frau Anna Sehnke was less than pleased to have another mouth to feed, already struggling to make ends meet with the ever-growing family living on the estate.

"Well, child, we will have to make the best of this and find a way for you to be useful," she offered.

Emilia's brother Ludwig, who was married and had three children, was living in Berlin. Werner was still single and made the Army his career. August ran the estate; he was married to Olga and they already had five children with another one on the way. Ludmilla, the youngest, had recently married and lived in Munich with her husband.

Anna Sehnke thoughtfully took in her granddaughter, who looked so much like the daughter she lost at sea, and wondered what to do with her. "I suppose Olga can use some extra help with all the children," she mused. "But you really should learn a trade, so you can support yourself, or, of course, get married."

Bertha shook her head. "Oma Anna, I know of no man to marry, I am too young to marry, but I will help as much as I can around the house and try to find an apprenticeship position somewhere."

Anna gave her granddaughter a quick hug. "Well, make yourself comfortable, then. You will have to share a room with two of Olga's girls, though—the rooms behind the kitchen are taken by some of the estate workers.

"August wants to build a separate house for them, but has not had time yet," she continued. "He has big plans to buy the estate next to ours, and then hire an estate manager. The work is just too much for one man."

"I could help with the books!" Bertha offered, a bit excited. "I did some of those things at the factory."

"Indeed. That most certainly could be something you can do. I will speak to August about that." Anna Sehnke was glad there would be something for Bertha to do.

Bertha was shown to her room, where a bed, along with a privacy screen, had been quickly put up. The two little girls, ages five and seven, were delightful and quite enjoyed the new addition in their room.

Chapter Five: 1877

Bertha's seventeenth birthday came and went with hardly a notice by anybody. The household was humming with activities, and Olga gave birth to another little boy; they now had six children under eight years. Olga was constantly exhausted, and August became more and more ill-tempered.

More than once, Olga left the dinner table in tears while Frau Sehnke threw disapproving looks at her son. It fell more and more to Bertha to tend to the children and, at the same time, to help August with the books. At night, she fell, exhausted, into her bed, not knowing how much longer she could keep this up.

A concerned Anna pulled her son aside one day. "It is time you hire a nursemaid for your brood," she admonished him. "You cannot expect to make one child after another and have your wife, your niece, and your mother take care of them all."

August shrugged his shoulders and grinned. "Can't help it, Mother. Olga is very, 'fruitful,' shall we say."

"You can leave her alone for a while," Anna suggested. "As a matter of fact, I think you should send her and the children to Olga's parents for a few weeks. Give all of us a break, and in the meantime, find a suitable nanny."

"Great idea, Mother—I'll get on it right away," August sounded sarcastic in his retort, but Anna decided to let it go.

"He is not a very loving boy, that son of mine," she sadly mused to herself. *"I really feel for his wife."* She tried to reason with him some more. "Son, six children are quite enough. Olga's health is already suffering; can you not control yourself a little more?"

August glared at his mother. "That is really none of your business, Mother!" he replied with a cold voice. "Olga is my wife, and I have the right to sleep with her as much and as often as I desire! Another child or two is of no consequence!" By now he was shouting at his stunned mother. He turned and left the room, slamming the door on his way out.

Bertha, having heard the loud voices, quickly entered the room, and saw her grandmother visibly upset. "Oma Anna, what is it?"

"Your uncle and I had an argument, just one of the many lately," Anna replied.

Bertha nodded knowingly. "I'll make you a cup of tea, and you can take it outside in the garden, Oma," she said quietly.

"Thank you, child," Anna smiled slightly. "Make one for yourself and we can sit and talk a little."

Half an hour later, the two women took a well-deserved break, sipping tea and enjoying the garden.

"It really is lovely out here," Bertha remarked, looking around the garden, now in full summer bloom.

Anna inclined her head in acknowledgement, still deep in thought about her son. "I suggested that August hire a nursemaid for the children," she turned to Bertha. "It is getting far too much for her and for you. I also suggested that he send Olga and the children on a vacation to Olga's parents. They have a place near the Baltic Sea, and it will give all of us a break."

Bertha let out a sigh of relief. "Oh Oma, that is a great idea! Thank you; I could really use a little time to myself."

"As a matter of fact, I think I may pay my sister in Berlin a visit," Anna continued. "I have not seen her since Hermann's death. I would have suggested that you go along with Olga and the children, but I truly think you need a break yourself."

With that, she rose, collecting the tea cups and slowly making her way back to the house.

Bertha lingered for a few moments in happy anticipation of some quiet times.

A few days later, August packed up his family and they all left by train towards the Baltic Sea while Anna Sehnke took another train to Berlin. Bertha spent the rest of the day in a hammock in the garden reading a book. It was a most precious time in her life.

A week later, August returned on his own. They exchanged pleasantries during dinner, August talking about his children, the times spent on the beach, the train ride, as well as wondering when his mother would be back. Bertha did not know; Anna was to send them a telegram when she needed to be fetched from the railway station.

The servant girl cleared the supper dishes, curtsied, and left the room. August leaned back in his chair, lit a cigar, poured himself a brandy, and closely examined his niece.

"You turned into a beautiful young woman," he declared. "It is time I pay some attention to my pretty niece," he added.

Bertha, acutely uncomfortable now, rose to leave. "I am very tired, Uncle August, please excuse me."

August quickly rose as well and then blocked the door. "Why do you want to leave already? Just when I want to get to know you better, my pretty niece."

Both, now standing, looked at each other, not sure of the next move. "Please Uncle August," Bertha suddenly pleaded. "Let me pass; I would like to go to bed."

"A very good idea," August roared. "I will escort you," and he stepped aside.

Bertha almost ran out of the room, up the stairs, and along the hallway. By the time she reached the bedroom, August was right behind her, breathing heavily. He pulled her into his arms. "Let me get to know you a little better, my dear Bertha," he whispered into her ear, wreaking of brandy. He pushed her through the door, slammed it closed with his foot, and started to kiss her face.

Bertha tried to wrestle away from him, kicking him, hitting him, biting his ear. These actions only seemed to make August more excited. "Oh, a little wildcat!" he murmured with pleasure. "I know just how to tame you!"

"Please, please, Uncle, let me go—you are hurting me!" Bertha whimpered.

"Oh, but my dearest, I will be very gentle with you," August assured her, while groaning with anticipated pleasure. With a sudden move, he had Bertha on the bed, pulling at her clothes while working the buttons on his trousers open. By now, he was moaning so loud Bertha was sure he was in dire pain.

"Maybe he is dying," she thought, almost with hope, while he fell on top of her.

Then she felt him fumbling between her legs and she wanted to die herself of shame. She felt a sharp pain when he pushed himself into her and she let out a cry.

"Oh, my lovely!" he panted. "You are so innocent, so sweet; I want to love you all night!" With a sudden loud cry, he slumped over.

Bertha felt something wet and sticky running down her legs, but as she tried to get up, August pinned her down again. "Not so fast," he told her. "This was just the beginning. Now the real loving starts."

He kissed her and began to caress her, nibbling on her budding breasts, stroking her hips, lingering along her thighs. "Oh, how I've wanted you for so long already," he kept groaning. Bertha was shivering and crying, pleading for him to stop, but it was useless. August kept her most of the night, forcing himself on her three more times before finally rolling over and falling into a deep sleep.

Finally, Bertha untangled herself from him, and crept soundlessly to the bathroom, where she vomited into the toilet several times. She drew a bath and soaked her sore and battered body in hot water. She must have dozed off because the water had gotten cold and she heard noises in the hallway. A door slammed and loud steps receded down the stairs; she hoped August had left.

She did not go down for breakfast but opted instead to spend the day in bed. Jamming a chair under the door handle and pulling a chest of drawers in front of the chair, she pulled the soiled sheets off the bed and finally collapsed on the bed, giving way to her tears.

The next couple of days passed with August and Bertha avoiding each other. Bertha temporarily moved into her grandmother's bedroom, the only room with a secure lock on it. She slept fitfully, jolted awake by the slightest noise. One night, she thought she heard footsteps passing by, and she wished more than anything for her grandmother to return.

The week was almost over when August accosted her in the breakfast room. Leaning against the doorframe, holding a cigarette in one hand, he leered at her. "How is my beautiful niece this bright morning?" he smirked. "How about spending a little more time together before everybody returns from vacation?"

Bertha stared at him in disbelief. "Do not ever come near me again, *Uncle*," she hissed, "or I will be forced to tell your wife as well as your mother."

Only a little flicker in his eyes let on that he was taken aback by that. "You will do no such thing, my dear. Do you really think they will believe you? And even if they did, you would have to leave—no room for the two of us under one roof," August mocked. "You seduced me, remember? Just like your mother, a little slut!"

It took all of Bertha's self-control not to slam her fist into his face as she speechlessly gaped at him. *"He is probably right,"* she thought disgustedly. *"He is the son, the father of six children, the heir of the estate. I will have to keep quiet and leave once I am eighteen."*

CHAPTER SIX:
THREE WEEKS LATER

WITH A CONTENTED SIGH, ANNA SEHNKE OPENED THE FRONT DOOR. "JUST LEAVE the suitcase in the hall," she directed the coachman as she stepped into the house. Looking around, she was surprised that nobody was there to greet her.

With a slight unease, she made her way up the stairway to her room to change out of her travel clothes. *"What a wonderful time I had with my sister,"* she thought with a smile as she took off her jacket and shoes. *"I should consider moving to Berlin. Elfriede offered for me to stay with her in her big empty apartment; there is just so much more to do there—concerts, operas, and the wonderful coffeehouses—not at all like here in the country,"* Anna reflected.

Deep in thought, she nearly ran into her granddaughter in the hallway. Bertha gave her a startled look. "Oma Anna, you are home already!" she let out a little cry.

"Yes, my dear, did you not get the cable I sent?"

Bertha shook her head. "I guess Uncle August forgot to tell me. But here, let me take your arm and we'll have some tea together and you can tell me all about Berlin and Aunt Elfriede." Trying to sound lighthearted, Bertha led the way downstairs.

Ringing for the maid, Anna asked where August was. "Oh Ma'am, he left early this morning to pick up his family from the Baltic Sea."

Bewildered, Anna looked from one to the other. "Did you know that, Bertha? I understood that they will be away for another week and then his in-laws were escorting the family back home."

The maid quickly excused herself while Bertha stirred her tea, trying not to look at her grandmother. "I am not sure either, Oma, he suddenly left yesterday," Bertha stammered in a low voice.

Peering closely at her granddaughter, Anna demanded, "What happened while I was away? Something is not right—you have been stirring this tea for at least twenty minutes, staring into space. So, let's have it, out with it!"

For a long time, Bertha was silent before answering, "We had an argument, Uncle August and I, and I don't really know how to deal with it. Please let me think about this for a while and work this out, I beg of you. Now excuse me, I have a terrible headache!" With that, Bertha left a very confused Anna behind.

When the maid returned to clear off the dishes, Anna stopped her. "Louise, what has been going on during my absence?" she inquired in a stern voice. The maid, trying to sidestep the question, replied with a murmured, "Nothing really, Ma'am." It was clear she wanted to make a quick getaway.

"Nothing?" Anna thundered. "*Nothing?*" She repeated with emphasis. "I don't believe you! Now tell me the truth."

Louise squirmed, chewing on her lower lip. "Well, the young master, he, um…" she stammered.

"Yes, and what has my son done now?"

"Well, Ma'am, the young master, he—he, well, he took a, a *liking*, to Miss Bertha," Louise finally whispered, her face turning flaming red.

Anna stared at her incredulously. "He what?"

"I saw him," Louise stammered. "He had been drinking and pulled Miss Bertha down the hallway into a room, Ma'am, and Miss Bertha was hitting him and crying and…and since then…well, since then—" at this her voice trailed off, and she averted Frau Sehnke's gaze.

Finally, Anna nodded. "Thank you, Louise, you may go now," she waved a very relieved maid out of the room.

"What in heaven's name has this boy done now?!" she drummed her fingers on the table. *"August always has been a troublemaker, a women chaser, but his own niece? That goes beyond anything I ever thought he was capable of. I must keep a cool head."*

"I hope nothing more serious happened," she continued in her thoughts. *"I will most certainly have to confront him immediately. In the meantime, I will wait if Bertha will say anything."*

With a deep sigh, Anna stood up; she suddenly felt cold and pulled her scarf a little tighter around herself. Now more than ever she felt the desire to move to Berlin, and leave August, Olga, and their children behind. But what to do with her granddaughter? So young, so vulnerable, and yet so strong—poor child. Anna acutely felt the absence of her husband now; he would have known what to do with that son of theirs.

"I must wait until he gets back home," she kept repeating to herself, before going upstairs to lie down.

CHAPTER SEVEN: ONE WEEK LATER

WITH EXCITED CONFUSION, AUGUST, OLGA, AND THE CHILDREN RETURNED FROM their Baltic Sea vacation. The little ones ran around their grandmother and tried to outdo each other with stories, hugs, and small presents in their grubby little hands.

"All right, already!" Anna laughingly tried to hug each one and admire the colourful seashells and necklaces. "Look, Oma, I have a piece of amber with a bug in it!" six-year-old Gretel boasted while her older brother was busy recounting a story of a big fish he had caught. Anna listened to all of them with tender interest, all the while trying to catch her son's eye. But August hurriedly ushered his family on to their own home, barely greeting his mother in passing.

"I would like a word with you, August," Anna stepped in front of her son sternly.

"I don't have time," August grumbled. "I have to help Olga get the children settled in."

"It's no problem, Gusti," Olga offered. "I have the nanny to help; you just stay and talk to your mom."

August groaned and then stared defiantly at his mother. "Well, what is it, Mother?" he snapped. "Trouble with the staff again?"

Anna came right to the point. "What happened between you and Bertha?"

August shrugged his shoulders. "Why, did she complain?" he leered.

"I see!" Anna exclaimed. "So, something *did* happen! I want to know what, and the truth—if you please!" Anna stared icily at her son, the son who was always so different from her other children, the son who had a cruel streak in him but could sweet talk any girl he wanted.

Again, August just shrugged before replying indifferently, "Well, Bertha is a pretty girl, and I thought it was time to make a woman out of her. Was there anything else, Mother?"

"How could he admit such a thing so callously?" Anna felt an unholy rage rise up inside her when she reached up and slapped his face with both hands. She hit him hard across the cheek and his head snapped from one side to another before he stepped away from her, his hand to one cheek, speechless.

"You are most despicable!" she roared. "Get out of my sight, NOW!" Her voice was cutting as she continued, "Do not come near Bertha ever again, and you are no longer welcome in this house!" With that, she turned and left a stunned August staring after her before he stormed out of the house, slamming the door behind him.

Anna sank into her chair, trembling all over before ringing for Louise to make her a cup of tea. Carefully sipping the hot brew, she began to consider options for Bertha and herself.

It was plain to see that Bertha needed to get away from August. As for herself, she had already toyed with the idea of moving in with her sister, and now the time had come to act on that.

"Perhaps there's room for Bertha in Berlin; maybe she can find some appropriate work," she thought with a bit of hope before her head lolled to her side and she fell into a restless sleep.

An uneasy quiet settled over the household the next few weeks. Bertha kept quietly to herself as much as possible; August avoided any contact with his mother and his niece. Only the children and an obviously oblivious Olga came and went.

One day, Anna sat at her desk, writing an answer to her sister, when Louise knocked on the door, entering with a hesitant curtsy.

"Ma'am, I…" she hesitated. "I—I really need to speak with you." She paused again. "It's…it's important," she stammered.

With a silent sigh, Anna put her pen aside. "What is it, Louise?"

"Well, Ma'am, it's…er…it's about, well, it's about—" she couldn't quite seem to get the words out.

"Yes, yes, please carry on," an impatient Anna waved her hand.

With a deep breath, Louise quickly replied before her brief courage gave out. "It's about Miss Bertha, Ma'am. I think… I think she is in the family way," she whispered, scuffing her feet and looking at the floor.

Anna stared speechlessly at her maid. *"Can it be?"* she questioned silently, feeling sick to her stomach. Mustering her poise, she dismissed a relieved Louise with quick thanks. "I'll take care of things from here."

"But how? What will we do?" she wondered.

A rather taciturn Bertha pushed her food around her plate at suppertime as Anna watched her granddaughter more closely. *"She does look pale, with dark circles under her eyes; why have I not noticed that before?"*

While Louise cleared the supper dishes, throwing sidelong glances at the two silent ladies, Bertha rose to leave. "Please stay a few moments, dear," Anna motioned to her. Slowly, Bertha sat down again, twisting her handkerchief into a knot. "Close the door, Louise," Anna instructed the maid.

"Now Bertha, you and I need to talk," she said in a straightforward tone as she turned towards a nervous-looking Bertha. "I know what happened to you, I—" she stopped talking as Bertha broke out in loud sobs.

"Oh, Oma, it was so awful!" she moaned, trying to catch her breath between weeping. "I tried to get away from him, I—I really, truly fought him!"

"I believe you, Bertha, and I've already had it out with August," Anna gently reassured her. "But now we need to deal with more urgent issues." She stopped to look at Bertha, a picture of misery, and continued. "I believe you may be with child, and that, of course, is a terrible tragedy."

Anna was interrupted by Bertha's loud wails. "Oh, I don't know what to do, Oma!"

"That is what we are here to discuss," Anna carried on, trying to maintain some semblance of composure. "It is out of the question that you will have a child without a husband. I will commission August to find you a suitable husband— that is the least he can do for you."

Bertha lifted her tear-streaked face. "A husband?" she stuttered, shocked. "I am only seventeen; I don't want to get married yet!"

Anna put up her hand to stop her. "As I said before, it is simply out of the question for you to have a child out of wedlock. I have no place to send you in this condition, and believe me, I have thought about it long and hard and want what is best for you. August knows plenty of eligible young men whom he can talk into marrying you. And who knows? You may even take a liking for him eventually."

Bertha stared at her grandmother, at a loss for words, as Anna continued with her plan. "I will move to Berlin soon to be with my sister. I had toyed with the idea for a while already and now it makes total sense to me to move. So, under these conditions, you can no longer stay here by yourself. Believe me, the only way out of this dilemma is for you to be married."

Anna rose from her chair and then gave Bertha a long hug, an unusual gesture from this rather stern woman. "It will all work out, you will see," she tried to reassure her forlorn granddaughter.

"You want me to do *what*?" August later yelled at his mother.

"Do not yell at me, son—you created this mess, and this is the least you can do for poor Bertha and your bastard child she is carrying!!"

A totally dumbfounded August stared at his mother in shock. "Bertha is expecting? Oh, dear God, I did not want *that*," he sputtered.

"You should have thought of the consequences before, my son!" Anna scolded. "Now you do your best to find a suitable husband for Bertha—and get on with it before she shows. It's also in your best interest to avoid telling your wife the circumstances of this quick development."

A rather subdued August left the room while going over in his head whom of his associates might be a suitable husband for his niece. *"This will take a good bribe,"* he thought bitterly. Most of his acquaintances were well off and many had been spoken for already. Save for her looks, Bertha was not a good catch for any of them, especially in her predicament. *"What should I do?"* His thoughts were going in circles.

"Watch where you're going!" he suddenly shouted at his estate manager bumping into him when turning the corner to the horse stable.

"Sorry, sir," the man quickly apologised and moved on. August suddenly stopped in his tracks, peering after the man. *"Now that might be a prospect; he is young, hard-working, still single, and can be persuaded."* August took another look at his manager. *"I will have to get him another position with one of my friends, somewhere far away from here, but that can be done easily enough."*

"Karl, please wait, I would like to speak with you." August followed the man into the stable.

Later, August shared the news with Anna. "Well, Mother, it's all set," he said rather smugly. "Bertha will marry Karl as soon as possible and…"

"Karl who?" his mother interrupted.

"Karl Hoffmann, my soon-to-be former estate manager."

"That's the best you could come up with?"

"Time is of the essence, Mother, and yes, he is willing," August replied curtly. "It cost me a tidy little sum for a dowry, as well as twisting Count Behrendorff's arm to take him on as estate manager in East Prussia, but this is a good solution!" A rather self-satisfied August stared down his mother.

Anna gave a deep sigh. "So be it," she agreed with a shrug. "And just so you know," she added, "as soon as this is over, I will move to my sister's and my request is that you refrain from visiting me. I have had more than enough of you; I'm done!"

"With deepest pleasure, Mother," August snarled as he left the room.

Three weeks later, Bertha and Karl Hoffmann were married in a quiet civil ceremony and soon thereafter left to begin their lives together.

CHAPTER EIGHT: 1878

THE MONOTONOUS CLICKETY-CLACK OF THE TRAIN RATTLING ALONG THE TRACKS made Bertha sleepy as she tried to shift her body into a more comfortable position on the hard, wooden seat. Staring out the window and taking little notice of the passing landscape, she replayed the events of the past week in her head. Glancing at the man sitting across from her, now her husband, she considered what her life might be like from now on. Karl was fast asleep, snoring slightly through a half-open mouth.

He was tall, slim, well-muscled, with short blond hair and a rather bushy moustache adorning a ruggedly handsome face. *"I can't remember the colour of his eyes,"* Bertha realised to herself, *"but everything is in such a haze."*

After the wedding ceremony, the family had gone to dinner at the most expensive restaurant in town—an unexpected and very rare treat indeed. She was not sure why her grandmother had chosen this setting; it had been very obvious that Karl was completely ill at ease in this environment.

Feeling uncomfortable in his suit to begin with, he withered under Anna's disapproving looks. He had no idea how to use the many different cutleries, he kept his elbows on the table, he quickly slurped down his soup, and he ended up drinking far too much alcohol. It seemed August, who was also there, took delight in showing up Karl's social shortcomings, and kept pouring more drinks for Karl, all the while grinning at his mother. *"I should have killed him then,"* Bertha brooded. The whole thing was an unmitigated disaster— *"just like our wedding night."*

Her grandmother had left for Berlin right after dinner, and with August returning to his home, they had the house to themselves.

Bertha had undressed slowly and quickly crawled under the covers when she heard her new husband stagger up the stairs. Bursting into the room, he stubbed his toe and cursed in frustration, kicking off his pants and tearing at his shirt. Throwing his clothes across the room, he fell into bed with a heavy thud. Bertha lay rigid with her eyes squeezed shut, wishing to avoid seeing her completely naked husband.

Karl turned to her, fumbling with her nightgown and finally ripping it off while trying to caress her breasts with his rough hands. His breathing became heavy as he tried to enter her. He was too drunk to consummate their marriage.

Seething with anger, he slurred, "Surely your lover had more fun with you than I am having," and with that, he left, bumping into furniture, cursing loudly when a vase came crashing down in the hallway.

Bertha, shaking with fright and horror, decided right then and there that she would not leave with him in the morning. *I will just quietly take a train to Berlin and find work there,"* she had mulled to herself.

But as she continued to understand the gravity of her situation, she realised she had no money, she was four months pregnant, her grandmother had left, and she would get no help from her uncle; it was hopeless. *"Maybe he is not that bad if he is sober,"* she tried to reassure herself through tears. *"All this was too much for him, as well."*

It was a very awkward first breakfast together as they sat across from each other while Louise served them their morning meal. They ate in silence, cautiously stealing glances at each other. Karl looked hungover and Bertha, tired and anxious. Finally, Karl reached for her hand and mumbled, "I am sorry Bertha; I should not have had that much to drink yesterday."

Bertha gave him an uneasy smile. "Let's not think about that anymore, Karl; we will have to get used to each other. But please, do not ever say such things to me again."

A somewhat relieved Karl nodded, but quickly reminded her that he was not only her husband, but also indeed her legal guardian until she was twenty-one years old. Bertha took a sharp breath but decided to swallow her anger and try to get along; she really had no other choice.

Two hours later, they boarded the train towards Stolp and Karl's new work as estate manager for Count Behrendorff's equestrian stud farm.

Karl started to stir in his seat and opened his eyes. *"They are blue,"* Bertha quickly noted as he gave her a quick grin. "We should be there soon," he offered while stifling a yawn.

Slowly, some passengers rose, grabbing their suitcases as the train huffed into the station. With a big puff of steam, the train came to a slow halt. Bertha rose stiffly while Karl collected their suitcases and they both disembarked. Their married life together was about to begin.

A coachman awaited them at the railway station. "*Guten Tag*, Herr und Frau Hoffmann," he greeted them, grabbing their suitcases and lifting them on to the horse-drawn open wagon. "I am Otto, one of the coachmen, and here to pick you up," he continued.

Karl just nodded while Bertha greeted him politely. "*Guten Tag*, Otto," she smiled, earning her a stern look from Karl.

"We have two crates of household items to be loaded," Karl turned to Otto.

"They can be picked up tomorrow," Otto replied. "We better get you home; it's a lengthy ride and it gets dark pretty early now." He pulled out a couple of thick blankets and handed them to his passengers. "Bundle up!" he added while he hoisted himself up the seat, loosened the brake, and spurred the horses forward.

Both Karl and Bertha looked around to take in the scenery of their new home while Otto began to whistle an old folk tune.

They drove through thick forests, passed some large pastures and even larger fields that appeared to be almost harvested. Occasionally, they saw some smoke rising from chimneys, but did not see any houses.

"It looks a little lonely here," Bertha remarked to Karl, who simply shrugged.

Two long and cold hours later, they finally arrived at the Behrendorff manor. "Here we are!" a good-natured Otto announced, then helped them off the wagon and carried the suitcases into the house.

"The Count will come by tomorrow to greet you; in the meantime, you should find all you need for this evening," Otto explained. "Have a good night."

The couple walked about the small but cosy house. It was adequately furnished, the beds with fresh linen and warm blankets on them. The hearth in the kitchen was burning and firewood was stacked beside it. The larder was stocked with food and several jugs of fresh water stood next to the basin. *"Looks like there is no running water in the house,"* Bertha mused. *"And the facility must be the outhouse in the backyard."*

"Well, my dear," Karl turned to his wife with a smirk on his face. "It looks like you will not have any servants looking after you here."

"Karl, please," Bertha sighed. "I am quite capable of running a household myself. And can you please try a little harder to be friendlier? I did not ask for this either, but now that we are married, we should at least get to know each other and get along," Bertha touched his arm while she spoke.

Karl slowly nodded. "I guess you are right—we need to make the best of it, at least for the time being."

"What did he mean by that?" Bertha wondered to herself. *"But best not to question him; I have a baby to think of."*

"Let's get some food into us," she brightly announced while rummaging around the larder and lighting the stove. Karl lugged the suitcases into the bedroom and a little while later they sat down to their first meal of sausage, potatoes, and cabbage.

That night, Karl demanded his right as a husband. Bertha endured the clumsy and rough interaction with no feelings, just a deep sadness as her husband rolled over and fell right to sleep.

Chapter Nine

Quickly a daily routine became established. Karl would leave the house early in the morning and Bertha would busy herself with the daily household chores of cleaning, cooking, and laundry. Water had to be carried in buckets from a community well and the outhouse was shared with several other estate workers and their families. She already dreaded the winter months.

Gradually, she got to know the other workers on the estate, as well as Count Behrendorff, his wife, and their four children. Christmas came and went, and a new year began, and Bertha grew heavy with child.

Karl now refused to sleep with her, much to Bertha's relief. Other than a postcard, she heard nothing from her grandmother, and most certainly nothing from her uncle.

She felt quite alone and looked forward to this child's arrival.

One evening, while adding some more wood to the stove, she turned to Karl and asked if he had inquired about a midwife.

Karl just stared at her blankly. "Why? That's up to you; it's not man's business."

Nodding, Bertha continued to try to engage him in conversation. "What should we name the baby?"

"Why are you asking me?" Karl became more annoyed with his wife's chatter.

"Because you are part of this child's life!" Bertha was becoming testy herself.

Now Karl was quite irate. "No, this is not my child—ask your lover what name he wants to give it, or better yet, send the child to him, I don't want it!"

Shocked, Bertha stared at him, mouth agape. "You know very well that Uncle August is not my lover! And why did you agree to marry me if you feel that way about it?"

"Because August is paying me and will continue to pay for his bastard until it is grown up!" Karl suddenly snapped, revealing the truth. "It was a good deal for me at the time; now I wish I had never agreed to that!"

"August is doing what?" An incredulous Bertha glared at Karl. "He is paying you for the baby? Don't you think you should give *me* the money?"

Karl laughed out loud. "I hope you are joking! I am still your guardian and I will keep the money," he said sternly. "Oh, and don't you dare call this bastard 'Karl'—I can make my own sons!" With that, he slammed the door shut as he stomped out into the snow.

Shaking all over, Bertha sat down in tears and frantically wracked her brain about what to do next. *"There is nothing I can do!"* she thought, panicked. *"I am trapped; where can I go at this point? I am due soon, I need to make the best of it."*

She resolved to write her grandmother as soon as the baby was born and ask her to have the money sent to her instead of Karl; as for him, she could simply tell him that August stopped paying. *"At least Oma Anna can save it for me when I leave Karl once I turn twenty-one."*

Two weeks later, Bertha went into labour and a midwife was summoned. After a few hours, the midwife placed a healthy baby boy into Karl's arms. "Here is your son," she said softly, and left a perplexed Karl staring at this baby while she tended to Bertha.

Watching Karl, Bertha noticed a small expression of tenderness and wonder in her husband's face as he held this newborn boy. *"Perhaps things will settle down between us and he comes to accept this baby as his son,"* she fervently hoped.

"Can't take your eyes of him, can you?" the midwife interrupted. "He is a handsome boy, that one," she carried on while piling the soiled linen in a corner to be taken away. "Now let me see how he latches on to feed," the midwife continued. "Ah yes, no problems here; he is a fine one." They all listened to the baby's suckling noises on Bertha's breast.

Karl, feeling somewhat overwhelmed and slightly embarrassed, turned to leave the room, but the midwife held him back while taking out a notebook from her bag. "I have to take down the details to register his birth when I go to Stolp next and, as his father, you have to sign this note as being truthful."

Shifting uncomfortably from one foot to the other, Karl glanced at his wife, grinning nervously, and shrugged as the midwife started to fill in the document. "Date of birth: April 16, 1878; name, Hoffmann—" she paused. "Er, what's his name, then?"

"We haven't decided yet," Karl muttered.

An irritated midwife looked up at him. "Well, you better decide in a hurry; I don't have all day and I need the name before leaving. I'll take out the laundry and when I come back, you better have a name, or I'll give him one," she sternly admonished the young father, picking up the sheets and slamming the door behind her, all the while shaking her head.

"Karl, what are we going to name him?" Bertha whispered in exhaustion.

"It's up to you, as long as it isn't Karl or August!" Karl angrily retorted.

Bertha ignored his anger and thought for a moment. "What do you think of Emil, after my mother, Emilia?"

"That's a name as good as any," Karl agreed, as the midwife returned.

"Well, do we have a name yet?" she asked, turning back to the document.

"Emil," Bertha answered proudly.

"Emil, and what else?" the midwife asked. "Every boy needs at least two names."

Once again Karl looked at Bertha as she quickly replied, "Emil Ferdinand."

"Good names," the midwife said and filled in the names Hoffmann, Emil Ferdinand; father, Karl Richard Wilhelm Hoffmann; and mother, Bertha Karoline Hoffmann, nee Holtzmann. She passed the document over to Karl to sign. Karl read it over carefully, flinching slightly at the father's name, and then slowly and carefully put his name on the document of birth.

"I'll bring you back the official birth certificate once it's issued," the midwife declared. "In the meantime, my young assistant will take care of you and the newborn for the next couple of weeks.

"And you," she said directly to Karl, "leave her alone for a few weeks! Birthing is tough on a body." If she noticed the couple's blushing, she did not mention it; she was used to the embarrassed discomfort displayed by young couples. With a "God keep you," the midwife retreated.

"I need some fresh air," Karl declared, leaving a sleepy Bertha and content Emil behind.

He headed straight to the Count's office to announce the birth of a son and join in a few drinks to toast this event. He basked in the congratulations and happily accepted a generous monetary gift from the Behrendorffs.

The celebrations carried over to the stables, and staff and farmhands drifted in and out for the free beer. In all that time, Karl never thought of Bertha or the child, choosing instead to enjoy all the attention focused on him—the father of a firstborn son!

Sometime during the night, a completely drunk Karl was brought home by farmhands who good-naturedly deposited him at the front door. Stumbling inside, he tripped over a chair and fell crashing to the floor, hearing a baby cry somewhere in the distance before passing out on the floor.

Bertha, startled awake by the noise, decided to stay in bed. *"Let him sleep it off; he will only get nasty if I say anything,"* she thought while cooing little Emil back to sleep.

Chapter Ten

May 18, 1878

Dearest Grandmama:

I hope that you and your sister are well and life in Berlin is agreeing with you. I would like you to know that on April 16th, I gave birth to a little boy; I named him Emil Ferdinand in honour of my parents. Karl did not want to add his name, saying it is enough the "little bastard" has his last name.

From this statement alone, you will have guessed that life is not going well with Karl. He certainly is not the man I would have married under normal circumstances, but I am sure you knew this all along. In fairness, I must say that Karl would have liked another woman as a wife as well, and so we carry on in the hope that we will find a path to each other at some time.

If he only would not drink so much. And his demands on me are not loving, but brutally angry. Perhaps the baby will temper him somewhat. Emil is a good baby; he rarely cries or fusses, looking at me with big blue eyes, almost as if he knows already that he is the cause of my misery. In truth, it is totally unfair to him, as he had no say as to how he came into this world, but I must admit that he will always be a reminder of last summer. I know I can tell you all this since you will understand. I am barely nineteen and life is already grim and somewhat hopeless.

I had asked Karl if I could visit you with the baby, and he started shouting that I only want to see August and so he will not allow this. Maybe you can find time to come here in the summer.

I should add though that the Count and his wife have been very kind to me after Emil's birth. The Countess sent her domestic apprentice to help me with the child. She is a little younger than I and in her second year of apprenticing; she comes every day for a couple of hours to help and give me some time to myself. I think the Countess has caught on very quickly that Karl is of no help to me. After work, he is off to his favourite pub and comes home late at night, demanding his rights as a husband even though he is to leave me be for six weeks. I shudder once the time is over and am also fearful of conceiving another child. I really would like to leave Karl but have no idea how to support myself and Emil.

The midwife tells me it is not uncommon for a woman to feel like this after giving birth, so I hope I feel much better soon.

Please write soon.

Your loving granddaughter, Bertha

June 27, 1878

Dear Bertha:

I sincerely thank you for your letter and congratulate you on the birth of Emil Ferdinand. I do like the choice of names and am sure your parents would have been proud.

Indeed, the circumstances of his coming into this world were far from pleasant, but you must not allow yourself to convey your feelings to the child; as he grows older, he will seek his position within the family, and it is my fervent hope that Karl will come to accept him and treat him as his own.

As for your hope, it is completely out of the question that you leave your husband. You must accept your fate; there is a reason for everything. It is of course most unfortunate you had to marry an immature man; however, you, too need to put some effort into this relationship. As to Karl's demands, I do remind you that it is a man's spousal right—a lady endures gracefully for the sake of peace and harmony. I hope you will have another child very soon, as this will certainly temper Karl's enthusiasm towards you, and you will live life as it is intended for a woman.

With that in mind, I shall plan for a visit later this summer once the August heat has diminished.

With love, your Grandmama

BY THE TIME ANNA HAD MADE HER WAY FOR A VISIT, BERTHA WAS PREGNANT with her second child. It was mid-October and an early frost had set in already.

Bertha was delighted to see her grandmother again—Karl was not. "Judging from all the baggage she brought along, I fear she will be here until next year," he grumbled under his breath as he lugged them up the narrow wooden stairway and into the second bedroom.

"I heard that, young man!" an indignant Anna responded curtly. "I will not stay until next year. I will, however, demand respect, courtesy, and decent behaviour. Your attitude towards me is extremely loutish, and it's time for you to grow up and be a man!" Anna was firm and stern.

Karl angrily turned around, but looking at Anna's face, he decided to swallow whatever he wanted to say, and with a red face, he picked up another case and trotted upstairs.

Bertha started to giggle while hugging her grandmother. "Oh, Oma, I am glad you told him off. He needed that!"

Anna just nodded. "How about a cup of tea and then you can show me around? And of course, I can't wait to see Emil," she added.

Bertha quickly put a pot of water on the stove and went upstairs to fetch little Emil from his nap and put him in Anna's arms.

"Oh, what a beautiful little boy," she crooned. "He has such serious blue eyes, and his soft dark curls—he looks so much like your mother looked."

"But of course—it runs in the family, after all!" a sarcastic Karl scoffed while hurrying out the door. "I won't be home for supper!" he added, slamming the door behind him.

Little Emil flinched, but did not cry out. "He is a very quiet baby," Bertha commented while pouring the hot water over the tea leaves. "I suppose he is used to Karl's outbursts."

Both women sat in silence for a while before they put Emil in his playpen. Bertha stoked the fire in the stove to generate more warmth, and then Anna spoke first. "This is a nice little place you have," she remarked. "You look quite settled."

Bertha, somewhat lost in thought, slowly turned to her grandmother. "Settled?" she asked, almost insulted. "Is *this* what you call settled? I live with a crude and hostile husband in a tiny house with furniture that are not my own. I have to lug buckets of water each day, trot through hot and icy cold weather to an outhouse, and now expecting another child!" she cried.

"I am only nineteen years old," she added, "and most likely have to endure more pregnancies in my so-called 'settled' life. I see these women each day as they do their duties with a gaggle of children running after them, looking old before they are forty!

"No, my dearest grandmama," Bertha shook her head, near tears. "I would never call this settled; I would call this a waste of me!" By now, Bertha was crying softly as Anna stared, open-mouthed, at her granddaughter.

It took her a while to gauge what may be an appropriate reply. Finally, she took a deep breath. "I, too, would have wished for a better life for you Bertha," Anna finally admitted. "Unfortunately, that is not the way God has planned your path; women over the ages—"

"God?!" Bertha suddenly shrieked, interrupting her. "Did you really say God? We both know who is responsible for this, but surely it was not God. If there really is a God, He would have struck August dead instead of condemning me to this."

Anna could not believe what she was hearing. "Bertha, Bertha, what are you saying?" she asked in bewilderment. "You are condemning yourself to eternal hell with these thoughts. What about your pastor, the church, have you talked to him about this? Are you even going to church on Sundays?" Anna was deeply disturbed.

"Yes, I go to church each Sunday," Bertha answered, lowering her voice a little. "Actually, we all go, as it is an unspoken requirement. I can't imagine not going, as my life would really and truly be a living hell.

"There is a Catholic family down the road, and their priest comes by once a month on horseback, for confession, I imagine," she continued. "Most people shun them, as they do not go to 'our' church. As to the pastor? Well, they have eight kids already, so you can imagine what his wife is like and what advice he would give to me. I do appreciate the two-hour church time as a time to rest and contemplate.

"But no, dear grandmama," Bertha again told Anna, as if to reinforce her position. "This is *not* the life I ever wanted to live. I would have liked to have had time to learn something, to read more, to marry a nice man, and yes, have a couple of children—but through love, and not violence."

"Oh, my dearest child," Anna sighed. "I wish so much to help you, but what can I possibly do?" She held her granddaughter in a helpless but comforting embrace. "I am sure God will find a way for you if you pray hard enough," she whispered to her.

Bertha just nodded at this rather feeble attempt by her grandmother to make her feel better. She quickly gathered her thoughts. "Right now, I must see to Emil, as he needs a change. I have a bucket full of soaking diapers needing washing. You can be a big help if you put the potatoes on." A weary Bertha picked up her son, letting out a defeated sigh.

"One more thing, my dear, before we put this unpleasant topic to rest," Anna quickly added. "We, particularly we women, are not on this earth for our own enjoyment. We are duty-bound to obey God, to work hard, and to raise God-fearing children. We must make the most of our situations, however dire they may be. You are married to a hard-working man and you, too, must put more effort into this relationship.

"Life on earth is not meant to be heaven; that will be our promised gift once we have fulfilled our duties."

An unconvinced Bertha stubbornly replied that she would leave Karl once she turned twenty-one. Anna decided to avoid arguing, knowing full well that a single woman of no skills, no wealth, and most likely three children by then would have no chance of any kind of life.

"She is a stubborn child, just like her mother was, but she will learn as she gets older, and I only hope both she and Karl will grow up soon," she thought to herself while starting to peel the potatoes for dinner.

CHAPTER ELEVEN: 1879–1880

WINTER CAME EARLY THAT YEAR, WITH SNOW PILED HIGH BY THE END OF OCTOBER already. Anna had returned to Berlin, and both Bertha and Karl were glad for that. A somewhat comfortable calmness had settled into their lives and Bertha was hopeful that their relationship would improve over time.

Being more housebound due to the unrelenting winter storms hammering the area, Karl took more of an interest in little Emil. He responded with smiles and happy babbles, shrieking with joy when Karl bounced him off his knees or played "horse" with him. Christmas and New Year's passed with a warmer glow than the year before, and Bertha happily awaited the birth of her next child.

"Do you think it will be a boy or a girl?" she asked Karl one evening. "It doesn't really matter, does it? But a boy would be practical—he can wear the hand-me-downs from Emil." Bertha had to smile, but then Karl had to spoil it by adding, "and I will have *my own* son."

"Just for that comment, I hope it will be a girl!" Bertha angrily retorted. "When are you finally going to leave that subject alone?"

"A little girl will be nice, too," Karl said half-heartedly. "Let's pick some names, shall we?" he looked at his wife with an almost apologetic grin. Bertha, still seething, slammed a cup of coffee in front of Karl, slopping some on the table. "Yes, let's!"

She then watched in amazement as Karl got up, grabbed a dishcloth, and wiped up the spilled coffee before picking up Emil and taking a closer look at him. "I know you are upset at my comment," he spoke rather calmly. "I really like this little boy, but he looks like a Sehnke through and through, and I just can't get the image of you and August together out of my head."

Bertha felt a wave of shame, anger, and disgust wash over her. "I never want to talk about that horrible part of my life," she growled, "and you will just have to accept Emil for who he is—your son as much as any future son—so stop comparing. You are no prince or wealthy businessowner who must pass on his bloodline.

"We are simple people and hopefully capable of raising all our future children with the same love and care they deserve," she continued firmly. "So please, for our future together, understand what can't be changed. And if I can add a nasty comment myself, you are getting an allowance for Emil, which you keep to yourself to spend on your own wants. No—" she put up her hand— "do not say anymore! This subject is closed! Now, let us return to our original topic—a name for this child."

Somewhat aghast, Karl put Emil down, picked up his coffee cup, and sipped for a few moments before settling down. "Fine, fine, let's do that," he conceded. "I like Karl for a boy."

Bertha nodded, unsurprised by his choice, and still upset from their squabble. "How about Karl-Heinrich?" she suggested. "That way it is not so confusing."

"Agreed, Karl-Heinrich it will be," he nodded. "And Karoline for a girl—what do you think?"

"That's the first time he asked me what I think! I must have really shaken him up. But then, of course, he gets Karl into both names—what a self-centred person," she thought. "Yes, and her second name will be Anna," she declared.

"Both are good names," Karl agreed before putting on his heavy winter coat and boots to return to his work duties.

On March 14, 1879, Bertha delivered another son, Karl-Heinrich Hoffmann, and this time, the midwife did not have to admonish them to come up with a name. And this time, Karl was overjoyed to have his own son, a spitting image of himself. A big, boisterous boy with blond straight hair and steely blue eyes. The contrast between the two boys—young Karl and Emil—could not be bigger. Emil was quiet and of slight stature, Karl-Heinz, as his name was shortened to, was tall, brash, and demanding. Bertha sure had her hands full with him.

One year later, almost to the day of Karl-Heinz's birth, Karoline Anna was born, March 20, 1880. Even the midwife became concerned—three children in three years was overwhelming for Bertha, and she took Karl aside to caution him.

"Give your wife some time to recover, or any future pregnancies may have dire consequences!" she admonished him.

"What do you mean?" Karl demanded.

"To put it bluntly, keep your pants on!" was her sharp reply, shaking her head as she left the house.

A furious Karl confronted his unsuspecting wife. "Did you complain to that old witch?" he asked her loudly. "I am fulfilling the duties of a husband! Is it my problem you keep getting pregnant all the time?" Karl's voice rose louder and louder. "It's no fun for me either to have you waddle around with a big belly and my needs not being taken care of!!"

A stunned Bertha tried to calm him down. "Please, Karl, the children are sleeping," she urged him. "Try not to wake them."

"Of course, the children!" he snarled. "It's always the children! I'll go seek some pleasure somewhere else!" he added, slamming the door on his way out and leaving a crying Bertha behind.

"I need to do something!" Bertha wiped her tears and resolved to make some changes.

When Karl returned late at night, he found the marriage bed almost empty, as little Karl-Heinrich was sleeping in the spot where his wife normally slept. Confused, but too drunk to care, he collapsed on the bed and immediately fell asleep. His crying son woke him, and he immediately felt the anger rise in him.

Grabbing the sopping wet child, he stumbled down the stairs. Bertha was in the kitchen, nursing baby Karoline, while Emil sat at the table dunking a crust of bread into a bowl of warm milk.

"What is the meaning of this?" his voice was dangerously calm. "Where were you all night?"

"The baby was fussy," Bertha quickly replied, "and so is this one—he needs changing. Karl, please, just take off the diapers and bring him to the outhouse; I'll take care of him as soon as I have fed Karoline. Anyway, it's time for you to go to work," she added, silently hoping he would just leave.

"I will deal with you later," he growled, picking up a piece of bread and gulping down his coffee before leaving. Turning around, he warned Bertha, "and you better be back in our bed tonight if you know what's good for you!" And yet again he stormed out.

"I will definitely leave that man when I am twenty-one!" she promised to herself while tending to the children and daily household chores.

By nightfall, Karl returned, again in a foul mood.

"Supper is on the stove," Bertha motioned to him. He ate in silence while glaring at her. The sight of her exposed breast while nursing the baby suddenly excited him. *"I need her—I need her right now!"* he thought, licking the last morsel of supper off his lips. "Put the baby down and get yourself up to bed!" he demanded, rising from his chair.

"Please Karl, not now," Bertha pleaded, sensing his fury as she tried to reason with him. "Karoline is not finished yet, and the boys—"

"Never mind the boys!" he growled. "Put the child down and get yourself upstairs!" He was becoming angrier.

"Please, Karl, I beg of you, calm down!" With two steps, he was at her side, tore the screaming baby away from her, and tried to drag her up the stairs. Bertha resisted, trying to put the baby into the playpen.

Suddenly Karl slapped her hard. He liked the sound of that slap, as it made him feel powerful, so he hit her again and again. Bertha, trying to protect the baby, started to scream, and then tried to hit him back.

Karl felt a new wave of excitement come over him. "Put the baby down. Now!" He could not wait any longer to get upstairs, so he ripped her dress, threw her on the floor, and viciously assaulted her, again and again. Bertha heard all three children scream and wail, the boys standing at the top of the stairs, howling.

Finally, panting heavily, Karl got up. "I will show you who the man of this house is," he snarled. "I have been far too lenient with you! From now on, you do as I say. And you two, get back to bed before I make you!" he yelled at the boys, who retreated immediately.

Bertha, bruised, battered, and bleeding, slowly rose and picked up the frying pan from the stove, and hit Karl over the head as hard as she could. "This is the last time you will have me!" she hissed. "I will leave you as soon as I am twenty-one. Go and seek your desires somewhere else."

A slightly dazed Karl just looked at her and laughed out loud. "I like it when you are wild," he snickered "We should do this more often."

"You come near me again, and I swear I will kill you!" Bertha stood like an avenging angel, wild-eyed, unwavering, holding a knife in one hand and a hysterically screaming child in her other arm.

Uncertainty flickered in Karl's eyes as he wondered how to withdraw with his ego still intact. Backing away slowly, he continued laughing while putting on his boots and leaving the house.

With a loud sob, Bertha sank into a chair, trying to calm the baby before turning her attention to the frightened boys.

Chapter Twelve: 1881

Bertha's twenty-first birthday finally arrived on July 4, 1881, and with that sense of freedom came the realisation that she was pregnant once again.

Other than verbal attacks, Karl had not touched her since that fateful encounter. She had quietly moved her mattress into the children's room, and Karl continued to drink heavily, and most nights, she did not hear him coming home or did not know whether he stayed out all night. She became frightened for her future, and her children's future, and decided to speak to their pastor.

If he was surprised to see her, he did not show it, and listened attentively to her grievances and resentments. "What exactly are your concerns, then?" he asked, confused.

"How can I accept a man who beats me?" Bertha was distraught.

"My dear child," the pastor replied with a sigh, "women are by nature sinful people and in need of discipline by their husbands to remind them to keep on the path of righteousness, just like children need the rod."

Bertha just stared at him, open-mouthed. "My grandfathers never hit my grandmothers!" she protested.

"This only means that your grandmothers knew their place and were not as obstinate as you obviously are," the pastor scolded her. "You must submit to your husband—it is your duty in life. And I suggest you pray more often." And with that he tried to stand to leave.

"But Herr Pastor!" Bertha was now in tears. "He forced himself violently on me and now I am pregnant again; this child, as all my children, was not conceived in love!"

"Bertha, you are married," he reminded her. "There is no such thing as being forced. Your husband is doing what he should be doing. As a married couple, you go forth and multiply; that is your God-given duty. And now I have to end this useless discussion and send you back to your husband and children." He stood up.

When Bertha made no move to do the same, he added, "I will talk to Karl and remind him of his duties with caring and not unnecessary force."

"I do not think that he will listen," she shrugged. "He is drunk most of the time." Bertha rose to leave.

The pastor frowned. "And where does he get the funds to indulge in drinking?"

"It's really Emil's money he uses," she admitted without thinking. "Poor child will never see a penny from what really is his."

"Emil? Is that not your eldest child?" The pastor frowned yet again. "I was not aware you had been married before."

Bertha realised she had revealed too much, but figured it was too late. "I wasn't," she said simply. "My uncle forced himself on me, and Emil came into being; my uncle pays a monthly sum to Karl to take care of the boy."

Now it was the pastor's turn to stare at her, open-mouthed. "Out, you get out of this house of God!" he thundered. "You are even more sinful than I guessed. A child out of wedlock? And to think I baptised him! I can't believe what I am hearing!" He pounded his fist on his desk, his face twisted in contempt.

Bertha, totally bewildered by this outburst, shouted back, "Emil was not born out of wedlock!" she retorted. "Karl and I were married before he was born!" She left with her head held high.

"Now more than ever I need to leave!" she resolved to herself. *"I just need to work out how to achieve this. This new baby will not be born here!"* She began to make plans in her head.

BOOK THREE
BERTHA BLOSSOMS

CHAPTER ONE: 1889

"EMIL, HURRY UP, YOU'LL BE LATE FOR SCHOOL IF YOU DAWDLE ANY LONGER!" Bertha pushed her eldest out the door; Karl-Heinz was next, running down the stairs, not missing the opportunity to give his older brother a shove from behind while racing by him.

Bertha just shook her head. *"Those two could not be any more different,"* she mused. They simply did not like each other. Karl-Heinz, even though a year younger, was much taller and stronger, and had the muscular build of his father. *"Not much between the ears either,"* she thought wryly. Emil remained a slight, gentle, dreamer, doing very well academically and destined for higher learning.

With a sigh, Bertha turned her attention to her daughter, a pretty nine-year-old, full of curiosity and life, and a real joy to have around. She was a big help to her mother and great-grandmother.

"I am ready to go, Mama," she gave her mother a big kiss and skipped out the door, down the stairs towards her all-girls school.

Bertha now focused on her youngest—her "problem" child. Eight years old, and still not ready to go to school. With some bitterness, Bertha recalled how he was conceived, and how she was unable to love this feeble-minded boy. *"I guess this is God's punishment for leaving Karl,"* she often thought, even though her grandmother chided her for these thoughts. Anna Sehnke was always patient and loving with him, and he, in turn, responded with bright smiles, sloppy kisses, and gurgling laughter.

Bertha pulled him to the table. "Let's have some breakfast, shall we?" she coaxed him to try to hold the spoon on his own. Happily, he grabbed it and started hitting his porridge bowl, splashing the contents all over the table, and Bertha's face and hair. "Stop it!" Bertha admonished him, already at her wit's end by eight in the morning.

"Bertha, dear, let me feed him," Anna had just come out of her bedroom and pulled up a chair next to young Eugen. "Here, here, young man," she cooed, "now let's eat like a gentleman." Eugen readily opened his greedy little mouth to eat.

Shaking her head in frustration, yet marvelling at her grandmother's patience, Bertha went about her daily chores.

Fluffing up pillows, straightening bedsheets, and folding blankets, her thoughts travelled back eight years earlier, a few months prior to Eugen's birth. That terrible row with Karl—Bertha still recoiled whenever she recalled the moment Karl hit her the last time.

He was irate when she told him their last violent encounter resulted in another pregnancy, accusing her of not being "careful enough," even though it was his own forced doing. Deciding not to reply to that, she continued to hang the laundry in the gentle breeze; Karoline was sleeping in the empty laundry basket, the boys playing quietly on a patch of grass.

Suddenly, Karl grabbed her from behind, trying to drag her into the house. "Stop it, Karl, the children are watching!" Bertha attempted to free herself from his grip.

"The children, always the children," he growled. "And now there will be another one to keep you from our bed!" His hot breath wreaked of alcohol. "Come to bed now!" he demanded. "At least you can't get any more pregnant!" he laughed at his joke.

"Please Karl, we will discuss this later," Bertha pleaded, trying to calm him down, but by now he was too aroused and angry, dragging her into the house while ignoring the wailing children.

Inside, a violent struggle ensued. He trying to yank off her dress, but Bertha grabbed a broom to try to fend him off. By now, Karl was beyond any reasoning and started punching her in her face and then in her stomach. Bertha cried out in pain and fury, when suddenly he let her go, at the same time falling like a tree. He had been felled by a well-placed punch from the coachman, Otto, who had driven by and saw and heard the wailing children as well as the commotion inside the house, and had stopped to investigate.

After knocking Karl out, Otto quickly deposited Karl outside and returned to take care of a bleeding and badly shaking Bertha. "Come Frau Hoffmann," he said gently. "It's only a superficial cut over one eyebrow, it will heal quickly." He handed her a wetted towel.

"Thank you, Otto," Bertha said gratefully. "I need to tend to the children now." She went back outside to calm the little ones and saw Otto leave, pulling a dumbfounded Karl behind him.

It was at that exact moment she decided to leave. Two months short of her twenty-first birthday, she figured it was safe enough that Karl would not force her to return so close to her age of majority.

Luck was on her side, or perhaps it was Count Behrendorff's doing after hearing of the events from Otto. In any event, Karl was sent to Hungary for a week to escort several horses the Count had sold. As soon as he was gone, Bertha searched the house for some money she knew Karl had hidden away, money that was to go for Emil's keep.

Few words were exchanged when Otto drove her, the children, and a few of her belongings to the railroad station in Stolp. It was late June and a hot day; the countryside was alive with fresh greens, blooming trees, and lush fields of yet-to-ripen wheat and rye. It was so very peaceful, even the children were relaxed and enjoyed the long drive.

At the railway station, Otto had helped her get settled into their seats on the train to Berlin. Bertha hoped her grandmother would understand and that together, they might find a way out of this dilemma.

It was a long ride. Tired and hungry children quarrelled, the baby cried, it was hot and stuffy in the compartment, and Bertha was acutely aware of her fellow passengers' discomfort and annoyance.

She was sure they were just as glad to arrive in Berlin as she was.

Standing on the platform of the large Berlin railway station, visibly pregnant, carrying a one-year-old girl and two little boys tucking at her skirt, several battered suitcases between them, she looked the embodiment of a lonely widow on her way to the poorhouse.

A while later, the station master considered her plight, hailed a hackney, helped her load it up, and she was on her way to her grandmother.

And Bertha was so glad she had decided to do so those eight years ago.

Finishing her morning chores now, all the while listening to the sounds of Eugen and her grandmother in the kitchen, she had to smile, recalling her grandmother's totally bewildered look when she opened the door and faced a dishevelled, bone-tired, and dirty young pregnant woman and three little children.

"*Mein Gott*, Bertha!" she exclaimed. "I had no idea you were coming! Come in, come in," she motioned to them all. "You should have let me know! How did you get here, and is Karl with you?" She continued her questioning as she stepped aside to let them all enter.

CHAPTER TWO

STILL LOST IN HER THOUGHTS, BERTHA SAT ON HER BED, WHICH SERVED AS A SOFA during the day. Taking in the small apartment, she wondered how much longer this arrangement could continue. It was crammed with furniture, which still looked the same as when it had been hurriedly pushed together and rearranged eight years ago. It was almost a blessing that her great-aunt had passed away a couple of years prior to Bertha's arrival, but it certainly was a huge adjustment for her grandmother.

One of the two bedrooms had been converted into the children's bedroom (Eugen had been added a few months later). Bertha slept in the sitting room while her grandmother had the other bedroom to herself. A small kitchen, an entryway, and a balcony enhanced the living space. A two-piece indoor toilet completed the flat. It was a major improvement from the outdoor facilities from the past number of years, but still a far cry from the comfortable surroundings she had been used to.

Bertha was still amazed and grateful at how easily her grandmother had adapted to these drastically changed circumstances, although neither one of them had believed it would last for all these years. Karl had made no effort to get his wife and children back after his demand for her to return was left unanswered. He did write an angry letter, accusing Bertha of his difficulties with Count Behrendorff, the loss of his "pocket money" (referring to Emil's support payments), and his eventual loss of work.

As far as Bertha knew, he was now employed as a seasonal helper in various horse stud farms close to the Russian border.

"Bertha, what is taking you so long?" Her grandmother interrupted Bertha's thoughts. "I have to take Eugen to the playground to work off some of his energy."

"I'll come, Oma," offered Bertha. "Let me tag along with you today; we can sit on a bench and talk while the children are in school."

Getting Eugen washed and dressed was becoming increasingly difficult. *"He is growing so fast and soon we won't be able to handle him,"* Bertha worried to herself.

Settling down on a bench in a sun-drenched park and watching Eugen running around among much younger children, laughing, waving his arms, and babbling incoherently, Bertha turned to her grandmother. "Omama, what are we to do about Eugen? He is becoming harder to handle—what on earth will happen to him?"

"I have spent many a sleepless night wondering the same," Anna Sehnke replied. "I think you might—"

Their conversation was suddenly interrupted by an angry, red-faced woman, screaming, "Can't you control your idiot son? He just threw sand all over my little girl! You need to discipline him!"

Lifting her head to look at the irate woman, Bertha remarked, "He's just a child. Perhaps your little one could stop kicking him."

"He's an idiot, that's what he is; you can't let him loose to attack other children!"

"My dear woman, if he is truly an idiot, then he doesn't know what he is doing, so how can he be disciplined?" Bertha snapped back.

"Well, I never! He must take after his mother!" The woman was furious.

"No, he actually resembles his father," was Bertha's cool and calm reply.

Fuming, the woman turned around and grabbed her screaming child. "Come, Lenchen, this is no place for little girls." They stalked off.

As soon as she was gone, Anna broke into full-blown laughter. "You really set her straight!" she chortled.

"But you see, Omama, this is what we have to deal with now!" Bertha was quite distraught. "The other children are teased mercilessly by their classmates—even Emil's teacher commented the other day how 'stupid' he was in mathematics and clearly comes from the same family as Eugen.

"It had my sensitive Emil in tears," she continued. "My Emil, who sings like an angel and plays his recorder with such devotion—it is a joy to hear him." Bertha was nearly in tears.

Anna put her arm around her granddaughter. "Perhaps you might like to speak to Pastor Werthmann; he may have an idea or even a solution. I heard that he also has a child that is not...quite right."

"I didn't know that!" Bertha was surprised. She paused for a moment. "I knew from the moment I held Eugen that something wasn't right; he felt kind of limp in my arms, he had troubles taking my breast, he hardly ever cried—but in many ways, he was a comfortable child while I had three other ones to deal with."

"I remember," Anna nodded. "I had mentioned a number of times how quiet he was."

Both watched Eugen, filling and emptying his little sand pail for probably the hundredth time.

Bertha rose with a sigh. "We need to take him home now. He has soiled himself, and there just are no diapers large enough for him anymore. Can you take him, Oma? I have some things to get for our meal today."

Anna nodded, took a compliant Eugen by his hand, and set off across the playground. Before they parted ways, Bertha quickly replied to her grandmother's suggestion. "And Oma—I will definitely make an appointment with Pastor Werthmann. I'll ask him after worship service on Sunday; I need to speak to him anyway about Emil's confirmation classes starting soon."

CHAPTER THREE

"Frau Hoffmann, please take a seat," Pastor Werthmann motioned for Bertha to sit. He quickly peeked at the sheet in front him to refresh his memory regarding the children's names and ages; after all, he led a very large congregation with plenty of children. It was very difficult to remember everyone's names and ages.

He remembered when Bertha first came to see him for the baptism of her youngest, eight years ago already, the grandmother—who came regularly to Sunday services—bringing one or three children with her. However, the pastor didn't remember ever seeing Eugen.

Bertha watched him for a few minutes as he sat back in his chair, lit a cigarette, and waited patiently for her to start. She liked him; he had a calm and reassuring demeanour, his sermons were non-condemning, and she sensed that he was well regarded by the people of his parish.

"I notice that Emil is ready for confirmation classes," Pastor Werthmann began. "Is that what you wanted to see me about?"

"Yes, that's one thing," Bertha finally felt settled enough to talk about Eugen. Pastor Werthmann listened carefully to her as she explained the situation, asking a question here and there, looking out the window deep in thought; Bertha could sense his compassion for her.

She started to relax when he spoke up. "You might not know this, but my wife and I have a daughter who is four years old now; she can't walk or talk, she eats and sleeps, and likes to be cuddled. We have prayed for a miracle, I have railed against God, I have argued, questioned, and tried to bargain. In the end, Elisabeth is unchanged, and we, too, needed to accept and come to terms with God and our mortal limitations."

He stopped to light another cigarette and Bertha felt his pain, a pain she shared with him. The difference, though, was that he had a partner with whom he could share and carry this burden together; she was alone, having to rely on her aging grandmother.

"But my dear, Frau Hoffmann, I believe I have an answer for you," he continued. "Last year, Berlin was fortunate to open Dalldorf, a mental asylum for underdeveloped children. My wife and I decided to investigate this further and found it to be wonderful place, well-staffed, children with varying degrees of developmental difficulties being challenged and kept busy within their capabilities. Our little girl has become a much happier child, and she now can sit unassisted already," he paused for a moment of reflection.

"She will most likely spend the rest of her life there, but then what are the alternatives? Just like Eugen, she will become too big for us to properly tend for her, and we can't burden our other children with her eventual care once we are too old or dead. I can only encourage you to seek them out. If you like, I will come with you," the pastor offered.

A slow smile of relief crossed Bertha's face. "Thank you, pastor; I'm very glad I came to speak with you. Yes, I would like to take you up on your offer to come with me." After a shared prayer for strength, the pastor promised to be in touch as soon as he had arranged for a visit.

Three weeks later, Bertha watched with mixed feelings as Eugen was fed his last breakfast at home. Oblivious to the upcoming change in his life, he happily opened his little mouth to each spoonful. *"Just like a little bird,"* Bertha mused. *"He opens his mouth to whatever is put in front of him, flaps his arms like wings, but will never take flight..."* and soon enough tears were flowing down her face.

Noticing her grandmother secretly wiping her face as well, Bertha quickly left the room to pack Eugen's few belongings. It wasn't much—some clothing, pyjamas, a pair of good shoes, already a little small, and his beloved teddy bear.

Pastor Werthmann was already waiting for them, and together, they took the streetcar towards Dalldorf asylum. While the pastor visited his own little daughter, Elisabeth, Bertha, together with a friendly young nurse, settled Eugen in a playroom with other children. After showing Bertha Eugen's bed in a large communal bedroom, putting his things away and generally assuring Bertha that Eugen would be well taken care of, Bertha sought out her son. He was already intermingling with other children, playing a game led by an instructor, laughing and jumping up and down, never even looking at his mother. Bertha smiled sadly.

The ride back was quiet, and both Bertha and Pastor Werthmann were deep in their own thoughts. "I hope I did the right thing," Bertha mused in a low voice.

"Frau Hoffmann, I can assure you, this is the best for all of you," the pastor encouraged. "My little one is so lovingly cared for and happy, though she does not know me—if she ever even did. It is truly a Godsend that a place like Dalldorf exists."

Over the next few years, Bertha tried to visit Eugen once a month, marvelling at the care her son was receiving, and the joy he was experiencing, even though he didn't recognise her any more.

Eugen died in the winter of 1894 of pneumonia. He was just twelve years old, and sadly was missed by only a few. Once a month, Bertha visited the cemetery to lay flowers on his grave; once in a while, she saw Pastor Werthmann's wife at their daughter's grave. Elisabeth had died around the same time as Eugen, as many children had succumbed to pneumonia that winter.

Chapter Four

Just about the time when Eugen was admitted to Dalldorf, Emil's life was about to take a major turn. Having been recently promoted to the next grade, he had to attend another school. It was there that his musical talent—in particular, his perfect pitch and clear, strong singing voice—was discovered.

It was not long before his music teacher sought out Bertha and discussed what career plans she had in mind for Emil.

"Honestly, I haven't given it too much thought," Bertha confessed. "After school, he will be drafted into the military, although I am unsure how he will fare there. He is quite small, shy, and a bit of a dreamer; I am a little worried about him."

"Frau Hoffmann, your son has exceptional musical talents!" the teacher told her, excitedly. "He needs the opportunity to expand his talent, to play an instrument, to study music and vocals," he went on, full of praise. "In short, you should send him to one of the excellent boys' choir boarding schools, and if he is in one of these schools, he would be able to apply for military exemption." He sat back and waited for Bertha's reaction.

Bertha stared, mouth agape, at this man. "My Emil? Exceptional talents?" she said, incredulous. "Yes, I know he sings well, and he is part of the youth choir at church, but exceptional?" Bertha tried to wrap her head around this.

"But practically, how will he earn a living when the time comes?" she wondered out loud. "And first, how can I, a woman with a no-good husband of no fixed address even afford such a school?"

She shook her head slowly. "Please know I want the best for all my children, but I also know my station in life, and cannot afford to put lofty ideas in their heads, pretend that they can achieve all their dreams, only to be reminded where they come from.

"We are working class, Sir, although I do come from a little better background," Bertha continued her explanation. "I have three other children, one in Dalldorf and two younger ones who need to be educated. No, no, I appreciate your visit, your kind words about Emil, but I fear there's nothing I can do to further any talents he may have."

The teacher took a deep breath to address Bertha's concerns. "I understand your arguments, Frau Hoffmann, but believe me, there are plenty of ways to assist you and Emil. There are scholarships and specific bursaries for gifted students, as well as waived school fees in exceptional circumstances—circumstances I believe will fit the criteria in your case. We can help you with all these requirements. I have connections to the Thomanerchor in Leipzig, an excellent choir and school I highly recommend. So, you see, something can be done."

Bertha sat there in stunned disbelief. "The Thomanerchor?" she gasped, as she had heard of the prestigious school. "I don't know what to say!"

She rose suddenly and called loudly for her grandmother. "Oma, come quickly, please, I need your advice!"

The music teacher patiently explained his vision for Emil's future to an astonished Anna, while Bertha slowly made some calculations in her head.

"Are there any other expenses that are not covered, payments we have to come up with?" Anna asked.

"I have to be honest, there are indeed some small extra expenses, specifically for personal needs that come more into play as the boys get older," the teacher answered. "He would need some regular pocket money."

"We need to discuss this a little more," Bertha finally said, excited yet wary. "I am very grateful you took the time to come by. If there is any way that we can afford this for Emil... Well, it would be simply wonderful for my son. Can you please let me know how you do with your suggestions before I speak with Emil?"

"Absolutely Frau Hoffmann," the teacher nodded as he stood up to leave. "As soon as I have a clear picture, I will meet with you again."

After he took his leave, Bertha exhaled and looked at her grandmother. "I think we can manage this!"

"August will have to forward a start-up sum for Emil, and the support money will then go directly toward Emil's extra needs," Anna, also excited, pointed out to Bertha. "We have put it aside for him already—or did you spend it?"

"No, no, Oma," Bertha shook her head. "I've saved it; it's in a small box in my night table."

Satisfied, Anna hugged her granddaughter. "Our Emil—what an extraordinary opportunity for him! Just think, the Thomanerchor Boys Choir! I can't believe it—my prayers are being answered one by one!" Anna was beaming.

"He will have to move to Leipzig to the boarding school," Bertha reminded her grandmother.

"Better than the Army!" Anna pointed out. Bertha nodded in agreement.

About a week later, the music teacher informed Bertha that her son had been approved for admission to the boys' choir and boarding school. He was approved for a scholarship, which included not only the tuition, but also a clothing allowance.

When the children came home from school that day, they were startled to see their mother and great-grandmother dancing joyously through the apartment. Laughingly, they joined in, not knowing the reason, but nevertheless happy to be part of the fun.

"Why are you so happy?" they all asked.

"Emil," Bertha turned to her firstborn, flushed and smiling, "you have been accepted by the Thomanerchor in Leipzig!" Bertha happily hugged her eldest.

A wide-eyed Emil stared at his mother in surprise. "I have? Really? Oh Mama, I can't believe this!"

Karl-Heinz and Karoline sat down in bemused wonder, looking at their brother with a newfound awe.

"Emil, do you have to move to Leipzig now, or do we all get to go?" Karoline excitedly asked.

"No, Emil is going to Leipzig to the Thomanerchor boarding school, but will come home for holidays and summer vacations," Bertha explained to the children. "And we have to start packing you up very soon, as they are expecting you within the next two weeks!"

"First Eugen, and now Emil," Karl-Heinz grumbled. "I'll be the only man in the house with three women now."

"Ah, but not for long, young man" Bertha reminded him. "Right after your confirmation, you're heading off for a carpenter apprenticeship your father has arranged for you."

Karl-Heinz jumped up in excitement. "Now *that* is news I like to hear—away from stuffy Berlin, into the country, living with my father... Yes, I look forward to this!"

"He is so much like his father," Bertha thought, a bit worried. *"The only one of the children who's close to him. I just hope Karl's hard drinking and womanising do not rub off on his son."*

A few days later, Emil was sent off to Leipzig and a year later, Karl-Heinz to Stolp, where his father now worked.

Suddenly it became rather quiet in the apartment, with room to spare, and attention focused on Karoline and her future.

Chapter Five: 1896

In 1896, Karoline turned sixteen and would finish middle school. She was a quiet, studious girl with ambitions of becoming a medical doctor.

"Your dreams of becoming a doctor are very lofty, my dear" Oma Anna told Karoline one evening. It was a particularly cold winter, and the women huddled together in the kitchen, the warmest room in the house, to discuss Karoline's future. "It's too bad you haven't met an eligible young man of the fellows Emil keeps bringing around here for a taste of Berlin," she continued, chuckling.

"Omama, I am much too young to think about marriage!" Karoline protested, waving her off. "If I can't be a doctor, I will look to studying to be a nurse. Down the street is the *Krankenhaus Moabit* (hospital) and just a couple of years ago, they began training young women to become nurses. I will apply for a position there as soon as I have my final report card from school."

Bertha looked intently at her daughter. *"She so reminds me of me at that age."* Karoline was a lovely young woman, tall and slender with thick dark hair, rolled into a bun at the back of her neck. "So, you don't want to wait around for a husband?" Bertha teased.

"No, Mama," an earnest-looking Karoline shook her head. "I want to care for sick people, I want to bring some comfort to them, and I want to be independent, just like you."

"You will not find a husband staying at home," Oma Anna smiled, "so follow your heart and all other things will fall into place."

Bertha could not agree more. "Men have been nothing but trouble for me, maybe it's best to stay away from them." Then she added, "so if you chose nursing as your profession, I have no objections at all. By working at Moabit, at least you can stay at home and I still have my girl around."

Deep down, Bertha was worried about her elderly grandmother and what she would do in an empty apartment with everybody gone one day. *"I am still quite young,"* she pondered. *"Perhaps I should look for something to do outside the home."*

"Oma," Bertha turned to her grandmother. "What do you think of me looking for some type of acceptable employment, now that I have very little to do around the house? After all, I am only thirty-six. I'm far too young to be finished with life."

"Mama, that's a splendid idea!" Karoline interjected with a squeal, Anna nodding in agreement. "One of the largest department stores, Wertheim, is just about ready to open and they'll be looking for staff," Karoline continued. "It supposedly has eighty-three elevators and a glass-enclosed atrium. It serves a high-class clientele—that's perfect for you with your knowledge in merchandising and sales!" Karoline gushed. "I suspect we will never go shopping there..." her voice trailed off with yearning.

Bertha turned the conversation back to Karoline's prospective nursing career. "I shall think of your suggestion, my dear, but first, let's return to you and your future. I was under the impression that nursing is more male-oriented work, that very few women are choosing this type of profession. Or am I misinformed?"

"You are right in some ways, Mama," Karoline spoke thoughtfully. "The care of the sick has been left mostly to military personnel and nuns, but there is a great movement to make nursing a more attractive profession for women. It's been observed that women are better caregivers and have more patience with sick people.

As a matter of fact, within Europe, nursing is being brought to the forefront and into modern age. They are called deaconesses and are basically in charge of providing healthcare for other women in the area," Karoline continued with her facts. "A few years earlier, I would have had to go to a deaconess motherhouse somewhere near the Rhine River, but now the hospitals have taken over most of the training locally."

Almost breathless from excitement, Karoline sat back in her chair.

Bertha was impressed. "How do you know all that?"

"I spoke to the pastor about this and he gave me advice and encouragement," Karoline replied. "Eventually, I can do some work as a deaconess at our congregation."

Until now, Anna had quietly listened, nodding from time to time. Her face shone with pride at her great-granddaughter's aspirations. "Pastor Werthmann is a good man," she spoke up. "He has been a great support to us with Eugen, poor little soul. He understands people, doesn't have lofty sermons, and he..."

"All right, all right, Oma," Bertha waved her hand to shush her grandmother. "Yes, you're right, but I'd like to hear a little more from Karoline about all the practical matters." She turned to her daughter. "How much does this cost? Can we handle it?"

Karoline took a deep breath before answering quietly. "I wrote to father and requested some financial help. Living at home during my training will help keep costs down as well."

Bertha was a bit taken aback. "Did he reply?"

"Yes Mama, he did," Karoline nodded. "He promised to send some money."

Karoline had very little contact with her father, so this was even more astounding to Bertha and Anna. Bertha just shook her head. "I hope you will not be disappointed, Karoline. You know he is not that reliable. That said, I think we will have to manage."

"I have a little money tucked away; I no longer have much need for it, so it is yours if you'd like," Anna offered with a smile.

Karoline, touched by this kind gesture, hugged her great-grandmother. "Thank you, Omama," she whispered in her ear. "I will make you proud."

"I know you will, my child," Anna replied warmly. "And now, let us have some hot soup to warm us all up." Bertha rose to set the table while Karoline stared out the window, watching a couple of sparrows on a tree branch. "I would like to work with children like Eugen," she spoke to no one in particular. "Yes, that will be my goal."

CHAPTER SIX: 1899

THE STREETCAR STOPPED IN FRONT OF WERTHEIM DEPARTMENT STORE AT THE Leipziger Platz and Bertha, along with several other employees of Wertheim's, exited and made their way towards the staff entrance. Dressed in long black skirts, white blouses, and wide-brimmed hats, they all looked more like their clients then sales ladies.

After almost two years working in the men's clothing department, Bertha still marvelled at the expanse and beauty of this department store, one of the largest and finest in Berlin. Chandeliers hung from high ceilings, the merchandise was arranged in a pleasant manner, and the whole environment was one of affluence, attracting rich, famous, and high-society clientele. At times, Bertha felt almost intimidated by the gentlemen asking for her advice and guidance on their purchases.

Her estranged husband, Karl, had not come through with any financial support for his daughter's education, as Bertha had expected, and it was now up to her to ensure Karoline's future in nursing. At the same time, she truly enjoyed working for Wertheim's; it was far superior to factory work that so many single women had to slave at in unhealthy environments.

It was October 1899, and there seemed to be an excited buzz all around, everybody was awaiting the turn of the century. Huge celebrations, along with fireworks, were being planned and many people looked forward to New Year's Eve to enjoy these displays and participate in grand galas, concerts, or ballrooms. Bertha was expecting to spend time with her grandmother, watching the events from their balcony, and hoped that at least Karoline or Emil would come home for a visit. From Karl-Heinz she received a short note saying he finished his journeyman year, he was living and working in Switzerland, he had met a woman, and he had no intentions to return to Germany for his military service. Emil had fortunately avoided conscription due to his slight build and educational deferment. He was looking for a career in music in Berlin with the hope of returning permanently.

These thoughts circled through Bertha's head as she walked over to her workstation, greeting people here and there on her way. She began another workday, ensuring everything was in order—shirts, ties, suits, and hats hanging straight, gloves and scarves pleasantly arranged in the display cases, and so on.

This particular morning had been very busy, with hardly a break in between, when she noticed a man, leaning slightly against a pillar and watching her. Bertha briefly wondered who he was, but quickly forgot him as she continued with her duties.

It was nearly closing time when the same man approached her. "Pardon me, madam, but I could use your advice about a shirt I would like to purchase."

"Certainly, sir," Bertha smiled politely, barely looking at him. "Let me show you some of our latest collection."

While leading the way towards the men's shirts, the supervisor suddenly appeared and stopped Bertha's customer. "Oh, Herr Graf, what a rare pleasure to see you here! Can I help you with something?"

A somewhat irritated Bertha stepped back to yield to Frau Scholz. *"Well, at least I now know his name is Graf, but he's my customer,"* she thought wryly. *"And I wonder what makes him so special for the supervisor to greet him with her syrupy smile."*

"Ah, Frau Scholz, good to see you," the man nodded politely, "but I believe Frau..." he quickly glanced in Bertha's direction.

"Hoffmann," Bertha jumped in.

"Yes, yes, Frau Hoffmann is already in the process of helping me, so thank you."

Frau Scholz gave a small nod and retreated, yet watched curiously from a distance.

"Now, Frau Hoffmann," Herr Graf turned his attention to Bertha. "Shall we look at some shirts? I prefer white, with a stiff collar and button cuffs."

Bertha hung up a few shirts for him to examine. "I will need to take your arm length measurements, just in case our tailor needs to adjust them," she said, pulling out her tape measure.

The man took off his jacket and held out his arms. Carefully, Bertha noted the required size and held up a few shirts for him. He chose one and Bertha accompanied him to the cashier for payment and proper packaging. "Auf Wiedersehen, Frau Hoffmann" he smiled at Bertha, who, to her sudden dismay, felt herself blushing as she bid him farewell.

"What a nice and good-looking man," she thought while returning to her workstation under the watchful eye of Frau Scholz.

Returning home, she was met by a beaming Karoline. "I passed all the exams, Mama!" she said excitedly. "I'm now a fully approved deaconess and the hospital has hired me to stay on in the children's ward."

"Oh, Karo, how exciting and wonderful for you!" Bertha praised her youngest. "I'm so proud of all of you and what you have achieved. I feel so very blessed."

A smiling Anna came out of the kitchen. "I think that deserves a little celebration, don't you? I'm inviting you all to *Aschinger*!"

Cheerful, the three women bounded down the four flights of stairs, Anna holding on to the railing, somewhat supported by Bertha.

Taking the streetcar to Friedrichstrasse, they settled in for an affordable meal of thick pea soup with sausages and limitless buns—a simple but delicious meal that made *Aschinger* famous and, with their many outlets all over Berlin, a favourite dining spot for students and folks on a tight budget.

"Mama, look, there is Dr. Feldmann—I work with him," Karoline pointed to a group of young men deep in conversation. One of them briefly looked up, recognised Karoline, and nodded a greeting before returning to his conversation.

Bertha had noticed a slightly blushing Karo and took a closer look at the young man. He had curly dark hair, wore glasses, and seemed of average height, although rather slender. "Are all of these men doctors?" she wanted to know.

"Yes, I have worked with most of them in different areas, but I like Dr. Feldmann the best," Karoline responded.

Anna raised her eyebrows. "Do I detect a blossoming romance?" she teased her great-granddaughter.

Once again, Karoline blushed, while shaking her head. "No, no, I just like working with him," she assured Anna.

"Hmm, well, he looks like a nice young man."

"Oh, Omama, let's just eat and enjoy the evening!" Karoline protested.

"I agree." Bertha piped up. "I'll tell you two about my workday."

Well-fed and content, the three women made their little journey back home.

Several days later, Bertha once again noticed the man, whom she now knew as Herr Graf, wandering through the menswear department. He lingered in the shirts section, often glancing her way. Finally, he made his way towards her, holding a shirt in his hand.

"I would like to buy this one," he announced. "Can you please make sure the sleeves are long enough?"

Bertha nodded. "Certainly, sir, I am pleased to do that for you." She again escorted him to the cashier for payment.

"Thank you, Frau Hoffmann," he smiled at her while waiting for his shirt to be packed.

This went on for several weeks in a row, always the same routine. Herr Graf would come to the store, walk around a bit, wait for Bertha to be free to help him, make a few more comments about the weather and general topics, and purchase another shirt. Bertha enjoyed his company and comments, but was quite perplexed.

After he purchased, by Bertha's calculations, his tenth shirt in just three weeks, she blurted out, "You do know these shirts are washable and can be ironed?" As soon as she said it, she regretted it, as she knew that could affect her job. She quickly apologised to him, but he just stood there, laughing.

"I do appreciate your comments," he managed to say in between gales of laughter, "but I don't care about the shirts. I have dozens of them hanging in my closet." He slowed his laughter a bit before continuing. "However, I come here to get to know you a little better."

Bertha was stunned.

"I see a beautiful woman, graceful and well spoken, and I hope you will honour me by joining me in a walk through the *Tiergarten* (park) Sunday afternoon," he went on, with an almost shy smile.

Bertha, suddenly tongue-tied, nervously took a closer look at him; it wasn't hard to do, as he was very nice to look at. Tall; dark, slightly curly hair; kind, gray eyes; a gentle look on his face; with a well-trimmed moustache. He was well dressed in a three-piece suit, shined shoes, holding his hat in one hand. She noticed he wore no wedding band.

Bertha took a deep breath. "I am most flattered, Herr Graf," she almost whispered. "I don't know what to say, I—well, I... May I please think about it?"

"Of course," he replied. "I will wait at the main gate of the *Tiergarten* at three o'clock on Sunday. I sincerely hope to see you then." With a quick smile, he turned towards the exit, leaving behind not only the shirt, but also an astonished Bertha.

In an instant, Frau Scholz, came up behind her, clearly upset. "What is going on? Herr Graf left his shirt behind! Did you anger him?" she demanded.

"I noticed you in a discussion; we cannot allow this in our establishment. And there is to be no fraternisation between staff and clients!" She was talking herself in a rage.

Bertha listened for a while until Frau Scholz ran out of breath. "He simply decided to return later for the shirt, and merely spoke of an engagement he had to hurry off to" Bertha quickly explained to defuse her angry supervisor, and before Frau Scholz could say any more, she quickly went to hang up the rejected shirt and help another customer.

On that day, she was in a hurry to leave work to avoid running into Frau Scholz once more.

Sitting in the streetcar on her way home, Bertha recalled the comments from Herr Graf. *"I have no experience with a gentleman caller,"* she thought to herself with a smile. *"I've never had the opportunity to meet anybody whom I might like and enjoy talking with..."* She felt a rush of joy at the possibility and a warmth spread to her cheeks.

CHAPTER SEVEN

ARRIVING HOME, FULL OF EMOTIONS TO SHARE WITH HER GRANDMOTHER, Bertha was somewhat disappointed to see Emil and his friend, Anton, sipping coffee and conversing with Anna.

She put her feelings aside and put on a smile. "Good evening, boys," she greeted them, placing a kiss on Anna's cheek. "Any coffee left for me?" she asked while taking off her gloves, hat, and shoes. She grabbed herself a cup and sat down. "Ah, that's better," she sighed. "So, what brings you boys here today?"

"Mama, I've found a position as music teacher at the Stern'sche Konservatorium, which is a private music school for..."

"I know what the 'Stern' is, son," Bertha interrupted, "but that is a wonderful opportunity for you! I'm very happy for you."

Emil had been a good fit for the choir, travelling all over Europe. As his voice changed, he became a passable tenor, but later opted for a teaching career in music and ultimately returned to Berlin. "Anton and I are looking for a place to live somewhere in the Schoneberg district," Emil added, all the time peering closely at his mother. "Well, that will certainly help with expenses," Anna laughed. "What are you doing now, Anton?"

"I am a ballet dancer, and hoping to become the principal dancer one day," Anton answered proudly.

Both women looked at the young man they had known as Emil's friend for many years. He was taller than Emil, well built, and muscular. "You certainly are well-built for a dancer," Bertha told him. "I wish you much success; it's definitely a physically hard profession."

"I hear Karo is smitten with a young doctor," Emil quickly changed the subject.

"Is she now?" Bertha asked, curious. "What do you know that she has not told me?"

"Nothing, Mama...but I have seen them a few times together at *Aschinger* and they have 'that' look," Emil grinned.

"Oh, Anton, I feel bad for you," Bertha said, a bit teasing and a bit concerned. "I always thought you had an eye on her."

"Oh, that's not a problem, Frau Hoffmann," Anton replied quickly. "As much as I like Karo, she is more like a sister to me. I am very fond of somebody else," he said, blushing.

Before anybody could say another word, Emil jumped up. "We have to go Anton, remember? We must look at the apartment today!" With hugs and handshakes, the boys took their leave.

"Who is Anton is fond of?" Bertha wondered. "Maybe a petite ballerina?"

"I'm sure he will tell us one day," said Anna, who then looked directly at her granddaughter. "So, how was your day today?"

"Oma, you will never believe this, I cannot wait to tell you!" Bertha exclaimed, and excitedly reported the day's events to Anna.

"Oh, my dear, that's indeed astonishing news!" Anna gasped. "What do you know about this man? I really hope that you will find a partner. With the children well on their way into life and me, well, God-willing, just a few more years left, I hate to see you all alone."

"Oma, please don't speak like this," Bertha pleaded. "You still have many years ahead of you!" Bertha suddenly became dismayed at the thought of losing her Oma.

"I will turn eighty in just a few months," she reminded her granddaughter, "but let's talk about you! Will you go on Sunday?"

"Do you think I should go?" asked Bertha. "After all, I don't know this man."

"Nobody knows anybody until they meet and talk, and the *Tiergarten* is a safe and respectable place for that," Anna explained. "If you are attracted to that man, I think you should go; you can always walk away—nothing is lost."

Bertha nodded. "I do feel some excitement, Oma," she admitted. "But I don't know how to talk to him, nor what to say. I really do not know how to speak to men!"

"Trust your instincts, and let your soul guide you," Anna advised. "He must have found something appealing about you or he would not have asked. Simply be yourself, and then you never have to remember who you had pretended to be later," Anna reassured her with a chuckle.

"Now I can hardly wait for Sunday!" Bertha exclaimed, rising to get ready to retire for the night.

Never was a sermon longer and a church service never-ending than on this early December Sunday in 1899. At least the weather co-operated; it was a beautifully sunny day with just the right amount of light dusting of snow to feel Christmas approaching. The air was crisp and cold.

Slightly nervous, Bertha exited the streetcar and sauntered towards the *Tiergarten*.

She saw him before he saw her. *"He looks very handsome with his fur-lined coat, gloves, and hat,"* Bertha thought.

He suddenly turned, and their eyes met. A big smile lit up his face as he rushed to her. "Frau Hoffmann! Oh, I am so delighted you came, I am half-frozen already," Herr Graf grinned, quickly greeting her with a kiss on her hand.

"It is just now three o'clock. I am right on time!" Bertha felt foolish for having to point that out. *"Please, can't I have a more brilliant comeback?"* she silently chided herself.

"I know, but I was quite early, just to make sure I didn't miss you," said Herr Graf, pulling her arm through his. Together they walked into the large park, enjoying the beauty of this early winter day. Not much was said during the stroll, as they occasionally pointed out a particularly pretty plant or watched the squirrels busily gathering walnuts to store for winter.

The sun started to fade, and the coldness became more noticeable when he suggested they stop at a café nearby and warm up with a coffee and piece of torte. As he helped her out of her coat and pulled an upholstered chair out for her, they both settled down to afternoon coffee, lavishly served on good china and silverware.

In one corner, a piano player entertained the guests with soft music. The large windows overlooked the park setting of the *Tiergarten*, now appearing jewel encrusted in the setting sun. It was a truly magical moment for Bertha. Leaning back in her chair, she relaxed in the warm and cosy atmosphere.

Herr Graf poured her coffee before his own and took pleasure in watching her enjoy her piece of torte, in an almost sensual manner. He had fallen in love!

"I would have brought you flowers, but I was afraid they would not last in this cold weather" he admitted, almost shyly.

"Thank you, that is so thoughtful," Bertha replied, also shyly and blushing slightly, "but you are right; they would have died."

Neither one knew how to continue the conversation, and they sat mostly looking at each other off and on.

Finally, he put down his serviette. "Would it be too forward of me if I asked your Christian name, Frau Hoffmann?"

"Oh, no, of course not, it's Bertha," she replied with a smile. "And how may I address you, then?"

She noticed a slight hesitation in his voice, a small tap with his spoon before answering "Leopold. I will be very pleased if you call me Leopold."

"Leopold Graf," Bertha repeated. "That sounds nice. May I know what kind of work you do?" Bertha had noticed by his hands that he was not a labourer; further, his manners and clothing pointed to upper class.

Once again, he hesitated, this time for a longer period. "I am in a managerial position of an agricultural enterprise based in East Prussia."

Bertha was unsure what that meant, and what exactly he might do there, but felt silly asking, so she just nodded. "Where in East Prussia? I was born there; my parents owned a factory for Christmas decorations, mainly nutcrackers and blown glass ornaments." This obviously caught Leopold's interest. "So, then, why are you living and working in Berlin?" he asked curiously.

"It's a rather sad story," Bertha admitted, and gave a brief account of her early life, leaving out Karl and her children for the moment. *"I need to know more about him before going any further. He seems to be fairly hesitant about himself, so be cautious,"* she reminded herself while talking.

At one point during her account, he put his hand on hers in a gesture of comfort. She enjoyed the feel of his touch.

Bertha suddenly realised the time. "It's getting dark out. I should be thinking of going back home. It was a delightful afternoon! Thank you, Herr—I mean, Leopold."

Immediately Leopold jumped up, pulled back her chair, and helped her into her coat. "Of course, I will escort you home," he offered, as they left to catch the streetcar.

Before bidding her good night, he once again kissed her hand. "It was a wonderful afternoon, Bertha. May I call on you again?"

Once Bertha consented, he quickly asked if she would like to accompany him to a "Sylvester Ball," or New Year's Eve gala. Bertha was torn on what to say. On the one hand, she would have loved to have gone with him and have some fun—something she sorely missed in her life. On the other hand, she did not feel it was fair to leave her grandmother all alone on that day, especially since her children would most likely be out with friends to celebrate.

Leopold reluctantly accepted Bertha's polite decline and decision to stay with her grandmother. Wishing him a "Merry Christmas and a Happy 1900," she entered the apartment building.

"I will see you before the holidays," he promised before slowly walking away.

Bertha almost ran all the way up the stairs, all four floors. *"Before the holidays, before the holidays..."* she kept humming to herself.

She was still humming when she entered the apartment.

"I can see you had a memorable afternoon," her grandmother greeted her with a smile.

"Oh Oma, it was so wonderful!" Bertha gushed like a younger woman. "His name is Leopold, and he wants to see me again. He invited me to a Sylvester Ball, but I told him no, I'd rather spend New Year's Eve with you!"

Anna gave her a big hug. "Oh, *Schatz*, you should have accepted, you need more fun!"

"No, Oma," Bertha shook her head, "I need to be with you. And anyway, it's better we get to know each other a little more."

The two women retired to some tea and *stollen*, and then lit the second candle on their Advent wreath. Two more Sundays before Christmas. Bertha opened a book of Christmas stories and read them aloud to her grandmother; it had been a most satisfying day.

CHAPTER EIGHT

MID-WEEK, KAROLINE SUGGESTED THAT THEY GO TO THE *CHRISTKINDLMARKT* (Christmas market). "We have not been for a few years now, and I would really like to go. How about it, Mama and Omama? Maybe I can talk Emil into it, as well," she added eagerly.

"Emil is not in town this week," Anna informed her. "He has some musical performance for Christmas in Leipzig. And I am too old to wander around in the cold with all the crowds. But thank you for asking, Karo, that was very thoughtful of you."

"Well, Mama," Karoline turned to Bertha. "What do you think, you and me?"

"That's a wonderful idea, Karo," Bertha smiled. "I would absolutely love to spend some time with you. And you are right, we have not gone for a few years now; it will be enjoyable

The following Sunday, the two of them set off for the *Christkindlmarkt*.

Arkonastrasse had been transformed into the *Christkindlmarkt*, a shantytown of wooden stalls filled with Christmas toys and sweets—a children's paradise. The pair made their way through the children clamouring around the displays of rocking horses, miniature trains, marionettes, dolls, Noah's ark, wooden swords, gilded bugles, and drums as well as nutcrackers. Other stalls beckoned with dried fruits, oranges threaded on strings, candies, fruitcakes, gingerbread, and mulled wine. The sweet aroma of caramelised almonds filled the air. Children choirs sang carols on one side while brass bands competed on the other side.

The sounds and smells undeniably heralded the coming of Christmas.

Bertha and Karoline happily trotted through the snow, taking in the sights and sounds, pulling their scarves tighter around them. It was a cold day for sure.

"Do you remember when we were small and all of us came to the *Markt*"? Karoline asked her mother.

"Of course!" Bertha smiled. "You all had red cheeks and shiny eyes..."

"...and Omama held Eugen's hand real tight so he would not get lost..."

"...and Karl-Heinz would try to snitch a candy..."

"...and Emil—oh, we could never get him away from the music!"

The spirited nostalgic conversation continued.

"I think we should treat ourselves to mulled wine to warm up—what do you think?" Bertha suggested.

"Great idea, Mama" Karoline agreed, and together they sat in the wind-sheltered hut to sip the hot wine.

"Mama, I miss Eugen, he was such a sweet boy," Karo reflected out of the blue. "Do you have any idea why he was born that way?"

That awful, fateful day with Karl came rushing back to Bertha's memory. She subconsciously put a hand to her stomach and slowly shook her head, twisting her glass in her hand. "No, *mein Schatz*," she said quietly to her daughter. "I have wondered about that many times. I have tried to protect him..." her voice trailed off.

"What do you mean by that?" Karo asked, suddenly curious.

Bertha, somewhat mellowed by the wine, was unsure how to answer that. *"She is old enough to know how her father truly treated me."*

Bertha took a deep breath. "Karo, I truly cannot say if this affected Eugen, but, when I told your father I was expecting again—Eugen—he became outraged. He yelled that he couldn't afford all these children I was producing and started to throw things at me."

Karoline stared, mouth agape, at her mother, unable to say a word.

"When I tried to calm him down," Bertha continued, "he tripped me, threw me to the floor, and kicked me all over. I held my hands around my abdomen for protection, but some of the blows landed there anyway. God forgive me, but I hoped I would miscarry. I was bruised, bloodied, and had wet myself."

Tears trickled down Bertha's face as she recounted this to her daughter. "Some neighbours finally came running and pulled him off me. The men yanked him outside and pummelled him into submission. The ladies helped me clean up." Bertha paused to still her voice. "Oh, my dear, it was simply awful."

Karoline quickly drained her wine and ordered another round. She put her arms around her crying mother. "I had no idea, Mama," she tried to console

Bertha. "Please don't cry anymore. It wasn't your fault—Father is a drunk. Please, please, Mama, stop crying. I love you, Mama."

The words just tumbled out of a shocked and dumbstruck Karoline, who wanted so badly to make things better.

Drying her tears, Bertha swallowed hard and took another sip of wine. "It was then and there I decided to leave him, but I had all of you to think of, and with no money and no idea of where to go, I spoke to our pastor.

"He was of no help," Bertha continued, with a hint of bitterness in her voice. "He just told me to stay with my husband. He talked with your father, telling him to keep his beatings to just light slaps, as a wife has to be disciplined once in a while—"

"He said what?!" Karo interrupted, furious. "A wife needs to be disciplined? He didn't really say that, did he?"

"Yes, he did!" Bertha nodded, now furious herself. "I walked out and never went back. I managed to be ill every Sunday for the next few weeks. When I received a letter from your Omama, telling me that her sister had died, and she was now all alone in the apartment, it felt like a sign from heaven.

"I got up enough nerve to speak to Count Behrendorff's wife, a very lovely and compassionate woman, who managed to get her husband to send Karl to a horse auction a few days away. She gave me money for rail tickets for all of us and had Otto, the carriage driver, take us all to the station where we made the long journey to Berlin. Not one of you ever asked about your father. I must say, your Omama was quite startled and astonished when we all suddenly appeared at her door."

Bertha's anger dissipated as she chuckled lightly at the memory. "She never hesitated to give us a home. She let her live-in servant girl go to make room for all of us. She was by my side when Eugen was born. She comforted me and took care of all of you, particularly Eugen. And that, *mein Schatz*, is why I left your father."

"Oh, my dear Mama, and Omama, of course, I can hardly take this all in!" said Karoline, who was still clearly astonished. "I have wondered and asked Omama why you are separated, but she said it was for you to tell me in time. I feel so badly for you, so much suffering."

"Please, please do not worry about the past!" Bertha beseeched her daughter. "One cannot change it. All of you have become fine adults, well educated, and our sweet Eugen is in a much better place now. I am happy and content with my life."

"Are you sorry you had Eugen?" Karoline asked quietly.

"Absolutely not," Bertha shook her head. "He was a ray of sunshine in our lives; no matter what happened, he was always happy. It was the physical care we no longer were able to provide properly for him and it would have been impossible had he grown into a man."

"Thank you, Mama. Thank you for telling me." Karoline hugged her mother again. "And, if we don't move on soon, my feet will freeze to the ground!" she added with a grin.

After their conversation, it was difficult to re-immerse themselves into the hustle and bustle around them, and they decided to look for a *Konditerei* (bakery) to warm up with a coffee and a piece of torte.

CHAPTER NINE

A FEW DAYS BEFORE CHRISTMAS, BERTHA RECEIVED A LETTER FROM HER SON, postmarked from Switzerland.

"What a nice surprise to hear from Karl-Heinz!" Bertha happily waved the letter at her grandmother.

"I am eager to know how he is making out and when he will be back," Anna remarked while waiting for Bertha to tear the envelope open and read it out loud.

Dear Mama, Omama, Emil, and Karoline. I am sending you my best Christmas wishes and only good things for 1900. Imagine, 1900—a whole new century, I wonder what it will bring us.

"I wonder, too," Anna interrupted.

"Shh, let's finish reading," Bertha said.

I am in Switzerland, in Geneva. My journeyman year is over, and I should return to Germany, but I will not. I have no interest to start my mandatory military service there. Anyway, I like it here and will make my home here. I have found a great workplace here as a cabinetmaker in a smaller factory. The owner took a real liking to me and I can make my 'Master Carpenter' here, which will allow me to run my own carpentry shop. The owner has offered me to eventually buy the factory from him. I cannot ask for a better life.

Oh, yes, one other thing—I am engaged to be married! I met Theresa at a local dance. Her father owns the local bakery and she is the only child. So, I have found the pot of gold at the end of the rainbow. And Mama, I'm sorry you can't come to the wedding, as you soon will be a grandmother and that is why we will get married in early January 1900. We're waiting for Theresa to get written permission from her parents, as she is only eighteen, and for a date at City Hall.

So, this is all the news from me. Hope you are all well. I will let you know when the baby is born. Merry Christmas and Happy New Year!

Your loving son, grandson, brother,
Karl-Heinrich Hoffmann.

Bertha had to take a deep breath to digest all this news.

"Just like our Karl-Heinz," Anna chuckled. "He is the one who can fall into cow dung and come up smelling roses. He has set himself up very nicely, good for him."

Bertha was still trying to get a handle on the idea of becoming a grandmother. "Oma, I am too young to be a grandmother!" she lamented, secretly wondering how that might sit with Leopold.

Anna, still chuckling, pointed out that Bertha had married very young herself, with a baby on the way, and could therefore expect to be a young grandmother. "But with them being in Switzerland, maybe you don't need to tell anyone," she suggested.

"*Ach*, Oma, I am very happy for him, as he never seemed to quite fit into our little family here. It is good he left to seek his fortune," Bertha mused. "I am even happier he wrote us a letter! It's a wonderful Christmas gift, and a new life in a new year and new century...such blessings."

Christmas Eve brought the rest of the family together. Emil and Karoline lugged a tree up the stairs, leaving behind pine needles all along the way. Laughing and teasing each other, they hung ornaments, clipped on candles, and put up the nativity creche. In the meantime, Oma and Bertha were in the kitchen putting the finishing touches on the *stollen*, rolling marzipan into balls and dusting them with cacao powder. Potatoes were peeled and ready to be made into salad for the traditional Christmas Eve dinner—potato salad and wieners.

"Mama, where would you like the nutcrackers?" Emil called out, and together they gently unwrapped the precious collection saved from Bertha's paternal grandparents, singing carols all the while. Bertha was glad the store closed at noon so that she could come home early and enjoy the happy banter of her children. *"Who knows how much longer we will all be together again at Christmas Eve,"* she wondered. *"I miss Karl-Heinz—and, of course, Eugen."*

Still absorbed in her reflections, she was startled when the doorbell rang. Emil was the first to answer. "Flowers for Frau Hoffmann," he triumphantly waved a large bouquet of flowers wrapped in tissue paper over his head. "I wonder who sends my mother flowers?" he teased her while handing them over with an exaggerated bow.

"Oh, Emil!" A blushing Bertha snatched the flowers and opened the attached card, surrounded by her very curious family.

"Wishing you a very blessed Christmas and a most exciting and wonderful New Year," she read out loud. "I will call on you when I return after the holidays. Affably yours, Leopold G."

"Oh, Mama, now who is Leopold?" Karo asked dramatically with a wink and raised eyebrows while Emil clapped his hands in glee.

"Mama has a suitor, Mama has a suitor!" he sang.

"Emil, please!" Karo shushed her brother. "Let's hear from Mama who this mysterious Leopold is."

Bertha didn't want to reveal too much. "He is a very nice man with whom I had coffee recently," she said quickly. "Now, let me finish the *stollen*." Bertha retreated to the kitchen, from where she could hear her children quizzing Oma.

She smiled to herself. *"What a nice surprise, Leopold!"* while humming "Joy to the World" to herself.

In the meantime, Karo dug out a vase, big enough to hold the flowers, and the gentle scent of roses mixed with the overall fragrance of baking, pine needles, and candles seemed to make everybody a little giddy.

After dinner, small gifts were exchanged. Newly knitted socks and mittens tried on, books almost reverently examined, and sweets nibbled on. Contented, the family lazily shared stories and events.

"Mama, don't be upset, but I have to leave soon," Karoline announced later. "I have the midnight shift today. And I will not be around for New Year's Eve either. Dr. Feldmann—Julius—has invited me for a gala event," she added as almost an afterthought.

"Julius?" asked Bertha with a raised eyebrow. "You are on first-name basis already?" Bertha was interested, watching her daughter blushing furiously.

"Well, we have been seeing each other for a while now..." Karo stammered.

"Did you kiss?" Emil interrupted with a sly grin.

"Oh, Emil, what a question!" Anna scolded him. "It's none of your business!"

"Yes Omama, but I still want—"

"No, Emil," Karoline decided to answer her brother. "At least not yet," she added shyly.

Now everybody laughed good-naturedly.

"My dear Karo," Bertha hugged her daughter. "Of course you can spend *Sylvester* with your friend, and I hope you have a wonderful time. Tell me all about it when I see you again!"

"Only if you tell me about Leopold!" Karo quickly shot back, grabbing her coat and laughingly hurrying off to work.

Now it was Emil's turn to apologise. "I am sorry Mama, but I have to excuse myself as well for New Year's. I will be going out to celebrate with friends," Emil explained apologetically with a smile.

"So, have you found a nice girl yet?" Anna prodded a little.

"No Omama, I am not ready for that yet!" Emil quickly shook his head "I am having far too much fun at the moment. A girl wants lots of attention—no, I don't need that in my life."

"Well, you are still quite young," Bertha admitted. "You are wise not to rush anything until you are well settled in your profession. Why don't you stay overnight and come to church with us in the morning?" she offered.

"I can do that, Mama. That would be nice," Emil agreed, and with a big yawn, signalled it was bedtime.

New Year's Eve came quickly, and both Bertha and Anna wondered what the new century had in store for them.

"The year 1900. Just think about that, Oma! A lot has happened in the past number of years. I feel like I have lived one hundred years myself already!" Bertha laughingly reflected.

"I invited my friend Hertha to join us this evening; I hope you have no objections," Bertha continued.

"Of course not, my dear!" said Anna. "I'm not even sure if I can stay up that long." Anna was feeling tired already.

"But you must! We have to watch the fireworks from the balcony, drink mulled wine, and pour lead to guess what the future year has in store for us!" Bertha exclaimed excitedly.

Pouring lead, or *Bleigiessen*, was an ancient and fun tradition for families to try to divine their fortune in the new year. A small bit of tin or lead was melted and then dropped in cold water. The design created by the metal was examined to determine the future. For instance, if a ball was formed, it meant good fortune rolled your way; the shape of a ship could mean a trip was forthcoming, but a cross could mean death. When the children were small, they had a lot of fun guessing what each shape represented and making up wild stories for the next year.

Around midnight, three women gathered on the balcony on Turmstrasse, wrapped in warm scarves and with a glass of mulled wine. They were enthralled with the fireworks, the ringing of all church bells and the throngs of people parading up and down the street wishing each other a "Happy New Year." Once back inside, they indulged in *Berliner Pfannkuchen* (a type of donut), a rare and special treat only baked for *Sylvester*, and sipping on spiced eggnog.

A lot of laughter and amusing banter accompanied the lead pouring, with each trying to outguess the other what the future year would bring. The bucket filled with water hissed and sizzled as the hot lead poured from a spoon hit the water.

"Mine looks like an angel," Hertha announced, pondering the meaning.

"More like a butterfly," Anna added, while holding something akin to a star in her hand.

"Yours looks like a *Pfannkuchen* with a hole in the middle!" Hertha kidded Bertha.

"...Or a ring," Anna said quietly.

"No, no, Oma, it's definitely not a ring!" Bertha firmly shook her head.

"Are you seeing a gentleman?" Hertha was intrigued. "Tell me more."

"Oh, stop it, you two! I have no plans to—"

"But you received a lovely bouquet of flowers from a gentleman!" Anna interrupted her slightly blushing granddaughter.

"Now I *really* need to hear more!" Hertha eagerly cut in. "Who is that man and where did you meet him?"

"Truly, there is nothing to tell, so please, no more questions!" Bertha decided to end this conversation quickly.

In her pocket, she carefully caressed a ticket for the traditional New Year's Day production of the operetta "Die Fledermaus" at the Staatsoper (State Opera). The ticket had arrived via a courier at her work the previous day, and she had not yet had time to tell her grandmother. Of course, she knew it could only have been Leopold, and she began to wonder what profession he had to afford such expensive treats. Even more, she wondered what she could wear to such an occasion.

"It's time for me to say goodnight—or perhaps good morning is more appropriate," Anna rose to go to bed. "But you two can stay up if you like, and Hertha, feel free to stay overnight; there is enough room."

But by 4 a.m., Hertha decided she would go home, just two streets away, and Bertha fell into bed, exhausted but intrigued about what 1900 had in store for her.

Chapter Ten

January 1, 1900 dawned, a dry and cold day. Somewhat bleary-eyed, Bertha and her grandmother sat down to breakfast, both yearning for a strong cup of coffee.

"I am not doing a thing today!" Anna declared. "I feel tired, almost achy. I will surely lie down again later. What might you be up to today?" she asked Bertha.

"Do you still have that elegant black dress from your sister?" Bertha asked.

"Pardon? What do you want that dress for today?" Anna was surprised. "And yes, it is still hanging in the closet, along with her fur stole. And yes, you may have it, but can you share with me what it's for?" Anna was clearly intrigued.

Bertha pushed her opera ticket across the table. "For that," she smiled.

Raising her eyebrows, Anna looked at the ticket and then at her granddaughter, then back again, remaining silent for a while.

"Bertha, my dear," she finally said. "This is a very expensive gesture! What do you know about this man? He seems to be well off. He is also rather persistent. I think you need to find out more about him. I know—" she brushed off Bertha before she could say anything. "I know you are a mature young woman, but you can easily be taken advantage of, and I can't bear to see you hurt again.

"I also do not know if you fit into his world, so please hold on to your heart and be vigilant. But," she added with a mischievous grin, "I do think you should go! One does not decline such a wonderful opportunity to see 'Die Fledermaus'—I hear all of Vienna is intoxicated with Johann Strauss and his music."

"I know, Oma, I had similar thoughts," Bertha admitted. "I hope he did not spend his month's wages on these tickets. There really is no need to be so extravagant to impress me. And you are right; he is moving a little too fast for me."

Bertha paused for a moment. "I think after the theatre, and if we go for a coffee, I will ask him a few things and hope he is forthcoming."

"Yes, do that dear, and I hope you have a wonderfully enchanting afternoon," Anna smiled gently. "Go try on the dress; I think it will fit you well. I also have a pearl necklace you may borrow."

Bertha rose, gave her grandmother a kiss, and proceeded to clear off the breakfast dishes, as well as the remnants of the prior evening. For a long time, she held the lead shape in her hand, thinking that it indeed looked a little bit like a ring.

A horse-drawn cab took Bertha to the opera house. She had decided to splurge on a cab rather than her usual streetcar. It was too cold to walk without a warm cloak and in her dress shoes—shoes she had last worn to her children's confirmation. Snuggled under the blanket that the carriage driver draped around her, she enjoyed the sights and sounds of a bustling holiday afternoon in Berlin. *"Such a rare treat with an even better treat yet to come,"* she thought to herself, leaning back in joyful anticipation.

The opera house was an imposing building, square with large columns in the front and stairways on both sides leading to the front entrance. Bertha had seen it from the outside many times but had never been inside. Emil had told her a few times how impressive the concert hall was and now she could experience it herself. She almost skipped up the stairs but decided to hold back and appear more sophisticated.

Inside the large foyer, throngs of people mingled about, smiling, talking, shouting greetings to acquaintances, sipping champagne from fluted glasses. Ladies held long cigarette holders and men puffed on cigars. The air was filled with happy sounds, heady perfumes, and cheerful laughter. Bertha tried to take all of this in; it was so new and unfamiliar, yet wonderful. A waiter pressed a champagne glass into her hand and a well-dressed gentleman brushed a kiss on her gloved hand. "Madam," he said quietly, then was gone in an instant.

Suddenly, she saw him. Leopold was leaning against a post as he watched her. She smiled at him and he returned the smile, taking her breath away a little. Slowly he made his way through the crowds towards her.

"He looks so handsome in his morning frock," Bertha marvelled, feeling as if she were dreaming.

On his way over, she noticed that quite a few people were greeting him by name as he walked over to her.

"Happy New Year, Herr Graf," she heard them say.

"Herr Graf, glad to see you!"

"Good to have you back in Berlin."

"How are the Hinterlands?"

With a huge smile, he took both her hands, held them longer than what was considered proper, peeled back her gloves, and kissed both her hands. "You look beautiful," he whispered. Bertha blushed furiously, particularly since she noted a lot of curious looks from other patrons, whispering "You are certainly well known here," and she immediately felt foolish.

Bertha had taken special care with her appearance, in particular her hair. Normally she had it rolled into a rather severe bun at the back of her neck, but for this occasion she let her thick, chestnut brown hair fall in soft curls around her face and down her back. Even after all her pregnancies and struggles, she did not have a single gray hair, and she could easily pass for someone ten years younger.

Leopold gently took her by her elbow. "Let's find our seats before the rush is on." He ushered her into the concert hall. Bertha stood still and took in the gorgeous sight, the huge sparkling chandelier, the stage, the orchestra pit, the plush seats, and the multi levels of balconies and separate boxes for royalties. *"What a splendid sight,"* she thought, mesmerised.

Leopold was swept up in her sheer pleasure without any false pretense. Slowly, people began to make their way and take their seats. A hush filled the auditorium when the first strains of the overture to "Die Fledermaus" began. Bertha settled back into her seat and let the music take over. The music, the atmosphere, and the handsome man next to her filled her soul to nearly bursting, and she felt tears rolling down her cheek. A concerned Leopold handed her a snow-white handkerchief, "Tears of joy," she whispered assuredly, and lost herself once again in the music and actions on stage of this lively and fun-filled operetta.

After the performance, Leopold and an exhilarated Bertha made their way to the exit. Bertha, humming one of the tunes, was completely enthralled with the music. They walked into a dark and cold wintery late afternoon, all the while Leopold doffing his hat to somebody, acknowledging their greetings. Bertha was rather puzzled by his popularity, but decided against asking any questions at this time; she was too caught up in the enchantment of the music.

Eventually, Leopold steered her to a small coffeehouse in one of the side streets. "I think we need a little libation now," he suggested with a smile.

Bertha nodded eagerly; she was in no hurry to let go of this day just yet.

Once seated in a cosy little corner, she turned to thank him. "What a lovely afternoon! Thank you so much, Leopold."

"I very much enjoyed it myself," he replied. They were interrupted by the waiter bringing their order of coffee with whipped cream for her and a cognac for him.

"Can I ask you something?" Bertha wondered after they took their first sips.

"Of course," Leopold nodded.

"Do you work in the theatre, or *Opernhaus*?" (opera house)

Surprised, he looked up from his drink. "No, no, why do you think that?"

"Well," Bertha paused, unsure how to proceed. "It just seems so many people know you and greeted you 'Herr Graf,'" she teased.

"Hmm, yes, that is true," Leopold admitted. "One makes a lot of acquaintances through one's business."

"And what kind of business may that be?" Bertha was truly intrigued.

But Leopold wanted to shift the focus. "Can we talk a little about you now?" he asked.

"But I asked you first," Bertha protested slightly, showing her stubborn side.

Leopold, twisting his now-empty glass in his hands, nodded slowly and ordered another drink. Bertha watched him with great curiosity *"I wonder what he will tell me now,"* she mused. *"Something is not quite right here, and I will be extremely disappointed if he tries to sweet-talk me. It will not fit his gentleman image. But perhaps I only see what I want to see..."*

Leopold took a deep breath, and then another sip of his cognac. "First, I must say that I am deeply attracted to you and want to ask your permission to call on you—no, don't say anything just yet," he held up his hand to stop her from responding. "I need to tell you that my name is not Graf."

"I knew it—he is a fake; it was too good to be true!" Bertha suddenly felt a great wave of disappointment wash over her as she slowly stirred her coffee, over and over again. "So, who are you then?" she finally ventured.

"I am Graf Leopold Friederich von Ullmannshausen-Hohenstein," he answered, searching her face for a reaction. "I own a 2,000-hectare hereditary estate in the Stolp area."

Bertha suddenly burst out laughing in amusement. "*Ach*, Leopold, you are too funny!" she smiled with a twinkle in her eye. "I am actually the Empress of Austria, here incognito, so don't tell anybody," she winked, still full of laughter. Clearly Leopold had expected a different reaction, but he nonetheless joined her in hearty laughter.

"Now that we have established our identities, can you please tell me who you really are?" Bertha was still chuckling.

From across the table, Leopold reached for Bertha's hand. "Look at me," he pleaded. "I am telling you the truth."

Bertha waited for more, but then looked into his eyes. *"He really is serious!"* A suddenly solemn Bertha contemplated what she had just heard.

"I...I don't know... Truly, I am more than surprised," she stammered, much to her own disdain. *"Pull yourself together!"* she chided herself, and with as much dignity as she could offer, she rose, and Leopold immediately jumped to his feet.

"I am going now," she told him firmly, standing upright and confident. "I am deeply disappointed. Surely you have a wife and children back home, and I will not be some plaything for you in Berlin!" She was near tears, stumbling out as fast as she could.

"Wait, wait, please—it is not like that at all!" Leopold called after her as he grabbed her by the arm firmly yet gently. "Please, Bertha, let me explain everything to you. And as to the married part, well, you have not told me of your status either.

"Come, sit down again and let us talk again," he begged. "Don't run away. I would only have to run after you," he finished with a small grin.

"He is right. I have not told him about Karl and the children, either. So why not listen to him and see where it takes us?"

Bertha silently assented and sat back down in the chair he had pulled out for her. With a deep sigh of relief, Leopold sat down again as well. They sat quietly, looking at each other for a long time, feeling a surge of magnetism they could not escape.

"Is this what is called 'love at first sight'?" Bertha wondered while looking at his handsome face and genuine expression of care. She almost sighed out loud. *"Oh, dear God, what am I getting myself into here?"*

Slowly, hesitantly, she began to tell him about her parents, her uncle's assault, the reason she had to marry, Karl, her children, particularly Eugen, and why she had to leave her husband—and that yes, he was still her husband in the eyes of the law.

"I couldn't divorce him legally," Bertha told Leopold, feeling shame. *"What can he think of me?"* she thought, worried. "Karl would have had the children, and it is unimaginable what would have happened to them in that case. He has never asked for a divorce and by now it does not matter anymore."

Bertha paused for a minute, before adding, "Women who leave their husbands are never awarded custody of their children," she said bitterly. "No matter how badly the men treated them and the children."

She spoke quickly, trying to get it all out and behind her as fast as she could, in between sipping on her now-cold coffee. All the while, Leopold held her hand, listening silently with thinly veiled anger at the people who did this to her.

He paused before speaking. "Bertha, I can see that this is draining you, and it is also getting late. I will take you home now, and we will find a quieter place to talk in the next few days. Will you agree to that?"

"What is a quieter place?" Bertha asked suspiciously.

"An absolutely honourable place, please, Bertha, I will never put you in a questionable position!" Leopold replied, slightly indignantly. "The most reputable restaurants have private dining rooms, just for two, where we can speak freely and undisturbed."

Bertha's fears were assuaged. "I will give it serious thought," she promised.

"Of course, I will meet him! I want to hear his story, and I think I am falling in love—or whatever this thing is called." She felt the tingle of anticipation run down her back while he hailed a motorised taxi cab, one of the first in Berlin, to take her home.

CHAPTER ELEVEN

By the time Bertha got upstairs, she was shivering without a warm cloak and looking forward to a warm and quiet evening. Anna had just boiled water for a cup of peppermint tea along with a piece of *stollen* and Bertha gladly joined her.

"Now, tell me all about it, did you have a good day?" she asked her granddaughter.

"Oh, Oma, it was absolutely splendid!" Bertha gushed. "The music—it was so wonderfully lighthearted, the atmosphere, the well-dressed people, and most of all, Leopold!" She paused for a moment. "You will never believe who he said he is, Oma—even I still have my doubts."

Bertha confided everything to her grandmother what Leopold had told her. Anna listened intently, shaking her head every so often.

"I don't know, my dear," she said. "This sounds a little peculiar to me. A man in his supposed position? What could he be looking for? Is he at least free to call on you?"

"Might I remind you that I am not actually free?" Bertha interjected.

"True enough, but Karl has no more hold on you, and even though a divorce is rather distasteful, not to mention what the church will say, at least you can be free in rather short time," Anna said. "So, what about him? Is he married?" Anna was pushing for an answer.

Shrugging her shoulders, Bertha had to admit she did not know; however, she assumed he was. "He wants to explain it all to me—he gave his word," she promised Anna, her voice trailing off, thinking about how that sounded once spoken out loud.

"If your friend Hertha were to tell you such a story, what would you say to her?" Anna pointed out.

"What a question!" Bertha retorted. "I would tell her to run the other way—she is courting heartache and misery."

"Exactly!" Anna declared. "All married men can explain, so to speak. I hope you will follow your own advice and don't let yourself be drawn into something you cannot handle."

Anna was watching her granddaughter closely now. "Please hold on to your heart, *mein Schatz*—he sounds like a very attentive man and you are vulnerable, never having experienced this thoughtfulness and these gestures. With all my heart, I wish for you to have love and happiness in your life, as you deserve it; I am just not sure if Leopold can give you that."

Both women sat in silence for a while before Anna piped up. "Now, let's talk about something else. Emil and Karoline came by today to wish you a happy new year and were most surprised to hear you had gone out to the opera!"

Bertha had to chuckle. "I suppose so! They are not used to their mother having other interests—usually it's just simple coffee with my friends. Did they both have great celebrations last night?" Bertha asked her Oma as she refilled their teacups.

Anna cleared her throat. "I think Karo wanted to tell us something, but since you were not home, she will come by tomorrow evening. I have a feeling she and Julius... Well, I don't want to say anything just yet."

Anna looked pleased at having surprised Bertha.

"Karo? Karo and Julius? My little girl?" Bertha was shocked, but then both women fell into laughter. "She's not so little anymore," Bertha admitted. "That would be wonderful news; I can't wait to hear it in person." Bertha was now elated. "Julius is a very nice young man, and a doctor—how marvellous for my Karo."

The rest of the evening just flew by before it was time to settle down for the night. Bertha had trouble falling asleep, going over the day, indeed the whole week, before drifting off, dreaming that she and Leopold were dancing to some of the music they had enjoyed earlier.

It had snowed overnight and was still snowing by the time Bertha was returning home from work. All of Berlin was covered by a thick blanket of snow and traffic had come to a near standstill. Men clad in thick coats and armed with shovels tried to clear roadways for the few horse-drawn carriages still driving. With no streetcar in sight, Bertha faced a long walk home. To her delight, she was met by Karoline at the entrance door of Wertheim department store.

"Mama, I came to pick you up, because I need to talk with you," Karo explained. "I have to work a night shift, so there is no time later. But it looks like we need to walk—the streetcar stopped at Potsdamer Platz and let all the people off because it was stuck in the snow."

"So, then we walk," Bertha shrugged. "It's only about an hour. Plenty of time to talk." Bertha hugged her daughter and together they trudged through the snow along the Helgolaender Ufer, crossed the bridge over the River Spree, stopped to watch some skaters, and continued towards Alt-Moabit and Turmstrasse.

"What is so urgent you need to talk about my dear?" Bertha finally prodded her daughter.

"Mama, I am so very happy!" Karoline squealed with joy in her eyes. "Julius asked me to marry him! We were dancing at the New Year's Ball, and when it turned close to midnight and they brought out the champagne to toast the new century, he took my hand in his and said he wanted to start 1900 together with me, and asked if I would marry him!"

By now, Karoline was all dreamy-eyed. "Oh, Mama, it was so romantic!" she gushed. "I love him so much, and I hope you have no objections. He wants to meet with you to officially ask for my hand. I am so happy!" Karoline had to stop her exuberant gushing to take a deep breath.

"Karo, slow down!" Bertha teased. "I am indeed happy for you! But my dear, why would I have any objections? I am overjoyed by your news; Julius is a great young man. I don't understand your concerns."

Karoline furrowed her brow. "Mama, you don't know?"

"Know what?" Bertha was genuinely confused.

"He—he is Jewish..." Karoline said quietly, her voice trailing off.

Bertha turned to her daughter, red-cheeked from the cold and excitement. "Yes, carry on, what else?"

"Nothing else, Mama, he is wonderful, and he is the man I want to marry."

Bertha failed to see the issue. "So, what exactly is the problem, Karo? I see my wonderful daughter wanting to marry a wonderful young man. I'm sorry, but I am quite confused."

"I just told you, he is Jewish!" Karoline said, now louder and a bit upset.

Bertha simply shook her head. "So, he is Jewish. What of it?"

"But don't you see Mama?" Karoline was clearly frustrated. "There will be no church wedding, just a civil wedding at the *Standesamt* (registry office). Your only daughter, not being married in church—is that not a big disappointment to you and Omama?" Karoline's mood had turned from excitement to frustration to worry.

Bertha continued to slog through the snow, all the while shaking her head, before stopping and facing her clearly anxious daughter. "Now, you listen to me, Karoline," she said sternly but lovingly. "You are my precious child. Your happiness is first and foremost in my life as your mother. I am not at all concerned whether you will or can marry in church. I am concerned about your future well-being, the kind of man you will share your life with and how he treats you. I am elated that you have found that man in your life!"

Karoline breathed a loud sigh of relief.

"And yes, tell your young man to come by—I will gladly give my consent," Bertha continued.

"But what about father?" Karoline asked, concerned.

"You should tell him, of course, but do not worry about him—you do not need his approval," Bertha assured her daughter. "Now, for heaven's sake, let's get home to warm up and tell the good news to our Omama!"

Smiling and laughing, both women locked arms and continued to tromp and slide through the snow towards Turmstrasse.

CHAPTER TWELVE

"KARO IS ENGAGED?" EMIL HAD COME HOME FOR A VISIT AND WANTED TO KNOW more. "Is it that doctor? The one she had made eyes at and he back at her?"

"Well, I don't know about the 'making eyes' part," Bertha laughed at her son. "But yes, I believe it is the same one. He came by a few days ago and officially asked for her hand in marriage and the engagement celebration will be... Wait, the invitation just arrived today!" Bertha picked through the mail on the table. "Here, read for yourself."

Dr. Rudolf und Ehefrau Lilly Feldmann
Are pleased to announce the engagement of their son
Julius Samuel to Karoline Anna Hoffmann.
You are invited to share this joyous occasion
with the couple and Karoline's family
On
January 29th, 1900
at 16:00 hours
Dinner will be served at 20:00
Evening dress is requested
The festivities will take place at the groom's parents' house at
12 Auerbach Straße, Berlin, Grunewald

A civil wedding will take place at Charlottenburg City Hall on February
15th, 1900, at 11:00 hours followed by a brunch.
Family members only please.

"Wow!" Emil whistled. "That's an exclusive area—our Karo did well for herself!"

"She followed her heart, Emil," Bertha gently chided her son.

"Yes, of course, Mama, and knowing Karo, she would have married a street cleaner if she loved him, but this is a much better catch!" Emil could not help but applaud his sister's good fortune.

"Please Emil, enough of this kind of talk!" Bertha said more sternly. "Karo and Julius are happy; that is all that matters. I do hope you can come to the celebration." Bertha turned back to cutting up the carrots for supper.

"Of course, I would not miss this for anything," Emil replied. He paused as if he wanted to say more but was unsure how. "Um, hmm, Mama? Hmm..." he hemmed and hawed some more.

"What is it?" Bertha took down a pot to put in the carrots. "Here, peel some potatoes while you sit and tell me what's on your mind." She handed him a knife.

"Um...hmm...Mama?" he asked, still stammering. "Can I bring Anton?"

"For dinner tonight?" Bertha was only half-listening to Emil as she prepared supper and was lost in thoughts of Karoline's upcoming marriage.

"Ah, no, actually—to Karo's celebration," Emil said slowly, looking down.

The sentence hung in the air for a while before Bertha turned around sharply. "What? Are you daft? What an absurd question. Absolutely no, you cannot bring your friend. Honestly, Emil, I must wonder about you sometimes. If you were engaged to a nice young woman, you could be bringing her, but your roommate and friend? What a strange request!"

"Now enough of that," Bertha continued as she turned back to dinner preparations. "You can start to set the table and keep Oma some company while I finish dinner."

Bertha shook her head as she was talking, mumbling to herself about such strange ideas and requests her son had sometimes.

Before turning to go, Emil asked, "Will Father be invited?"

"Well, we can hardly disregard him, can we now?" Bertha replied, shrugging. "But Karo does not want him there, so our idea was to send him the invitation the day of the celebration. He will receive it too late to attend!"

At that, Emil laughed out loud. "Good plan, Mama!" Then he paused before asking, "Is he Karo's father?" he suddenly blurted out.

Bertha just stared at him. "What in heaven's name has come over you today with all your odd questions? Of course he is Karo's father!" she exclaimed.

"Well, he isn't mine, is he?" Emil stared back at his mother.

Bertha was taken aback but tried to cover it. "What—why do you say that?" she stammered, quickly busying herself with dinner.

"Mama," Emil sighed. "You don't need to hide this from me. I have known this for a long time. When I saw father with Karl-Heinz a few years ago, and he made a point of calling me his 'bastard son' and how lucky I was to keep receiving money from my real father—whoever he is—so I can go to school and all that, things he could not afford for his real son. That made Karl-Heinz upset and jealous."

With her heart pounding, knees shaking, and tears welling up, Bertha slowly sat on the closest chair. "Oh Emil, my dear son," she said softly and sadly. "I did not know that happened—why didn't you tell me?"

Emil shrugged. "Because it didn't matter, Mama," he admitted. "Father never was much of a father to any of us and you and Omama were everything to us—well, perhaps not to Karl-Heinz!" he added sheepishly.

Then he looked down before continuing. "And Omama told me later that you had been...well...um...violated," he almost whispered, blushing in embarrassment for this mother. "And in order to give birth to me, you needed to find a husband quickly."

"*Ach*, my dear Emil," was all Bertha could think to say. "We can talk more about this at some other time if you like, but right now I don't know what else to say."

"No, no need, Mama," Emil quickly replied. "I don't want to know any more, and I won't tell Karo either—this is between you and me," he assured her.

Bertha could only nod. It was a rather quiet supper the three of them sat down to, each of them caught in their own thoughts. After helping with the clean-up, Emil quickly left to go home.

Once Bertha and her grandmother settled down with a cup of tea, Bertha recounted Emil's strange conversations, as well as his request to bring Anton to the engagement dinner. Anna sat very quiet while Bertha talked.

"He needs to find a nice girl," Bertha said. "I am not too fond of Anton; he used to be a very nice boy, but now he seems a little odd," she shook her head. "I just can't quite figure out what it is."

Anna just nodded, while thinking, "*I hope our Emil is not involved in these ungodly activities people have whispered about. This would be totally unthinkable, and ruin Karo's future, as well.*"

She must have looked deep in thought. "What are you thinking about, Oma?" Bertha asked.

"Oh, just that you are right with your hopes of Emil finding a nice girl and settling down," she answered quickly.

"Yes, of course," Bertha nodded. "But I wondered if Emil knows about August. Do you think I should tell him?"

"Did he ask?" Anna wondered.

Bertha shook her head.

"Well, then don't offer any information unless he does ask," Anna advised. "It will do no good, particularly since he has been to see his cousins on different occasions."

Bertha nodded. "I suppose you are right," she sighed. "Oma, I feel completely drained right now, it's time to get myself to bed. Thank goodness tomorrow is Epiphany and we have a day off." She rose, took the teacups to the kitchen, wished her grandmother a good night, and went to bed.

CHAPTER THIRTEEN

THE NEXT FEW DAYS FLEW BY IN A FLURRY OF ACTIVITIES. AN INFORMAL MEETING between Bertha, Anna, and Julius' parents had been arranged prior to the official engagement celebration. They met on a Sunday afternoon at Café Kranzler and thoroughly enjoyed each other's company.

Dr. Feldmann was a surgeon while Frau Feldmann was an ardent follower in theories of Dr. Sigmund Freud, who had the medical community abuzz with terms like "psychoanalysis." Bertha found her discussion on the subject most interesting while Dr. Feldmann only raised his eyebrows, looking quite unconvinced. Anna listened carefully and wondered silently if one or the other theory could be applied to her extended family.

"Now, my dear, that is enough of this," Dr. Feldmann interrupted his wife a while later. "We are here to discuss our children's future life together and not bore our guests with unproven theories. I say if something bothers you, cut it out."

"Yes, you would say that!" his wife laughed. "But you are right; let us get to know each other better and let us look forward to hopefully many grandchildren." The mood became light and with good-natured banter, they parted to look forward to January 29.

The next day, Leopold was waiting for Bertha as she left work. Well dressed as always, and with impeccable manners, he greeted Bertha with an almost shy smile. Tucking her arm under his, as if this was the most natural thing to do, he suggested they walk towards the Potsdamer Platz from where she could get a horse cab to take her home.

"I needed some time to think about things." he finally spoke after some silence, with Bertha wondering what was going through his mind. "My feelings for you have not altered, and I need an opportunity to talk and explain things to you."

Bertha did not reply, but she did move closer to him for some warmth as a cold wind had picked up and blew some of the snow around. "Please Bertha," Leopold implored. "Please let me take you out to a quiet place where we have time in a warm and relaxed atmosphere to talk."

Bertha looked at him; his eyes were big and pleading. "And where would this place be?" Bertha threw him an apprehensive glance as she tried to maintain her composure.

"A nice place to have dinner—will that be acceptable to you?" he asked.

By this time, Bertha was so cold she felt willing to go anywhere to warm up. "Yes, Leopold, I accept," she finally answered. "I admit I am both cold and hungry!"

He let out a hearty laugh. "All right, then, let's go. It's not far from here."

As they entered a warm and cosy restaurant, they were immediately ushered to a corner table, nestled behind a large potted plant. Bertha noticed an air of elegance as well as white tablecloths, sparkling silverware, crystal wine glasses, and candlelight to complete the picture. A pianist provided soft background music.

With a satisfied little sigh, Bertha let herself settle into the plush seat that an attentive waiter had pulled out for her. "Ah, I think I might finally thaw out a little," she smiled at Leopold seated across from her. She watched as he ordered a specific wine before handing her the *carte du jour. "He is so handsome, so poised, so intelligent,"* she thought to herself again while soaking in the atmosphere.

"Now, tell me how you spent New Year's Eve," Leopold looked intently at Bertha, who was sipping on her wine.

"Karoline became engaged to Julius!" she blurted out, describing to him the happy developments, as well as the upcoming arrangements. By the time dinner was served, Bertha had been doing all the talking. Leopold was enthralled, asking for some clarification here and there, but mostly captivated by her fascinating conversation and eloquent account of events.

By the time dessert was being offered, Bertha finally had the courage to ask him, "What did you do over the holidays?"

Leopold took a deep breath before answering her. "I spent it back home at the estate," he paused for a moment, "with my family."

Bertha's heart sank, but she sat still and waited for him to continue. "I have parents who like to see me once in a while," he carried on with a little chuckle before becoming serious again. "...and yes, you are correct in your assumption that I am married. I have a wife and a son—but at the same time, I do not have a wife nor a son."

Bertha was genuinely confused. "Please, Leopold, please explain," she requested, a bit upset. "That does not make sense to me."

"I know, it sounds strange," he admitted, "but you need to know the circumstances of this arrangement, and hopefully you will understand." He took another deep breath before continuing. "My father inherited the sizeable estate, along with the titles of 'Count.' As you may know, aristocratic titles are inherited, along with the estate. Once the estate is gone, so is the title."

Bertha nodded in understanding.

"So, this large estate was passed on to my father, to be passed on to me," Leopold continued. "But I also have a younger brother, and once our grandparents passed away, it was divided into two—still very large—manors. One half to me, the other to my brother Ulrich.

"Ulrich quickly married his childhood sweetheart, Ludwiga," Leopold went on, as Bertha tried her best to process this deluge of information. "Ludwiga is from Polish nobility descent, the youngest of nine children, and therefore with a tiny dowry. Her prospects of marrying into a well-to-do noble family were very slim, so it was of great benefit to her and her family that Ulrich was enamoured with her. Soon thereafter they became parents to a son, Franz-Ludwig."

Leopold stopped when Bertha interrupted him. "It all sounds rather interesting," she admitted, still puzzled, "but what exactly does that have to do with you being married or not married?"

"Patience, my dear Bertha," Leopold took her hand and smiled. "I am trying to explain everything. Please forgive me if I digress a little; it will all make sense soon enough."

Bertha sipped her wine and nodded again.

"Ulrich, being the younger brother, and as is customary for a second son, became an officer in the Imperial Army. He had his own horses and he had money, and that was of course mandatory," Leopold went on. "Unfortunately, Ulrich was a happy-go-lucky person, prone to drinking and gambling—and he did both to the fullest. An officer has to cover his debts—that is an understatement. He was way in over his head, and..." Leopold's voice trailed off for a moment before he continued with yet another deep breath.

"One day, Ulrich had to take the only honourable way out—and shoot himself." Leopold looked down and Bertha gasped, staring at him. It slowly dawned on her what he was going to say next.

"Our father could not cover his huge debts and Ulrich's portion of the estate had to be sold. With this, it would leave Franz-Ludwig, my nephew and godson, without title or property. Of course, they would live with my parents—the property is large enough for that—but that did not solve the boy's dilemma.

"Ludwiga and I, the boy's godfather, eventually came to an agreement that would solve this issue of inheritance. To everybody's relief and with their blessings, I married Ludwiga and adopted Franz-Ludwig. We call him Fra-Lu," he smiled now, thinking of him. "Fra-Lu is now five years old and the official heir to the title and inheritance. I love him as my own, but Ludwiga and I are not in love. But should we divorce, Fra-Lu would be excluded and any male I would legally sire will become the legitimate heir.

"I just cannot do that to the boy, nor to his mother," he sighed. "Since I am now over forty, it is most unlikely that I will have my own children anyway. I must add though, that Ludwiga is a very fine person, a most likeable woman—"

Bertha felt a sudden stab of intense jealousy but tried to hide it as she continued to listen.

"—and she and I have agreed to lead separate lives, but united in raising our son."

Leopold leaned back in his chair, downed the last bit of wine, and waited for Bertha's reaction.

They sat looking at each other for a long time, Bertha trying to digest all she had heard and Leopold waiting for her reaction.

Finally, Bertha responded carefully. "You are a very honourable man, Leopold. Ludwiga and Fra-Lu are most fortunate people to have you in their lives. I do not know what exactly you like to hear from me!" Bertha was near tears and looked away.

Leopold quickly took both her hands in his, gently turned her chin, and looked deep into her eyes. "I would like to hear that you can accept what I can give you. I will give you my love, my commitment to you, basically all of me!" he exclaimed passionately. "The one thing I cannot give to you is my name. I would like to hear from you that you can accept that!"

"You mean, as your mistress?" Bertha cried, heartbroken and incredulous.

"No! Absolutely not!" Leopold replied. "Do you hear? Not my mistress, but my wife in God's eyes, and not the law!" He was still holding her hands, and now gently dried her tears. "Don't you see? *You* are the one I love, *you* are the one I want, *you* are the one I want to spend my life with." Now Leopold started to sound heartbroken and desperate. "Bertha, oh Bertha, I love you, I want you, I need you!"

Bertha's heart was pounding madly; she could hardly believe what he was saying and what was happening. Her entire body started to tremble. Finally, she managed to answer him. "You—you love me?" she whispered, shaking. "I—I don't know what that means, how that feels, I have never been loved by a man before..." she paused for a moment before continuing.

Leopold was looking anxious, but still holding her hands.

"I feel overwhelmed," Bertha continued slowly, "but I also feel happy, I feel confused, I feel my soul singing, and yet I feel frightened."

"Do—do you think you can love me back?" a nervous Leopold asked in a hushed tone.

"I think..." Bertha trembled, "...I think I already do!"

Leopold let out a loud sigh of relief and even laughed. "Oh, my dear Bertha!" he exclaimed in pleasure. "You have made me the happiest man alive! Now, let me take you home and I will call on you in a couple of days. I will count the minutes until then!"

Bertha was overcome with emotions, particularly when he kissed her lips lightly at her front door. They both wanted more, to linger in the embrace, but they held back; there would be plenty of time ahead of them.

CHAPTER FOURTEEN

A DAY LATER, KARO, WHO SEEMED TO BE ON ETERNAL NIGHT SHIFTS, WAS HOME long enough to accept the delivery of a large bouquet of roses.

"Oh, Omama, look what has arrived," she excitedly turned to her great-grandmother. "I did not think Julius to be so romantic!" She was flushed with emotion.

Anna waited to comment; she had her own thoughts about the sender of such a lavish gift in the middle of winter. "Are you sure they are from Julius? Is there not a card along with them?"

With a baffled look on her lovely flushed face, Karo asked, "But for who else, Omama?" Then she found the card inside the flowers. "Quick, let me see what it says."

She was ready to rip it open, when Anna interrupted, "Karo, to whom is it addressed, my dear?"

Karo shrugged. "It must be to me from Julius. Who else?" Then she turned the envelope around. "It says to Frau Bertha Hoffmann on it!" Karo was stunned. "To my mother? Who sends roses to her?"

"I think you may have to ask her when she gets home," Anna answered with a little smile on her face. "Why don't you put them in a vase in the meantime; it will be a lovely surprise for your mother."

Obediently, Karo headed to the pantry for a vase, confused about the sender. Suddenly, it dawned on her. "Wait! Is that the same man who sent her flowers before?" she asked her Omama.

Anna just shook her head and chuckled. "I do not know—I did not read the card, and it is not for us to know," she gently chided Karo. "Your mother will be home in a little while, and you can ask her, perhaps she will tell you."

"And here I thought they were from Julius," Karo said with a slight pout. "I must admit I am a little disappointed, and even a little jealous!"

At this Anna laughed out loud. "You will just have to train your young man a little better!" She was still chuckling when Bertha came home.

"Well, you two are in good spirits," Bertha smiled as she walked in the door. "And Karo, so nice of you to come by—oh, what beautiful roses, are they for you, dear?"

"No Mama, they are for you!" her daughter exclaimed. "And now you must tell me who is that man who sends you roses? I simply must know!"

"Do you now?" Bertha winked.

"Yes, you are my mother, I need to know! And here, there is the card that came with them." Karo was practically giddy now.

"Oh, Karo, Karo, can I please take my coat off first?" Bertha laughed. "And can I read the note in private first?"

Reluctantly, Karo agreed.

"In the meantime, you can start dinner," Anna instructed Karo.

Bertha hung up her coat and gently stuck her head into the flowers and inhaled their fragrant scent. Gingerly, she took the sealed envelope and retreated to her room.

Nearly breathless and with a pounding heart, she opened it, took out the card, and read the short message:

My dearest Bertha, you have made me the happiest man alive. I love you with all my heart. If you will allow me to call on you on Sunday, I will be delirious with joy.

Yours forever, Leopold

With her knees trembling, Bertha had to sit down. *"What did I get myself into?"* she wondered. *"Can this really be happening to me?"*

When she had composed herself, she slowly made her way back to the sitting room, back to two women eagerly waiting to hear what she had to say. Looking from one to the other, Bertha decided to be open and disclose the proposed relationship.

"He is not going to marry you, Mama?" Karo was incredulous. "I know what you would have told me if the roles were reversed!"

"I know, my dear, and most certainly I still would tell you the same," Bertha agreed. "You are very young, you will have children, your Julius is free to marry, so I am grateful I do not have to apply any restrictions on your relationship. However—" she held up her hand to quiet her daughter— "I am a mature woman, Leopold is a mature man, and we know what we are facing. We both want something we never had before—love, tenderness, and affection. I believe we have found a special gift in each other, something almost divine... It defies any explanation."

"But Mama, what will people think?" Karoline gasped. "You will not really be able to go anywhere together! And, oh, my God, my wedding!" she suddenly realised. "You cannot possibly come with him to the engagement celebration or the wedding, especially if my father will be there!" Karo was beside herself.

"Shh, daughter—do you really think your mother would be so tactless?" Bertha scolded her. "Leopold and I have not progressed to any such state yet, and when or if the time comes, I am sure we will be going places together. People will *always* talk, but in his case, it may well be tolerated.

"I hope you will understand, Karo, and I hope I can continue to be in your life after you are married," Bertha said to her daughter, quietly and genuinely. "I promise we will be discreet; my friend Hertha has had a married friend for a number of years now and they are doing just fine.

"And please remember, I, too, am still married and can do little about it, since your father never agreed to a divorce," Bertha reminded Karo. Almost breathless now, Bertha stopped and waited for any response. She knew Anna was on her side; the two spoke half the night the prior night.

Karo rose slowly and gave her mother a hug. "Mama, I wish you love, just as Julius and I have found love," she smiled. "I wish that everything will eventually work out for you. As long as that man treats you well, with the respect and caring you deserve, I will accept the situation as it is. After all," she added with a laugh, "you are old enough to make your own decisions; I do not have to approve."

"But Karo, I need your approval," Bertha protested, "because if you did not, I truly would have to decide against this relationship with Leopold."

"No, Mama, please," Karo shook her head. "I want you to be happy, I will never ask for you to sacrifice your happiness; you have done so much for all of us already; it is time you get something in return. Be happy, and let us meet this special man soon!"

In the meantime, Anna had gone to the kitchen and finished supper, set the table, and brought out a bottle of wine. "Let us toast to all of you and your happiness!" she suggested. "It is such a special blessing for me to live long enough to see all your lives unfold."

The trio raised their glasses before beginning their meal, chattering happily all throughout. After clearing the dishes, Karo bid them a good night. "I need to go off to work now. If I'm lucky, I will catch a glimpse of Julius before his shift is finished."

As she put on her coat, she looked at her mother. "I will say nothing to him, Mama," she promised. "What we talked about will stay here, until there is something to talk about, if this makes any sense." With a little wave, she was off, and they heard her running footsteps down the stairway, fading to the thump of the front door being shut.

"What will you tell Emil?" Anna asked Bertha after they had settled down for the evening.

"Emil? What is there to tell?" Bertha wondered. "There is nothing to talk about with him at the moment. I wonder if he is even remotely aware of anything that does not concern himself these days."

Anna agreed, and both allowed themselves to get lost in their thoughts and events of the past several days before retiring for the night.

CHAPTER FIFTEEN

SUNDAY AFTERNOON CAME TOO SLOWLY IN BERTHA'S MIND, BUT LEOPOLD, TRUE to his word, picked Bertha up. He had one of the new motorised taxis waiting downstairs while he ran up the stairs to greet her.

It was the first time for him to come to the door, as well as to meet Anna Sehnke. Politely greeting the older lady with a customary hand kiss, he introduced himself.

Anna liked what she saw—a handsome, mature man with perfect manners. *"If only he wasn't married,"* she couldn't help but think to herself.

The mere presence of a man in the apartment seemed to fill the space completely and made it appear smaller than it was. Leopold did not notice; his eyes were fixed on Bertha. The two were preoccupied with each other in that moment in time and were startled back to reality when Anna asked, "Where are you going this afternoon? It is too bad that it is not summer, and you could go for long walks in the *Tiergarten*, or along the rivers."

"I am thinking of the Café Instanz, an intimate little place near the Alexanderplatz," Leopold answered Anna while holding his gaze on Bertha, something Anna couldn't help but notice. "Their food is terrific, and with only a few tables, it is a quiet place to talk."

"May we go now, Oma?" Bertha asked.

"Of course, my dear, have a wonderful afternoon!" Anna turned to Leopold. "And it was a pleasure meeting you, sir." He returned the sentiments and bowed off with another hand kiss.

As soon as the pair were outside the door, Bertha's neighbour hurriedly opened her door, pretending to be leaving at the same time.

"Frau Hoffmann, so nice to see you again," she greeted them politely. "How is your grandmother and the children? Oh, and I see you are in company! Are you going somewhere special today?"

"Good afternoon, Frau Baum," Bertha acknowledged her, thinking of how to respond. "Thank you for your interest, my family is just fine, and have a nice Sunday!" She had to suppress a giggle as she grabbed Leopold's arm while they descended the stairs.

Once outside, Bertha could no longer hold back her giggles. "Oh, she is such a nosy person," she chuckled in explanation to Leopold. "This will give her something to gossip about for the next few weeks!" They grinned at each other while entering the taxi. Bertha was sure Frau Baum was watching from behind her curtains upstairs.

"This is indeed a very nice and hidden place," Bertha commented once they arrived at the *Instanz*. "I am so cold—I am already wishing for summer to come back in a hurry!" she continued, rubbing her cold hands together.

"You don't remember how cold it is back in East Prussia," Leopold teased her. "Almost Siberian cold! But this will warm you up very quickly," he said, motioning to the cup of coffee topped with a large scoop of whipped cream, as well as a glass of brandy.

Bertha felt the warmth slowly making its way throughout her body as she sipped the brandy. With a grateful and contented sigh, she leaned back in her chair and watched Leopold as he ordered their dinner.

"I have a solution for your winter doldrums," he offered with a grin.

"I'm all ears!" she laughed.

"Come with me to Italy!" he almost blurted out, surprising Bertha. "We can easily spend ten days or so in Venice; it is a lot warmer there than here."

"You cannot be serious—or are you?" Bertha began to giggle, feeling the effects of the brandy. "How do you propose we get to Italy?"

"Easy," Leopold replied with a wink. "We board a train in Berlin and then get off in Italy!" Now they were both laughing.

Bertha, with a dreamy look on her face, spoke softly, almost to herself. "Italy... Oh, how much I would like to see Italy. Venice, gondola, St. Markus Square, the Lido..." her voice trailed off. She felt lost in a dream.

Leopold's voice quickly brought her back to reality. "Did you hear anything I said?" he asked good-naturedly.

Bertha felt sheepish. "Oh, my, not really!" she admitted. "I was a little lost in my thoughts."

"Well, let me repeat then," Leopold offered. "You and I will go to Italy, just the two of us, for at least ten days. We will take the time to get to know each other better, walk in the sunshine, take in the sounds and sights, sit by the water, hold hands, kiss, and simply be together. What do you say?" He eagerly looked at her.

"You look like a little boy on Christmas!" Bertha had to smile.

"This is much better than Christmas, trust me," he smiled back.

The thought of spending a number of days together, in another country, no less, deeply excited Bertha, but there were too many things to think of. She got right into it.

"What about my work? My Omama, my children—oh Leopold, I would love to go with you, but I am just not sure how I can manage all that."

She continued, "I get only one week of vacation time in the summer. Also, there's Karo's engagement celebration, as well as her wedding coming up, and..."

At that, Leopold cut in. "You can ask for your week holiday now, your children are grown up, your grandmother looks to be in good health and can easily take care of herself. And, let me continue please, and it is obvious that you will be here for your daughter's important days. We will go in February or March."

"Oh, Leopold, that is so—" Bertha clasped her hands to her face. "I'm at loss for words, but, yes! I will go with you!" she watched Leopold's face break into a huge grin. "I am so very excited," she continued. "I will ask for vacation time tomorrow."

She thought for a moment. "Oh yes, I have an appointment with our pastor tomorrow evening, as well."

Leopold, with a slight frown, questioned her motive.

"You know that Karoline and Julius will be married, but Julius is Jewish and therefore they cannot be married in our church. Karo and I need to talk to our pastor and how he feels about that," Bertha explained. "I might even mention that I have met a man I care very much about," she added shyly.

At that moment, the waiter arrived with their dinner plates, as well as some light, white wine to go with their repast, and for the time being, he was relieved of an answer. Bertha chose not to dwell on this.

"I need to know if a relationship proposed by Leopold is at least somewhat acceptable by the church," she told herself. *"But I will not forgo the love this man offers me."* For the moment, she let the romance of the evening engulf her senses.

Some days later, Karo and Bertha met with their pastor.

"So, I hear congratulations are in order," he turned to Karoline, nodding his head.

"Yes, Julius and I are very happy," Karoline answered, "but he is Jewish, and the wedding will be a civil one." Karo came right to the point with her usual self-confident poise. Bertha could not be prouder of her daughter at this moment.

"Are you considering converting to Judaism?" the pastor prodded.

Karoline shook her head. "No. We have talked about this in depth, with each other, as well as our families, and there are no objections to our union."

"And what about any future children?" the pastor inquired.

Bertha noticed Karo's slight embarrassment and a sudden thought hit her. *"I wonder if my little girl may be with child; perhaps that is why there is no long engagement."* She peered at her a little closer.

Karo, now visibly nervous, replied that she and Julius had decided to have their children baptised and any boys not circumcised. At that statement, she blushed.

"As long as you are both of one mind, all should be well for you and your future." The minister rose and shook her hand. "I hope to see you in church once in a while and I give my blessings to you and your young man."

Rising as well, Bertha turned to him. "Can I have a word with you, as well?" she asked.

"Of course, please sit down again," he offered.

"I'm going off to work now, Mama," Karoline bid her farewell. "See you tomorrow!" and with that, Karo left the church office.

"A fine young woman, your Karoline," the pastor noted. "And now, what can I help you with, Frau Hoffmann?"

After a few minutes of silence, Bertha finally blurted out that she, too, had found a new love in her life and needed to talk to him about that.

The pastor cleared his throat. "Now this is a little more complicated," he began. "You are still married, aren't you?"

"Yes," Bertha nodded. "If one can call it a 'marriage'—it really never was one, but—"

The pastor held up his hand. "If you are married, you are married!" he interrupted. "There are no ratings as to marriage satisfaction. Are you planning a divorce then?"

"Karl won't give me one," Bertha admitted, feeling beaten already.

"So, then, what of this new man in your life? Is he still married, as well?"

Bertha nodded in silence, feeling the pastor's disapproval and judgment.

"And how are you envisioning this to unfold?" the pastor asked quite sternly.

"We would like to be together," Bertha answered simply but quietly, slowly regaining her composure.

"If you are asking me to sanction a relationship outside of marriage, you are mistaken! It is contrary to the church's teachings."

"But it says nowhere in the Bible one has to be married," Bertha suddenly countered, speaking more firmly. "As a matter of fact, it says, 'and he took her as his wife'; there is no mention of an official marriage that I can find!" Bertha was now visibly agitated.

"Quiet!" the pastor thundered. "If you live in sin and shame, then you can no longer come to the Lord's table! I will not ban you from church services, but—"

At this Bertha rose in anger. "I was hoping for some understanding and some grace from you, but sadly, I leave very disappointed. You, of all people, know what I've been through—you could at least understand my human desire to be loved and cared for, but instead you condemn me!"

"I am not condemning you, please don't feel that," the pastor tried to explain. "I am merely trying to point you back to the path of goodness, to save you from your sinful choice."

Bertha shook her head. "No, I don't agree with you, Pastor," she told him. "I believe God wants His creation to be a happy one—after all, He made us in His image, and I don't think He is an unhappy God when two people love each other!

"Why, He even gave Adam a wife, and there was no church involved!" she continued, rose to leave, and left a silenced and stunned pastor behind.

CHAPTER SIXTEEN: MARCH 1900

At last, the train pulled out of Anhalter Bahnhof headed for Vienna. Bertha snuggled blissfully into the soft and cosy seat in their compartment, with Leopold across from her.

As she watched Berlin pass by on her way to Venice, she still could not believe this was happening. It was a snowy early March morning, with the wet snow beating against the window, the sky a dull gray.

"I am so looking forward to some sun and warmth," she turned to Leopold.

"So am I," he agreed. "First, we'll go to Vienna where we will stay for one night—there is no direct connection to Venice from Berlin—and tomorrow, we carry on to Venice," he explained to her.

"Yes, you mentioned that before, but do we get to see a little of Vienna then?" Bertha wondered.

"Not this time around. Vienna in the winter is no better than Berlin, but we will go there in the summer, I promise," Leopold smiled.

"But I can't take off work all the time!" Bertha declared. "I had a hard enough time to get two weeks off now." Bertha then looked at Leopold, puzzled. "How do you manage it? How do you get away like this all the time? And—I'm sorry, but I must ask—what did you tell your wife?"

"My dearest Bertha," Leopold reached across and took her hand in his. "I have told you before, and I will tell you again, and you must believe me! Ludwiga is not my wife in the traditional sense. This was, and is, a marriage to safeguard Franz-Ludwig's rightful inheritance.

"Both my parents, as well as Ludwiga, have agreed to this arrangement with the understanding that we live our lives separately," he continued earnestly. "We do not need or wish to tell each other where we are going or what we are doing.

Ludwiga is like a sister to me, as she was when she was married to my brother, and..."

At this point, he stopped and looked closely at her before continuing, "...and we have never consummated this marriage. I am not in love with her, as she is not in love with me. I sincerely hope she has found her own discreet relationship, but that is her business, not mine. As to your time off work, well, we will discuss that at a later time. Does that answer all your questions for now?" Leopold searched Bertha's face for a sign of acceptance.

"I know, I know, you have told me before," she finally replied, "but please understand that this is a most unusual situation—not only your status, but mine, and then going away with you in an unmarried state."

Bertha paused before continuing, as Leopold tried to listen patiently. "At the same time, I have made a conscious decision to bypass conventional conduct to be with you, to experience and taste love in my life, even if it's for a little while." By that time Bertha had tears in her eyes.

Leopold now tightly grasped both her hands. "Bertha, I promise to you that this is not for a little while!" he declared. "I promise to be with you forever. I promise to love you and care for you as long as we both shall live."

With that, he pulled a little package out of his side pocket, opened it, and took out a ring while an astonished Bertha watched.

"I was going to wait for this until we reached Venice, but this is a more appropriate time, I believe," he smiled at her, took her hand, and slipped the ring on her finger. Bertha gasped. It was a beautiful, exquisite ring, with two sparkling blue sapphire stones embedded next to a gleaming diamond.

Bertha just stared at it, wide-eyed and with disbelief at this special token of Leopold's love. "I—I—oh, Leopold, I don't know what to say!" she stammered.

"Please, say yes, please be my wife," Leopold pleaded. "Please accept this ring as my commitment to you as a husband."

"Yes, Leopold, yes and yes, I also commit myself to be your wife," Bertha replied a bit shakily, as she was still somewhat bewildered and overwhelmed.

Leopold stood up, pulled Bertha to her feet, and took both her hands "Bertha, I love you, I will be faithful to you, I will protect you, I will be there for you in sickness and in health, until the day I die," he promised. "This is my vow to you." He was very serious when he iterated the common wedding vow.

A big smile spread across Bertha's face as she replied, "Leopold, I love you, I will be faithful to you, I will be there for you in in sickness and in health, until the day I die."

For a long time, they stood holding hands, gazing at each other, swaying a little back and forth as the train rumbled along, before Leopold finally took her in his arms and kissed her, lightly at first but becoming more passionate as the kiss lingered. "Bertha, I love you so much," he murmured into her ear. "I can't wait to have all of you!"

Bertha shivered with joy and anticipation as she eagerly returned his kisses.

A loud rap on the door quickly brought them back to earth, and a slightly embarrassed porter announced that breakfast was now being served in the dining car.

All during breakfast, Bertha was gazing in awe at her hand, admiring the ring that she vowed to wear from now on. "It is so beautiful, Leopold, I can't stop looking at it. You have no idea how happy I am!" she gushed.

"Oh, not any happier than I!" Leopold grinned.

"Now, you must tell me all about Karoline's wedding," he deftly turned the conversation around as more people entered the dining car.

"It was quite the engagement celebration, Leopold," Bertha told him. "Everyone all decked out in evening attire, sipping champagne, and the many guests congratulating the young couple, as well as his parents and me along with Oma. Emil played a beautiful composition on the grand piano, a composition he had written especially for his sister—it was a most touching moment."

She stopped for a minute to pour another cup of coffee for Leopold and herself. "The meal was splendid, but we did not get home until well after midnight. The civil ceremony was eloquent, with only the closest family members present. Thankfully, Karl did not come, and neither did Karl-Heinz, as his wife is expecting their second child any time now.

"But once again, Emil played some music, along with his friend Anton, who played the violin," she continued. "Afterward, we all went to Hotel Kaiserhof for a lovely meal and some time together. Karo and Julius stayed overnight there, a gift from his parents, and the next day, they both returned to work!"

Bertha paused again, now deep in thought. "My sweet and spunky little girl is a Frau Dr. Feldmann, it's hard to believe. I wished I could have spent more time with my children when they were little," she said wistfully, "but with all the problems with Karl and poor little Eugen, as well as the cramped apartment, well, it was so difficult.

"I don't know how I would have coped without my grandmother," she continued to a still-listening Leopold. "She is such a solid, earthbound woman, having had many hardships in her lifetime and yet never turned bitter like some people. She is always cheery, always understanding. I dread the thought of losing her one day—she is in her eighties, after all."

Absentmindedly, Bertha stirred some sugar into her coffee, while gazing out the window at the fast-moving and rather bleak landscape.

A white-gloved waiter removed their breakfast dishes and Bertha and Leopold rose to vacate their table to other waiting travellers. Joyfully, they returned to their compartment. Two more of the six seats were now occupied by another couple who boarded at the last stop. They exchanged courteous pleasantries, but otherwise refrained from more conversation. Feeling somewhat mellow but content, Bertha leaned back into her seat and lost herself in her own thoughts. She quickly noted that Leopold looked mellow and content himself.

CHAPTER SEVENTEEN

IT WAS LATE AT NIGHT WHEN THEY FINALLY ARRIVED AT THE HOTEL STEFANI IN Vienna. Even though it was a most comfortable train ride, Bertha felt quite tired and secretly wondered how the rest of the night would unfold.

She certainly was familiar with the inexplicable desires of a man. To her, it never was a time of pleasure—rather like something a woman had to endure because it was a part of married life. Recalling Karl's drunken and carnal attacks, she once more pondered if she was doing the right thing. *"What will happen with Leopold?"* she wondered, suddenly nervous.

To her surprise, Leopold had rented two rooms across from each other at the hotel. The porter opened her room, stowed her luggage, and departed, all the while Bertha stood somewhat uneasy in the doorway.

"I thought you might be more comfortable on your own," Leopold explained with a smile, handing her the key. "You are tired from a long day of travel, and tomorrow is an early start and another several hours more on the train." Bertha couldn't believe his consideration.

He put his arms around her and whispered, "Good night, sleep well, my love," kissing her gently. Bertha sighed contentedly, and the longer they kissed, the more urgent his kisses became, and Bertha began to feel some stirring within her that was completely foreign to her, something that made her want to continue with the kisses and caresses.

Suddenly, Leopold, breathing hard, pushed away from her. "Bertha, my dearest," he said rather hoarsely. "I do have to go now before I do something you're not ready for. I want you so much, but—" With that, he quickly turned and shut the door to his room.

Bertha was somewhat bewildered at his abrupt departure but entered her room with a dreamy smile on her face. Once she was in bed, even though tucked under a warm duvet, she still felt little shivers up and down her spine. Staring into the semi-darkness of the room, she asked herself if this is what physical love feels like. A gentle yearning, light touches, and oh, those kisses! She could still taste his lips and feel the searching of his tongue—how strange and wonderful it all was.

"I can't remember Karl ever kissing me like that!" she suddenly realised. She remembered, as a young wife and mother, watching the birds outside mating, and envied how the young males courted the females with tenderness and how they fed each other and took turns sitting on the eggs until they hatched. It was what she imagined a loving family looked like. Bertha had desperately craved the attention the bird received; she was so jealous—of a little bird! *"Maybe, just maybe, I finally found someone who treats me like that, as well,"* she thought. She giggled quietly to herself, picturing herself and Leopold as birds, and hugged her pillow, soon asleep.

Morning arrived quickly, and somewhat drowsy, the couple began the last leg of their trip to Venice.

After a delicious breakfast in the dining car, they settled into their seats, and Bertha eagerly watched the rapidly changing scenery passing by. Every so often, Leopold would point out something of interest, but mostly there was a pleasant, quiet calm between them. He had asked for a newspaper and was studying it diligently.

"There seems to be unrest all over the world," he commented. "The Japan-USA war, Boxer uprising in China, another *pogrom* (attack, persecution, genocide) in Russia," he sighed. "The news is indeed very depressing."

He closed the paper and turned his attention to Bertha "Let's forget the world for a while and think about our time together," he suggested. "What would you like to do first in Venice?"

"Oh, that's easy, a gondola ride, of course!" Bertha answered quickly.

Leopold nodded, "Of course, and then?"

"Have an espresso in St. Mark's Square?"

"We will do that, among all the pigeons," he laughed.

"And one more important thing, please," Bertha added in excitement. "The Venetian Glass Museum—the Murano!" She began to tell Leopold about her grandparents' factory and how she decorated the glass ornaments for the Christmas markets in the United States. She described her love for the nutcrackers and how her fingers were always sticky from the glue and paints. Leopold listened with great interest and time just flew by as she chatted.

In the early evening, they finally arrived in Venice. Bertha was nearly jumping up and down with excitement as they exited the train. A porter took their luggage to a waiting water taxi, something completely new to Bertha, and her excitement mounted.

The sun was just setting, but it was still warm enough for the two to take off their overcoats, and Bertha breathed in the fresh fragrance of Venice. The taxi was open on all sides and she had a grand view of the city. Leopold was enchanted with her childlike pleasure, as she took in the sights and sounds of this most romantic spot. On the way, gondolas passed them with young lovers on board and a costumed gondolier singing folk songs as he stoked the gondola along the canals.

Soon they reached the Hotel Daniela, a grand hotel in the middle of Venice, right along the main canal and close to St. Mark's Square. A few steps led them up to the narrow pier and right into the beautiful and architecturally stunning hotel foyer.

This time, a porter took them to one room—a full suite. Leopold gave Bertha a slightly uneasy look. "Are you comfortable with this, or would you rather have separate suites?"

Bertha, recalling the kisses from the night before, smiled and shook her head. Looking somewhat shyly at him, she remarked that it would be a waste of money to have two suites.

At that, Leopold burst into a roaring laughter, and all tensions were wiped away. He opened the double doors to their balcony and they both stepped out.

"How absolutely magnificent," Bertha whispered, leaning close to Leopold, who quickly put his arms around her. By now, the sun had set, the sky had turned into a velvety deep blue, and stars began to glisten. "I must be in a dream," Bertha continued. "I could live here forever."

From across the canal, they heard music, the laughter of people walking along the narrow aisles, and even the many church bells ringing all over the city.

Finally, Leopold gently pulled away. "Are you hungry?" he asked Bertha. "Would you like something to eat?"

She chuckled. "No, not at all—we ate a lot on the train," she suppressed a little yawn.

"Well, then I'll go downstairs for a little bit, and you can get prepared for bed," he said as casually as he could, but Bertha did not miss the hint of excitement in his voice as he made his way to the door.

Hurriedly, Bertha went to the bedroom where the porter had placed her valise. Opening it, she took out her brand-new *negligée* and matching dressing gown. A quick look in the full-length mirror reflected a still youthful-looking woman with a well-proportioned body, her full chestnut-coloured hair curled around her face and down the nape of her neck.

Leopold had given her plenty of time to prepare for bed. Slipping into her gown after a refreshing bath, she settled into the comfy high wing chair by the balcony and tried to calm herself by deeply breathing in the cool night air.

At last she heard him open the door, and he was carrying two glasses and a bottle of wine, along with a big grin on his face. "Bertha, you look beautiful!" he gasped, giving her a quick peck on her cheek.

Taking off his jacket and tie, he went towards the bedroom to "get into something more comfortable myself," he said with a smirk.

"I have never seen him without his suit," she mused, nervously taking a sip of the wine. *"Karl would just take off all his clothes and prance around naked! I hated that! I had to remind him that we had children and he needed to look decent."* The memories of that made her quite anxious now and she got up and went out to the balcony. It was truly a gorgeous night—a night made for lovers.

She felt him close to her before she heard him coming, and she need not have worried. He looked splendid in a deep red half-length dressing gown over his shirt and long dress pants.

A deep and contented sigh escaped her while he began to lightly kiss her neck, nibbling at her ear and slowly caressing her arms and along her body. She started to shiver, and little quivers ran up and down her spine.

"Are you cold?" he whispered. "No…" Bertha felt flustered. "Or maybe, oh, I don't know!" she stammered, feeling a little foolish. *"Why have I never felt like this before? Perhaps I am coming down with a fever?"* The thoughts were racing through her head, all the while Leopold kept kissing and caressing her, pulling her closer to him. "Let's go inside and warm up," he murmured, and pulled her to the large, soft bed.

They could not get enough of each other, and Bertha finally understood what physical passion truly was. He was a tender and considerate, yet passionate, lover. As they cuddled close, Bertha whispered drowsily that she had not anybody sleep next to her since likely Emil. "He had lots of nightmares as a child."

Leopold chuckled softly. "I have never slept with anybody before, so, you are the first."

"What?" Bertha propped herself up on her elbow to look at him. "I don't believe that! You must have had some women before me."

"Well, certainly, but nobody I slept with all night long," he murmured while kissing her again. "And I want you next to me forever."

Completely exhausted and feeling almost drunk on each other's love, they finally fell to sleep.

Chapter Eighteen

The following days were spent exploring Venice and exploring each other as a couple. A gondola took them along the Grand Canal, and they sat close together and took in the sights and sounds. The famous Rialto Bridge, under which the gondola passed, fascinated Bertha.

"It's also called the Bridge of Sighs," Leopold told her. "It is called such since prisoners were led across this bridge to their executions."

"Oh, how terrible!" Bertha exclaimed, shivering a little at that thought.

Quickly, Leopold pulled her closer. "Let's look at something else," he suggested, pointing towards the Doge's Palace, the little shops hugging the very narrow sidewalks. "Over there, see, there is the Campanile bell tower, and coming up, the Piazza St. Marco with the Basilica."

Bertha was enthralled. They made their way to the famous Lido Beach and watched some hardy people taking a dip in the water. Barefooted, Leopold and Bertha ran through the warm sand and sank happily into some beach chairs that had been set up all over the Lido.

In the evenings, they watched the colourfully lit gondolas going up and down the canals while eating foods Bertha had never before heard of. They became giddy on the light, sweet Chianti wine, and could not get back fast enough to their hotel suite, where Leopold continued to introduce Bertha to the rapture and ecstasy of love.

"Oh, Leo, I never knew such joy exists," Bertha exclaimed. "I have missed so much in my life..."

"We'll make up for it, I promise," Leopold whispered in her ear. "I love you with all my heart, *mein Schatz*." He held her close, while covering her with little butterfly kisses and gentle caresses.

Far too soon, their time in Venice came to an end. On their last full day, they sat in St. Mark's Square over espresso and fed the hordes of pigeons that had descended all around them.

"We need to talk a little about our future," Leo finally broached the subject both of them had tried to avoid these past glorious days.

"What are you thinking of?" Bertha lazily stirred her second cup and picked on the cake the waiter had just put on the table. "I think we should just stay here forever and ever, no work, no winters, no demanding children, just you and me." Bertha smiled at the thought even as she spoke it.

Leo laughed. "That would indeed be wonderful, but..."

"I know," Bertha interrupted, disappointed already. "It will remain a dream."

"No, not really," Leopold told her. "We will come back here, again and again, if you like, but in the meantime, we have to return to Berlin, and—so, we do need to talk about our future."

"I am listening, really Leo, I am," Bertha sighed. "But I have no idea what our future looks like."

"So, then, here is what I propose," Leo took her hand. "I will buy or rent a house somewhere in Berlin, perhaps the Grunewald area, somewhere that is a very good neighbourhood, and you can move there. I, of course, must go back and forth regularly to the estate to take care of things. Sometimes more often than others, depending on the seasons.

"There is a very capable estate manager on the premises, who, along with my father, run the horse breeding as well as the agriculture and forestry very efficiently," he continued, "and in a few years, young Fra-Lu will learn all aspects of estate running."

Leopold paused for a moment, watching Bertha's reaction. She remained silent. He continued "Of course, you will stop working at Wertheim, my wife does not need to work. I will be in Berlin, in our new home, for at least two weeks every month or more. How does that sound to you?"

"He looks like an excited little boy," Bertha thought. For a long while, she watched the pigeons waddling around the square, pecking at morsels of food, squawking for more and generally being a nuisance.

"Please, Bertha, please say something!" Leopold begged. "Do you have any other idea or thoughts?"

Finally, she answered him. "To begin with, Leo, I am quite overwhelmed— living in a house, in the Grunewald area no less, I am not sure I even fit in there." She quickly raised her hand in protest before Leopold could cut her off.

"Nevertheless, I will not move from the Turmstrasse apartment. You and I may be married in our eyes, and perhaps even in God's eyes, but as far as society is concerned, we are not. And if I live in your house, by your benevolence, I will feel like your concubine. I love you too much to enter into that kind of arrangement. I truly hope you understand that."

"My *concubine*?" Leo exclaimed in disbelief. "Bertha, Bertha, how can you even say such a thing? Never, never would I ever think of you in that way. I consider you my wife; we need to be together on a regular basis. I don't want to make love to you in many hotels—that will absolutely ruin your reputation!

"No, and double no," he shook his head vigorously. "I will find a place and we will work it out from there—and that is final!" He almost shouted near the end.

Bertha had to smile at his insistence. "Dear, dear, Leo, of course you are completely right that we need a place just for us," she conceded. "But how this will work in practice? I cannot imagine it."

"It will work; we can make it work! I am completely confident," Leopold said firmly, looking determined. "Now, let's enjoy our last evening in Venice. Look, there is an empty gondola! Do you feel like a romantic evening?" he grinned at her mischievously.

Bertha rose immediately and arm in arm, she and Leopold strolled to the steps leading down to the canal and settled into the gondola. It was another beautifully warm evening, with a light breeze, stars twinkling above, the moon rising over the city, and two lovers tenderly embracing each other. Bertha hoped this night would never end.

But of course, the magical night ended and, after another exhausting train ride with another stopover in Vienna, Leo and Bertha arrived back to Berlin in late March. The weather had become a little more pleasant, the snow was gone, the air was much milder, and the trees had begun to bud.

Standing on the platform of the train station, they held each other tightly for a few minutes before parting for the time being. Leo promised to come by her apartment within the next few days and Bertha prepared herself to return to work the following day.

BOOK FOUR
LIFE WITH LEO

CHAPTER ONE

THE DAY BERTHA RETURNED HOME FROM VENICE, SHE FOUND HER GRANDMOTHER clearly upset, beside herself.

"Bertha, my child, am I ever so glad to have you home again!" Anna cried, on the verge of tears.

"Oma, what on earth has happened?" Bertha was very worried. "Please, just try to relax, I'll make us a nice cup of tea and you can tell me all about it," she offered. "I am sorry I was not here to help," she added. *"Well, just a little sorry, but not very much,"* she thought, immediately chastising herself for her selfishness.

She quickly ran to the kitchen to boil the water for the tea, and in the meantime, took her valise to her room. Once she returned with the tea on a tray her grandmother had visibly calmed down already.

"I am so sorry to welcome you back like this my dear," Anna apologised. "But I fear I am getting too old for so many things all at once."

"Now Oma, please tell me what I have missed!" Bertha insisted as she sat down to join her grandmother.

"First, I am glad you are back. I am glad you obviously had a wonderful time, judging from all the postcards you have sent... Though I was a little surprised you had time for postcards," she offered a weak smile.

"I had the most wonderful time of my life, Oma, but please, don't keep me on pins and needles here—tell me why you are so agitated!"

"I don't quite know how to begin," Anna started, "so I'll just tell you the good news first. Karo and Julius are expecting a baby! I will be a great-great-grandmother. Now how about that?"

"I guessed as much, with the very fast wedding date after their engagement," Bertha admitted. "But you already are a great-great grandmother from Karl-Heinz's children."

"True," said Anna, "but they are so far away, and we have never met them, so it is a little unreal. But now, let me continue. Emil has moved back, and it is best he tells you himself once he comes back from work."

Bertha just shrugged. "He is a restless soul, so moving back here is not a great concern."

"Perhaps, but he most certainly is a troubled soul," Anna warned. "But now to the other news...my son, August—" Anna stopped when she saw Bertha freeze up. "Yes, *him*—he suddenly died. He is said to have been with another woman at the time—I guess it was a little too much for him at his age," Anna said sarcastically, shaking her head.

"August? He is dead?" Bertha felt shocked, and strange. "He was not that old yet. Did you go to the funeral?"

Anna shook her head. "No—by the time I was notified, it was already over and done with. In any event, he left several thousand marks for Emil in his will," she added. "I have not told him yet, since this will clue him in on who is father is."

Bertha sat in silence, thinking back to the awful circumstances that led to Emil's conception. Meanwhile, Anna continued to share other news with her granddaughter, until she noticed she wasn't paying attention.

"Did you hear what I just said?" Anna asked.

"Yes, Oma, you told me about Uncle August..."

"Yes, but you did not hear what else I said?"

"There is more? Please, Oma, I can barely take all of that in!" Bertha put her hands on her face.

"Karl is also dead—you are now a free woman!"

Bertha looked up and just stared, mouth open, at her grandmother.

"Oma, slow down," she begged, her mind whirling with thoughts. "Did you say Karl is dead? My legal husband, Karl? Dead? How? When? Do the children know?" Bertha's mind was now racing.

Finally, she stood up. "Oma, I think I need a stronger drink than tea!" she announced. "Is there still some of your medicinal cognac around?"

"Yes, and please make that two," Oma replied.

Bertha listened to her Oma as she unravelled all that she had learned while Bertha was away. Karl was thrown from a horse and broke his neck. Of the immediate family, only Karl-Heinz had attended his funeral service. It would have taken Karl-Heinz at least one day of travel to get there. Anna noted that Emil simply refused and Karo had been persuaded by her husband not to travel so early in her pregnancy.

Yet while all this sunk in, Bertha couldn't help but think, *"So now I am truly free to marry Leopold!"* she was ashamed at how jubilant she felt at that thought.

"Is there any more news, Oma?" Bertha said. "Because I don't think I can take any more today."

Anna shook her head. "But now you know why I was in such a state when you came home"

"Well, then, I have some news of my own to share, dear Oma," Bertha smiled. "Leopold has asked me to be his wife, and I said yes! Look, he gave me this beautiful ring!" she held her hand out to her grandmother.

"Oh my, it is indeed beautiful," Anna mused. "I honestly did not believe he was so serious. Well, now you are free, but what about him then?"

Bertha began to explain the reasons that Leopold could not be free to marry legally at this time. Oma listened carefully, nodding here and there, before remarking that this could be a long wait.

"It will work out Oma, wait and see," Bertha replied confidently, sounding overly optimistic.

"Well, I don't think that his wife will do him the same favour that Karl did!" was Anna's somewhat acerbic remark.

"Oma, please!" Bertha protested. "Leopold is the man I love, and he loves me, and we will work out something that is good for both of us. Now, with your permission I will get out of my travel clothes and start on making some supper. I suppose Emil will be home by then?"

"Maybe," Oma said quietly. "And by all means, get into something more comfortable. There are still some leftovers in the kitchen you only need to warm up.

Chapter Two

Bertha was just ladling the stew on the plates when Emil appeared.

"Just in time for dinner," Bertha smiled at her eldest. "You look thin, my boy, sit and eat."

Emil picked listlessly at his food. "Mama, I am so glad you are back home," he finally said. "I...er...well, I need to live here for a while."

Bertha nodded. "Of course! This is your home. Now eat, please."

As soon as the dishes were done, Anna announced that she was off to bed, exhausted from the past week's events. Bertha motioned to Emil to join her, explaining they needed to have a talk.

"Oma told me about your father's sudden death," Bertha started.

"He is not my father," Emil interrupted sullenly.

"Well, that may be so, but—"

"Please Mama, don't say much more, that subject is closed for me, he was a brute, and uncaring and such a—"

Bertha shot him a warning glance. "No swearing here, you know better than that."

"Pardon me, Mama." Emil hung his head.

"Now, I have another matter to discuss with you," Bertha moved on. "As you know, your Great-Uncle August recently died, as well."

Emil nodded glumly. "I hardly remember the last time I ever saw him," he admitted, looking off into the distance. "Just nothing but death around here..."

"Now, you listen to me Emil," Bertha quickly continued, wishing to get this conversation over with. "August left you several thousand marks in his will."

Emil's head shot up. "What? Why would he do that?" he was genuinely confused. "Doesn't he have at least seven children of his own? I don't understand." He stared at his mother, who silently but calmly watched his reaction.

After what felt like an eternity to Bertha, she noticed a slow awareness creep over her son's face. "It's him, isn't it? *He* is my father? Uncle August? Oh Mama, I can't believe this! Please tell me this is not so!" he exclaimed, shaking his head.

Bertha allowed him to express his feelings.

"Why did you never tell me?" Emil continued, lashing out at his mother. "How could you and your uncle—no! That's just, no! I don't know what to say!" he suddenly burst into tears.

"Emil, my dear son, please," Bertha quietly pleaded. "You are a grown man. You can hear the truth now," she paused before saying the ugly words she knew had to come out. "Your great-uncle, he...he took advantage of me when I was just seventeen."

Emil was stunned into silence. "He *raped* you?" he finally blurted, horrified and incredulous. Then a look of utter sadness washed over his face, and he sat by his mother's feet and put his head in her lap. "Mama, I am so, so very sorry that you had to have me, that you had to marry that man who pretended to be my father. Oh, Mama," he sobbed and sobbed.

Bertha just stroked his head gently, over and over again, until he calmed down enough to hear her out.

"Now, you listen carefully young man," she instructed. "I loved you from the moment you were born, and I will always love you. I would never ever not have wanted you. It matters nothing how you were conceived. What matters is that you are my son, my precious boy.

"I never, ever regretted having you," she continued, assuring him. "Please stop all that blubbering now. At least August was decent enough to pay support and schooling for you all these years, and even remember you in his will. Try to be thankful for that kind of father."

Slowly Emil nodded. "It's just such a surprise, Mama."

"I know, son."

Both sat in silence, absorbing everything.

"Now, tell me why you came back home," Bertha said, breaking the silence and changing subjects. "What is going on with you?"

"Anton and I are finished—we are no longer together," he mumbled, swallowing hard. "He has found somebody else and I have moved out."

Bertha frowned, confused. "Honestly, Emil, I don't understand how you can hang on to a school friend like Anton for so long," she said, furrowing her brow. "He has always mistreated you—he is not a good friend to you. Why does this upset you so much?"

"I guess you don't know, then, do you?" Emil looked at his mother carefully.

"Don't talk in riddles, Emil! What don't I know?"

"Mama, I love Anton," he confessed. "I have always loved him!"

"Yes, yes," Bertha replied impatiently. *This boy takes everything so seriously,* she thought, bewildered. *"Sure, one loves their friends, but..."*

"Mama!" Emil almost screamed. "You don't understand, do you? I love Anton the way you love Leopold! I am not attracted to girls, and I never have been!"

Bertha was completely stunned, and a heavy silence hung in the room.

"Emil, my sweet Emil," Bertha finally murmured. "How you must suffer! I have always puzzled why you and Anton were so close, and now I understand."

"I will pack my stuff now and leave," Emil got up to leave.

In a flash, Bertha blocked his way. "What on earth are you saying?"

"You would not want somebody like me around," Emil hung his head.

"Now, stop this immediately!" Bertha instructed. "This is your home, and it will always be your home.

"I am so proud of you son," she continued warmly. "I am proud of your achievements, and I love you dearly. I do not understand that kind of attraction," she admitted. "I do not know if this is something you will overcome or outgrow—I honestly do not know. But the one thing I do know is that you are part of the family and I will love you and protect you for as long as I have breath. All I ask is for you to be careful—careful of the company you choose."

Emil breathed a sigh of relief. "I will, Mama, I will!" he exclaimed. "Thank you for trying to understand. I don't understand it either, but there are many of us out there, hiding in darkness, shunned by family, kicked out of university, taken advantage of—oh, I don't want to talk about it. I will stay here for now.

"If there is some money available for me now, perhaps I will move to another country. I don't know yet."

"Go to bed son, and get some rest," Bertha suggested. "Please do not make rash decisions at this time."

"Thank you, Mama, I will. Good night!" Emil hugged his mother as hard as he could before going to his room.

Bertha sat for a long, long time deliberating what or how she could possibly help her dear Emil. *"I wonder if I should talk to Leo."* She hoped fervently he would understand. She yearned for him to be beside her and missed him already.

It was another four days before Leopold came back. All throughout that painful waiting time, she had a tight knot in her stomach, fearing that Leo had walked away from her and that their beautiful trip to Venice had indeed been just a dream.

On the third day without him, Bertha's work supervisor, Frau Scholz, called her over and reprimanded her for her disposition. Bertha apologised profusely and let her know that there were some deaths in the family, which might have accounted for her inattention to her work duties.

Frau Scholz frowned. "Under the circumstances, I will let it go this time, but please, put more effort into your work. There are many other women who are looking for a position such as yours," she warned sternly. Bertha gritted her teeth while Frau Scholz continued. "After all, you just had the extraordinary privilege of a two weeks' vacation. Did you go anywhere special then?"

Bertha quickly shook her head. "No Ma'am, as I just said, we had two deaths in the family, now may I please be excused?" a few tears trickled down Bertha's cheeks.

"All right, then," Frau Scholz sighed. "I offer my condolences, and you may return to your station." She waved her off and Bertha retreated quickly.

"I must keep my mind on my work. I must keep my mind on my work," she repeated over and over again to herself as she politely served an especially fussy customer.

On the fourth day, she was tempted to leave her job. Only her grandmother persuaded her to keep going. "Leopold will come," she assured Bertha. "You know he has many things to take care of. He would not have given you this beautiful ring if he did not mean it. Please pull yourself together—it is not like you to let yourself go like this!"

That day was one of the longest days Bertha endured at work. Under the watchful eye of her supervisor, she smiled, served customers with exquisite politeness, paid attention to every little detail, and noted the satisfied nod of Frau Scholz. She was never so happy to see that workday end.

When she exited Wertheim amidst a flock of laughing and chattering women leaving work, she saw Leopold standing next to a taxi, waving to her. At first, she wasn't sure it was even him. Dozens of curious eyes followed her as she slowly made her way to him.

"Leo, where have you been?" she asked, surprised and delighted. "I have waited so long for you!" she sighed with relief.

"I am here now, my love, and I have a surprise for you, so please join me," he replied with an impish grin. Leaving all doubts and thoughts of work behind, she cuddled close to him as the motorised taxi made its way along Leipziger Platz.

"Where are we going?"

"Wait and see." he answered, all the while kissing her hand. Little shivers of pleasure ran down her spine and she exhaled slowly.

"I know, I want you, too," Leopold murmured, his voice thick with desire. "I missed you terribly."

Very reluctantly, Bertha broke this tender spell. "Leo, I am free!" she suddenly exclaimed. "There is no more Karl or August!"

Leopold, very startled by this sudden and unexpected outburst, requested clarification, and Bertha told him what all had happened while they were in Venice. Almost at loss for words, he pulled her close to him. "One day, you and I will get married legally," he whispered. "I promise you, one day it will happen. Will you wait for that day?" he anxiously peered into her eyes.

"I will, Leo, you know I will," Bertha promised, settling back into her seat, when she realised how far they had already travelled. "Where are you taking me?" she asked once more.

"Soon—you will see shortly."

Finally, the taxi turned into a small road, rumbled towards the end, and turned once more before coming to a stop. Leopold gave the driver a generous tip, asking him to go for a meal somewhere and return in two hours. With a bow and a "Thank you, sir," the driver obliged and turned back.

Bertha stood waiting, still unsure what was going on. Looking around, she took in the dead-end road they stood on, the dense forestry and shrubs all around, as well as some narrow sandy pathways. She was clearly puzzled.

Leo, with a huge smile, took her hand and led her down one of the pathways. Once they reached an opening behind the many trees, she saw a house—white stucco, big veranda, plenty of windows, and even more flowers. It was April, and the spring flowers were in full bloom and birds were singing in the trees, giving the whole house an enchanted aura, particularly since it was already dusk.

"Whose house is this, Leo?" Bertha begged to know.

"Well, it's yours—if you like it," was his feigned nonchalant reply.

Speechless, Bertha stared at him, back at the house, and back at him. "Please explain," she finally said. "I don't understand."

"It is quite simple, my love," he replied. "This can be our together home in Berlin, provided you like it, of course. It is very quiet, with few neighbours. Most only come during the summer months, and we can live here rather discreetly as Herr and Frau Graf."

Bertha gasped. "Oh my, Leo, you most certainly succeeded in surprising me!"

"Let's go inside and see so you can check it out for yourself," he suggested. "I have spent the past four days driving all estate sales people insane with my request, looked at a number of possible places, but fell in love with this place. I sure hope you feel the same."

He pulled her to the door, fishing for the keys in his pocket and unlocked it. Bertha held her breath in anticipation. Before she could rush inside, he firmly put his arms around her, lifting her up off the ground and across the doorstep.

"Leo," she protested, giggling. "You will hurt yourself!"

He only laughed. "You are so small and light, and it is only appropriate we enter our married life in this manner." Bertha nearly exploded with love for him.

With eyes big as saucers, she wandered around the house, which seemed like a mansion to her.

"This was a *datcha* (summerhouse) for a Russian diplomat who returned home, and his replacement wants to live in the city, so my estate agent offered it to me—furniture and all."

"This is already yours?"

"No, not quite yet, my dearest, but as of tomorrow, it will be—that is, if you like it."

"If I like it?!" Bertha exclaimed. "This is a magnificent place. What is there not to like?" She was almost breathless.

"Come, let's look around at the whole house," Leopold suggested. "It's not that large, but there's plenty enough for us and perhaps a visitor or two," he chuckled.

The small sitting room had a big window to the back, overlooking a lovely garden. Off the hallway was a well-furnished kitchen, a small room for a maid, and a large bedroom. A stairway led up to an attic room that had obviously been used as a children's room. Then there was a most incredible part of the house— an indoor toilet and large bathtub. Bertha could not believe her eyes. *"No more sharing a toilet with lots of family, no more pulling out the big tub and filling it with water boiled on the stove—this is too good to be true!"*

"And there you have it" Leo announced with obvious joy in having found this very private house.

Bertha was too dazed to say a word. She kept looking around at this cosy little home and at Leo, and tried to grasp what was happening. Finally, Leo put his arms around her and gently pulled her into the bedroom, and with a twinkle in his eyes, suggested they try out the bed to see if it is a good fit. Bertha did not need much persuading, and they fell onto the bed, embracing each other hungrily.

Afterward, they lay back lazily. By now, it was almost dark out. "The bed fits!" Leo declared with a laugh.

Bertha started to giggle and laughed until her sides hurt. "Oh, Leo, you are incorrigible!"

Leopold, leaning up on one elbow, looked down at her with so much love and tenderness that she was awestruck. Finally, he got up, pulling her up with him. "Let's look more respectable—the taxi will be back any moment."

Sure enough, they could hear the rumble of the automotive already. "Now we need to eat somewhere. I am very hungry—you wear me out," Leo teased her with another kiss. Bertha couldn't stop laughing, "Then I'll explain how we will make this house situation work."

Chapter Three

Once settled comfortably in a restaurant neither one of them had ever been to before, they placed their order and Leopold raised his wine glass. "To us, my dearest!" he toasted.

"To us!" Bertha chimed in, still feeling like she was living in a fog. "You know, Frau Scholz criticised me yesterday for my inattentiveness at work," she told Leo. "Other than apologising and promising to do better, I could not tell her I am in love—all my thoughts have been with you every hour of the day."

Leo, twirling his wine glass in his hand, spoke up. "I would like you to leave there," he told her. "You do not need to work. I will set up an account for you to use as you see fit. I want you to be free for us to travel whenever I have the time. I want for us to spend time together in your soon-to-be home."

"Surely you mean our home?" Bertha tried to correct him.

But Leopold just shook his head. "No, Bertha, this house will be in your name. I want you to have some security in this relationship. One never knows what tomorrow brings."

"But—" she tried to interrupt.

"No, no, please do not say anything just yet," Leo stopped her. "I am very well situated, and my son will inherit everything when the time comes. I have always thought I need a home for myself in the Berlin area. I no longer want to keep staying in hotels all the time when I am here on business. And at some point, Franz-Ludwig will get married and he needs the space of the estate for himself and his family. If something were to happen to me, I need to know you are taken care of."

Before Bertha could say anything, their dinners arrived. Silently, they ate their food, and Bertha hardly knew what she was eating while she was deep in thought.

After dinner, over espresso and a cognac for Leo, Bertha had pulled herself together to share her thoughts. "Leo, this is more than a dream come true, that little house is so beautiful and yes, I will love sharing it with you."

She paused a moment before adding, "one thing though, I will need to keep the apartment on the Turmstrasse. After all, my Oma still lives there, and it's still the children's refuge if they need it—in particular Emil," she explained. "I do need to talk with you about that boy, but not at this moment."

She stopped to gauge his reaction, and he simply nodded as she continued. "And then there is the issue of work, as well as transportation and all that goes with it. I am not sure the house will be warm enough in the winter months; it may well be snowed in. At my present home, I have all that one needs— the breadman, the milkman, the mailman, the vegetable stalls, the butcher, everything one needs for daily life. So, I do have difficulties imagining myself living there all week, especially alone."

"I have thought of that myself, as well," Leo admitted, "and I am glad you brought this up. For the moment, we will live in the house only when I am here in Berlin; this makes everything easier for you. And, if you want to continue to work at the store, that's fine—I have no objections for now, but this will change soon.

"I want to take you to Vienna this summer," he continued, "so you will need to take time off again, which is something Wertheim will not give you."

"Vienna? This summer?" Bertha asked, surprised. "You did not tell me that!"

"I did, just now!" Leo chuckled. "So, you see, I am demanding all your time from now on." He winked at her.

"I am more than delighted to agree to your demands," Bertha pretended to be serious.

"Tomorrow you will accompany me to the notary public, and we will finalise the purchase of the house," Leopold instructed. "Please bring along all necessary identification papers, along with the death certificate of Karl," he paused briefly at that. "I must say that I was relieved to hear of his death—I know one should not say that—but it makes putting the house in your name much easier. He can no longer put a claim in for it."

They left the restaurant well past ten o'clock, and after a long embrace and an even longer kiss, he hailed a carriage for her to go back to her apartment. She could hardly wait to tell Oma about her day.

By the time she reached home, she was nearly bursting with excitement, and hoped Oma was still up and awake. *"I'll simply wake her; this is impossible to keep inside me all night,"* she thought, almost bouncing into the apartment. To her surprise, not only was Oma still up, but Karoline was sitting with her, as well.

"Mama, you sure are late coming home!" she jokingly chastised her mother.

"Is there any tea left?" she asked the women. "I have big news to share with you!"

"Yes, I will make some more," Karoline answered, "but funny that you should say that—I have news too, Mama." Karo got up to heat some more water.

Bertha, settling herself comfortably in the big armchair, gratefully sipped on the hot cup of tea, beckoning Karo to share her news.

"Julius and I are expecting a baby," she bubbled with excitement, "in July," she added, blushing a little.

"Ah, yes, a seven-month baby," Bertha acknowledged a bit teasingly. "I had a fairly good idea why your wedding followed so soon after the engagement."

"Mama, I wanted to tell you, but—"

"Don't worry, you've told me now," Bertha interrupted. "I am so very delighted by this news."

"Of course, Julius is hoping for a boy, and he picked Samuel for a name."

"Samuel?" Bertha frowned a little. "Isn't that pretty unusual for a name?"

Karo agreed. "I'd rather have a more popular German name, but Julius says the firstborn son of Jewish faith should be named after a recently deceased close relative, like his grandfather, whose name was Samuel. It also Julius' middle name," she explained.

"So how about a little compromise," Bertha suggested. "If it's a boy, call him Walther-Samuel. Walther is a very popular name right now."

"I personally favour Rudolph or Peter, perhaps even Erich," said Karo.

"Oh, you still have a few months to think about this," Anna reminded her, trying to stifle a yawn. "You have something to share as well, Bertha?" she turned to her granddaughter. But before Bertha could answer, Karo told them she needed to stay at the apartment for the next couple of weeks.

She explained that there was a measles outbreak in the paediatric unit where she and Julius were working, and she had orders to stay away from both work and her husband during her early pregnancy.

"Oh dear, that will make things tight around here again!" Anna laughed. Somewhat puzzled, Karo suggested that she could simply move into her former room.

"Well, Emil has moved back," Bertha explained.

"Emil moved back?" Karoline shook her head. "Does that brother of mine ever settle down? So now what?"

"For tonight, you simply sleep in my room, Karo, and I'll sleep on the sofa," Bertha offered. "Tomorrow we'll figure out something. I agree, Emil should be back on his own, but that is another story."

Bertha settled back in her chair with her tea. "And now to my big news!"

Anna and Karoline perked up their ears and said, "Let's hear it!" almost in unison.

After Bertha related her day and how the events unfolded with Leopold, the two women were enthralled. "Where is it?" Anna wanted to know of the house.

"Near the Mueggelsee in Treptow," Bertha answered.

"Oh, my!" Karo exclaimed. "That is a beautiful area," Karo exclaimed, "perfect for a summer house." Excited chatter filled the apartment and it was well past midnight by the time they all made their way to bed.

"Really, Frau Hoffmann, this is most unacceptable!" Frau Scholz scolded Bertha the following morning when she arrived at Wertheim, bleary-eyed. "Not only are you over one hour late, but you are not even in uniform! I am afraid I must ask you to leave immediately and return properly attired, at which time we simply must go over the requirements of your employment again." Frau Scholz was trying to keep her voice low, but her anger was unmistakable.

"I know, Frau Scholz, and I must apologise for not having told you sooner," Bertha quickly and calmly replied, "but I am here to tender my resignation, starting immediately. As soon as I have washed and ironed my uniform, I will return it. I do thank you for the opportunity to have worked here; it truly helped me on my future path of life," she added, while thinking, *"and you will never know how much."*

With a huge smile and sigh of relief, Bertha left a speechless and still-fuming Frau Scholz behind. Once outside, she had the urge to jump for joy. *"Free, free at last, and life ahead looks wonderful,"* she hummed a song as she walked on this gorgeous early spring day to the notary public's office where Leopold would wait for her.

She was planning to spend the next couple of weeks at the house while Karo stayed at the apartment during the measles outbreak. She hoped that Leo had time for her and that they could indeed live like a couple. The mere thought of that excited her and she could hardly wait.

Leopold was thrilled at her suggestion, and promptly arranged whatever needed to be done to make the place liveable. Two days later, Bertha took a taxicab, loaded with some of her clothing, a supply of food, and some other odds and ends she thought they might need.

Proudly she had shown off the deed to the house to her family—it was in her name, just as promised by Leo—eliciting oohs and aahs from them. Karo was relieved to know her mother did not have to sleep on the sofa for the next couple of weeks. Emil, still withdrawn and silent, hugged his mother, whispering "I wish you well, Mama" in her ear, and Anna hoped for some peace and quiet returning to her life.

Like two children let out of school, Leopold and Bertha, holding hands, ran down the walk towards the house.

"I hope you brought the key," Leo teased her.

"What do you think?" Bertha laughed, holding the key in her other hand, trying to pass it on to Leo.

But he shook his head. "It is your house, your key—you have the joy of first opening it. But I do hope you'll let me in," he added with a wink.

Bursting out in gales of laughter, they entered the house.

"You look around some more while I help the taxi driver unload," Leo suggested. For a solid minute, Bertha just stood in total silence, breathing in the clean smell of her very own house. Making her way to the kitchen to see if she could heat some water for tea, she noticed with absolute pleasure that it was fully stocked. Pots and pans hung gleaming in the sunshine from hooks, the drawers had the required cutlery, there were cups and saucers, as well as plates—a fully functioning kitchen. She lit the fire in the stove and put the kettle on when Leo came and put his arms around her.

"Phew, it is all done!" he grinned. "We are alone, just you and me." They embraced for a long time, kissing tenderly and simply enjoying being together, with nobody around. While Leo brought the suitcases and boxes to the bedroom, Bertha set the table by the window overlooking the garden. He had taken off his jacket and loosened his tie, pushing the comfortably upholstered chair behind her to sit. He took his place opposite from her and they simply looked at each other. It was an overwhelming moment—a moment they would never forget. The love they shared filled them with such awe they glowed.

These two weeks were most magical. Bertha enjoyed cooking for Leo, and he enjoyed eating her meals. They went for long walks exploring the area, hardly ever seeing another person. In the cooler evenings, they rested comfortably in each other's arms in front of a fire, listening to fire's crackle or soft rain falling, and shared stories and events in their lives.

CHAPTER FOUR

IT WAS THE END OF MAY WHEN BERTHA SUSPECTED THAT SHE, TOO, WAS CARRYING a child. The prospect of another child stunned and alarmed her.

"Maybe it's the change of life—I can't be having a baby at the same time as Karo!"

By now, Karoline had moved back home with Julius, Emil was coming and going, and Leopold had returned to his estate but was expected to return within the next couple of days. They had agreed on a two-week rhythm in order to meet all the other needs in their lives. So far, they had only gone through May, and Bertha was eagerly looking forward to the next two weeks with her husband.

"You are very restless today," Anna looked at Bertha intently one day. "Is something troubling you?"

Bertha decided to be upfront. "Well, yes, sort of—I don't really know," Bertha began. "But, oh Oma, I don't know how this could happen, but I think I could be having a baby!"

"You don't know how this happened?" Anna snickered. "You've had four children and you don't remember how they came into being?"

"Oma, please, this is not funny," Bertha pleaded. "Maybe it's not a baby. Do you think it may be the change that a woman goes through?" Bertha was anxious while her Oma peered more closely at her granddaughter, only to slowly shake her head.

"No, my dear, you are too young for the change, and not too old to conceive. Looking at you, I would swear you are indeed in the family way."

"What will I tell Leo? How will he react? Perhaps he does not want a child!" Bertha nervously rambled on.

Anna, always the epitome of calm, simply said, "What is done is done, it cannot be changed, so even your Leo has to accept that."

"And what about Karo and Emil?" Bertha worried next.

"What about them? They will also have to accept whatever happens."

"Oma, how can you be so calm?"

"How do you want me to react?" Oma teased. "I am an old woman now, and I am happy you have found true love later in life. I can assure you that you will love this child with all your heart; it is a very fortunate child to have two such loving parents."

"But I am not so sure of that part, will we be loving parents? I am so confused, because of our situation..."

"Enough of this talk, child," Oma replied in a firm voice. "As I said before, what's done is done, and you best prepare yourself and that man of yours!" With a softer, gentler voice, she added, "Don't worry; it will all work out, you will see."

Two days later, Leopold returned and picked her up for their time together at the house. "You look so tanned, Leo, so young and healthy," Bertha noted.

"I should be," he replied. "I spent most of my time outside on the back of my horse, taking note of the state of the terrain, the pastures, and the newborn livestock. It was so much fun this time, because Fra-Lu rode with me on his pony—that was the first time and he was quite excited. He will be a fine rancher one day."

Bertha heard the pride in Leo's voice and felt a little stab of resentment. *"Now stop that!"* she scolded herself silently. *"It is his son after all—well, sort of, anyway,"* she corrected herself. *"What will happen if I carry his real son?"* She was afraid to think any further.

The next few days went by rather quickly, with Bertha acting fitful and jumpy. Several times, Leo looked at her sharply without comment. She knew she should tell him, but she felt uneasy on how to broach the subject and how he would react. What if it changed their relationship? Or his feelings for her?

One morning, the sight of breakfast suddenly made her feel queasy and she refused to eat anything. But when she had to run to the bathroom to retch and came back white-faced, Leo put an end to her indecision.

"Now, my dearest Bertha, you are going to lie down on this sofa, and you will tell me exactly what is ailing you," he said firmly. "You have not been yourself the past week, and if you are sick, I will get a doctor. If there is something else you need to tell me, please do so, we have promised to be always honest with each other, so please, tell me."

"I am not ill, but we are going to have a baby!" Bertha blurted out. "I did not know how to tell you; I was so worried—"

"A baby?" Leo interrupted. "We are going to have a baby?" Leo shouted this time, excitedly. "A baby? Together? You are having my child?" A huge grin spread across his face as he grabbed Bertha, laughing and hugging her. "Oh Bertha, my darling, why did you not tell me sooner? I am beyond happy! My own child with the woman I love!"

By this time, Bertha was sobbing with relief "I— wasn't sure...how you would take it," she cried. "I am in shock myself and so far, I don't even know how to handle all this."

"What is there to handle?" Leopold asked. "We are having a child—the most beautiful gift one can have. Oh, I am so elated I could shout for joy!"

Through her tears, Bertha watched Leo's proud jubilance. "I will be a grandmother and mother, all in the same year," she reminded him, with a chuckle. "Can you handle that?"

"My dearest wife," Leopold said, now solemn. "We can handle everything, as long as we are together."

"I think we might not make it to Vienna this year," Bertha teased him, still a little weepy.

"Oh, there is always next year and the next year and many, many years ahead of us..." he paused. "A baby. I still can't believe it!" Leo was ecstatic.

The next few days passed in blissful joy, with Leopold being most gentle with her.

"I will try to come home more often now," he promised, but Bertha declined.

"You need to be at your estate at this time of year. You also need to spend time with your growing boy," she reminded him. "Nothing will happen to me with Oma and the kids around. By my calculations, I am not due until late November with our little Venice surprise," she said, trying to dispel his concerns.

"November is good; I can take at least the whole month to be with you," he said. "Venice surprise, indeed!"

"Now do you trust me?" Leo wanted to know with a little smile.

Bertha nodded. "I do, Leo, I do. I should have told you earlier."

Several days later, Bertha went to see her friend Hertha, who was delighted to see her. "Come in, come in," she greeted her warmly. "It seems like a long time since we saw each other. Aren't you at work? Are you still seeing your noble man?"

Bertha laughed. "Go slow, Hertha. I must admit I have been quite preoccupied," she admitted. "No, I no longer work, and yes, I am still with Leopold."

Over a cup of coffee and a slice of homemade cake, they chatted and caught up on the past few weeks of events. Finally, Bertha, who was not too sure how to approach this, asked her friend if she was well. "I'm not sure how to ask you this, except straight up," she said cautiously. "You looked to me as if you were with child the last time I saw you; perhaps I was wrong, and if so, I apologise."

Hertha nodded slowly. "You were correct, I *was*."

"Oh, my dear, I am so sorry I brought this up," Bertha said with concern. "It must be very painful for you. I only asked you because I am expecting myself."

"No... Wait, you are? Do you need some help? Surely you don't want to burden yourself with a baby at this age and time in your life!" Hertha said. "I didn't!"

Bertha stared at her friend in shock. "Don't tell me—I can't believe this. You got rid of your baby?"

"Oh, be sensible, Bertha," Hertha chided her. "Who wants a child at age forty?"

"Well, I do," Bertha huffed. "And Leo, too," she added rather defiantly, still not sure what Hertha was exactly talking about.

"You are fortunate then," Hertha said sadly. "My Hugo took off as soon as I told him, he went back to his wife, telling me not to expect any money from him and to never tell his wife. It seems he never had any intentions to leave her. He gave me enough money to see a certain doctor. I must admit I was relieved when it was all over."

Bertha was completely dumbstruck. "How could you?" she finally said, clearly upset. "You could have died; you could have been sent to prison, and the doctor could have been executed! Hertha, I am completely at loss for words!" she exclaimed to her friend.

"I know what you are saying," Hertha admitted. "It frightened me half to death, as well, but now that it is all over, I can only repeat that I am glad I did it. I cannot see myself with a child, unable to care for it, no prospects of finding another man—I am not as strong as you are, my friend," Hertha lamented with a forlorn look on her face. "I truly wish that it all works out for you and you continue to be happy."

Bertha could only nod, feeling quite upset at what she had heard. Trying to change the subject, she told her about Karo, about the house Leo had bought, and the reason she quit work. But the normally easy banter between the two now seemed strained, and both knew in their hearts that their friendship was no longer what it once was.

"I think I will move to my daughter's in Hamburg," Hertha finally said. "There really is nothing here for me anymore, and she has asked me several times already."

"I wish you well," Bertha hugged her friend, who now seemed so distant from her, before making her way home.

She felt like crying, but at the same time, she felt unbelievably blessed with Leo and the inner peace she felt, along with the joy of giving Leo his own child. A smile spread across her face and with a new bounce in her step, she arrived back home.

It appeared her nosy neighbour had made a point to wait for her return. "Good afternoon, Frau Hoffmann," she greeted her.

"As well to you, Frau Baum," Bertha replied, trying to slip by this meddlesome woman. "It looks like you had a good holiday with your husband," she gestured pointedly at Bertha's stomach along with a sly smile.

Momentarily disoriented by this comment, Bertha realised it must have been Karl she thought of, and at that she laughed out loud. "Yes, Frau Baum, it was a very good holiday!" Still snickering, Bertha quickly opened the door to her Oma's apartment, leaving a slightly confused woman behind.

The next few months flew by. By mid-July, Karoline and Julius became the proud parents of a little girl, whom they named Martha.

And in late November, Bertha delivered a healthy girl, as well. Leo was in seventh heaven with his precious daughter. They decided on Ella-Friederike for a name, eventually Elfi for short. Ella for Bertha's little sister who died so very young, and Friederike as a tribute to Leo's middle name, Friederich.

Leopold registered his daughter's birth at City Hall, naming himself the father. However, little Ella was given her mother's last name, as the new child had to be registered as "illegitimate," which greatly vexed Leo. He vowed that at some point he would legally adopt her so that she could carry his name. He also immediately set up a trust fund for her since, as a legally illegitimate child, she was not entitled to any inheritance.

Bertha did not particularly care what name Ella would be known by; in a way, she was glad it was simply "Hoffmann" as it would not stand out later in school or work.

As another year ended, Christmas was celebrated in the Turmstrasse, with Anna, Emil, Bertha, and Ella. Karo and little Martha came by on Christmas Day. Leo went home to his estate and to tell Ludwiga, his parents, as well as Franz-

Ludwig of the birth of his daughter. He returned just before New Year's Eve, filled with the happy news that Fra-Lu wanted to see his new sister.

"He was most excited to hear about Ella," Leo recounted, "as were my parents. Ludwiga is happy for me and wishes us all the best. She feels very guilty to be responsible for me being in this position."

"You did it for your nephew," Bertha reminded him.

"Well, yes, but he is now my son, and yes, it was for him as well as the family. It cannot be undone, so we carry on the best we can. All I want to tell you over and over again—I love you and nothing will change that," said warmly. "We will raise our daughter together, alongside my son, whom, I hope with all my heart, you can embrace, as well. I would like to bring him along, perhaps over Easter."

Bertha, nursing her tiny infant, was unsure how to answer that. Gently blowing the beads of sweat from the furiously suckling baby, she did not answer immediately.

Leo, sensing her hesitance, quickly sat next to her, stroking both the infant's brow as well as Bertha's, feeling the need to add a little more. "My dearest Bertha, *Schatz*," he implored, "Fra-Lu is starting boarding school after Easter and I will see very little of him—only during his vacations. I think it will be wonderful for him to spend some time as a family with his new sister."

Slowly Bertha nodded. "I hope you are right," she told Leo. "Eventually Ella will know her big brother, and that will be a good thing."

On Easter morning in 1901, both babies, Martha and Ella, were baptised and Bertha met her stepson for the first time.

Franz-Ludwig was a delightful young boy, very well mannered, just as handsome as Leo, and completely smitten with Ella. He would have carried her everywhere if he could. For that matter, he was just as tender with little Martha. Bertha's life was joyful and content. Most of her time was spent in her own home, as Emil now lived permanently in the Turmstrasse with Anna.

Chapter Five: 1906

Bertha sat in her backyard, enjoying a late summer afternoon. Inhaling deeply the fragrant scents of the last of the roses, she watched Ella trying to put together a kite with Fra-Lu. The boy was so patient when holding the paper for her to glue and tying bows on the rope of the tail. Ella was a picture of curiosity and concentration, nose slightly wrinkled, mouth half-open, and strands of her thick, dark blonde hair continually falling into her face, only to pushed aside with harried gestures.

Young Martha was quite opposite; slight and dark-haired, she was an inquisitive child, serious, analytical, and meticulous. *"Already a doctor in the making!"* Bertha mused, as she watched the child lying on her stomach observing a few ants struggling under their loads. All the while she rocked a restless and teething one-year-old on her lap.

Young Peter-Samuel was Karoline's and Julius' second child, and Karo was presently in labour with their third. *"This looks and feels like a nursery,"* Bertha thought wryly. *"The only one to talk with at the moment is Fra-Lu."* Bertha sighed heavily. This was the first day she was out of black mourning clothes, the traditional requirement when a member of the family had passed away, and after more than a year, she finally donned a light gray frock.

She secretly yearned for those carefree times with Leo that seemed so long ago, and resented always having to tend to her daughter's children. *"Why can't Julius' mother take them once in a while?"* she wondered. Karo had hinted of some dissention between her and the Feldmanns, but Bertha found it difficult to understand why that would include their own grandchildren. When Peter-Samuel was baptised, they did not attend, even though Karo tried to appease them by naming him Samuel, as well.

Julius had become somewhat withdrawn and quiet over the past few years, clearly not wanting to confront his parents. He immersed himself completely in his work.

Just now the baby had fallen asleep and Bertha carefully put him down on a blanket and in one motion pulled over her basket with the mending of clothes. With a quick glance, she made sure the other children were happily occupied before she allowed her thoughts to wander.

The past few years have flown by like a fast wind, blowing the months away like leaves in a winter storm, she mused. It was one year ago when her beloved grandmother died peacefully in her sleep. Emil had found her in the morning and became hysterical. Troubled, sensitive Emil was still near tears when he recounted how he had discovered her. Her funeral had been a quiet event. Karoline had just gone into labour with her little boy. Leo had rushed to Bertha's side as fast as he could; he was still in mourning over his father who had died several months prior and currently he was back to bury his dear mother. He had decided to keep Fra-Lu with Bertha rather than take him back for another funeral. He could see that Bertha could use the help of his earnest son.

Sudden footsteps on the gravel walkway to the house startled her out of her pensive mood. Emil hurried down the walk, around the house and stopped short on the patio. "It's a girl!" he announced triumphantly of Karo's third child. "I hopped the streetcar as soon as I heard; they are calling her Anna, in honour of Omama." At that he almost choked up again, but quickly caught himself when Ella and Martha stormed him, jumping up and down.

Both vied for his attention, with Ella being the more aggressive one, declaring, "He is my brother!" and Martha shouting back, "But he is my uncle, and that's more important!"

"No, it's not!" Ella stomped her little feet as hard as she could.

"Girls, girls, please, behave like little ladies!" Bertha intervened.

"But, Mother," asked a rather indignant Ella, "a brother is more important than an uncle, is that not true?"

"Now Ella, stop that nonsense instantly, nobody is more important." She turned to Emil. "Now, let us hear about Martha's new little sister."

"Ha, I have a new sister and you don't!" Martha stuck her tongue out at Ella.

Bertha was quite ready to ban them inside the house, but Emil quickly defused the situation by picking both girls up and putting one on each knee as he sat down. Franz-Ludwig came to shake Emil's hand in greeting and moved towards little Peter-Samuel, now crying with the commotion.

"This is a little like a madhouse at the moment!" Bertha spoke to Emil. "Seriously, I can't look after another baby. But now tell me, is everyone well?"

"Yes Mama, all are well, according to Julius. His parents are disappointed it's another girl; they had hoped for a boy."

Bertha just nodded, not really surprised.

"There is always next year," Emil teased.

"Oh, for heaven's sake son!" Bertha scolded her eldest. "Karo needs a little space now! Three is really quite a handful."

"But you had four," Emil reminded her, "and all very close in age as well. They will manage."

The young girls were bored enough to slide off Emil's knees and run down the garden path to chase a butterfly. Fra-Lu had quietly gone into the house and brought out Peter's bottle.

"Can I feed him please, Mama Bertha?" he asked.

"That would be such a relief for me, Fra-Lu, thank you for your help!" Bertha truly was relieved.

"He is such a mature eleven-year-old, a true joy to have around," she told Emil, as Fra-Lu's ears burned with pride.

"Are you staying overnight?" she asked Emil, who looked around, uncertain. "I could..."

"We'll make room," Bertha assured him. "Now tell me what is going on in Berlin and in the world, I have been almost in hiding for the past couple of weeks."

"There are more *pogroms* in Russia," Emil spoke with great concern. "More Jewish people are fleeing to America if they can. It is very worrisome, and I have detected that worry in Julius when he told me. The Feldmanns have some relatives in Russia as well as in America."

Bertha was shocked. "Why are they doing these massacres? I don't understand that."

Emil shrugged. "Neither do I, Mama. let's just hope it passes again and does not have bigger repercussions."

Both sat in silence for a while, trying to take in the last bit of sun in a peaceful setting. But that tranquil moment was short-lived; both girls came out running, flushed and dirty, holding a frog in their hot little hands to show Emil.

With a sigh, Bertha rose. "Time to make something to eat and get these two little savages washed up."

"I'll stay outside for a little longer," Emil said, as he was enjoying the garden and peaceful surroundings. Offering to hold the baby and give Fra-Lu a break earned him a grateful smile from his mother. He watched his stepbrother take out some school books and settle down to some studying. "I have a school exam after summer vacation—I am to go to officer school when I am twelve," he explained to Emil in a proud voice.

After a simple supper of milk noodles for the girls and ham sandwiches for everyone else, and a little quiet reading time, the sleeping arrangements were set up. Emil and Bertha stayed up in conversation for a long time, during which the baby had to be changed and fed once more. But Bertha greatly relished her time with her eldest son, and neither one was in a hurry to retire. Sharing stories and events, going over the past six years, speculating a little into the future—it was a precious time for both.

Finally, well past midnight, Emil rose, yawning. "So, when is Leo coming back?" he asked.

"Hopefully this week yet," Bertha replied. "I would like to take Martha and Peter back to Karo and try to spend a little quiet time with him. It seems to be harder and harder lately."

Stretching his tired frame, Emil muttered that she should not be so good-natured and always looking after everybody. "Let Julius' parents do something once in a while!"

Bertha laughed. "You sound just like Leo. I feel badly because he comes home to me and the house is like a rabbit hutch."

At that, both of them started to giggle uncontrollably. "*Ach,* time to go to sleep," Bertha finally said, and hugged Emil good night.

"*What a wonderful day today. Spending time with Emil was particularly special,*" she thought as she got ready for bed. "*I think he may be over Oma's death, and I so wish he would find a nice girl and get away from that Anton and his crowd.*" She would never understand his interest in men, but she loved him nonetheless.

CHAPTER SIX: 1910

THE YEAR 1910 DAWNED ON A RESTLESS WORLD. THE NEWSPAPERS COULD hardly keep up with new editions being printed as fast as possible with headlines screaming, "Boutros Ghali assassinated, Egypt in turmoil." "Portugal's king deposed, the monarchy making room for a republic."

And again a few months later: "In Portugal state and church are finally separated." "More *pogroms* in Russia, Tsar Nicholas on shaky footings."

And so, it went, on and on, from Japan, Korea, and Thailand across America and Eastern Europe.

Leo shared his misgivings with Bertha that he feared the end of monarchies all over Europe.

"Since Crown Prince Rudolf's suicide, the whole Austro-Hungarian monarchy is unstable," he mused.

"Will this affect you at all?" Bertha was curious.

Leo weighed his answer carefully. "I'm not sure, my dearest," he admitted. "Nobility is and will not be looked upon the same way anymore. However, I doubt it will affect me so much, as we estate holders are not looked on as leeches. We are feeding the people and are very necessary." He smiled when he saw her worried face. "Don't worry, I will not lose my head over this!"

"Don't make fun of that, Leo!" Bertha cried in sudden panic.

"*Schatz, Schatz*, please, calm down," he assured her. "An Ullmannshausen-Hohenstein is not important to the proletarians." Bertha remained uneasy and was silently grateful Ella was a Hoffmann.

Nineteen ten was also the year both Leo and Bertha turned fifty—Bertha in July and Leo in August. He used to tease her for having fallen for a younger man, something she did not really appreciate hearing. For that special event, Leo decided they needed to go away and spend some time alone again. It has been far too long for time together, and he surprised Bertha with a two-week stay in Vienna and Budapest.

The thought of spending two blissful weeks alone with Leo excited Bertha tremendously and Leo basked in her unabashed enthusiasm. He felt the same attraction and sensual affections for her as he did the first time he laid eyes on her in 1899. Noticing the unashamed desire in her eyes, he felt like a young man again.

Holding her tightly, he whispered, "Do we have time before Ella comes home from school?" She gave a quick glance at the clock and a hurried nod, and both tumbled on the sofa, clutching each other with such passionate freedom, it left them breathless. "My darling *Schatz*, I can't wait to have you all to myself again," Leo breathed, still hoarse with desire. "I can leave right now!" Bertha admitted. She loved this man beyond all reason.

During the school year, Bertha had moved back to Turmstrasse, so Ella could attend the nearby school. But whenever Leo was in Berlin and either Emil or Karo could look after Ella, they spent as much time as possible at the little house. That was where they could indulge in each other, in their love and forget all the other cares in the word. While at Turmstrasse, they needed to be more restrained as decorum dictated. One never knew when either Ella or Emil might come home.

However, on this particular day, even at Turmstrasse, their passion overpowered their self-discipline. They sat up, somewhat dazed, looking at each other in wonderment. "After all these years Leo," Bertha breathed.

"Yes, my love, after all these years," he laughed. "We have something so special." They held each other silently for a long time before Bertha pulled away. "Ella will be home soon," she said, and fussed with her hair and straightened her clothes.

In late July, Ella was sent off to Karoline for a couple of weeks. Karo was glad for the help from her young ten-year-old sister, since she was carrying her fourth child and Ella, along with Karo's eldest, Martha, enjoyed playing with the little ones.

All was set for Leo and Bertha to travel to Vienna and Budapest. The train ride was comfortable, and they arrived at the Hotel Sacher early evening. Leo had booked them as Herr and Frau Graf, which gave them the anonymity and propriety necessary to occupy a suite together. After a light dinner and some wine, they retired, both slightly tipsy enough to immediately fall asleep.

Bertha awoke to a beautiful summer morning, with the curtains drawn and the balcony door wide open. She drowsily squinted against the sun, while leisurely stretching her body. She was fortunate to still have a slim and supple body, even at nearly fifty, and having birthed Ella at forty. Kicking off the duvet, she relished the pleasure of staying in bed a little longer. Her shockingly flimsy *negligée* revealed more than it covered, and she revelled in Leo's obvious longing looks. He was carrying a breakfast tray, which he quickly put down lest he might drop it. She noticed him swallow hard. "Good morning, my sleepy one," he greeted her. "You look ravishingly beautiful." His voice was husky. "Good morning Leo, my love," Bertha replied softly and smoothly. "Breakfast smells delicious! I am famished."

"So am I, but not for breakfast!" Leo was clearly ready to rejoin her in bed, and began to kiss her neck. "Oh Leo, the coffee smells so good, let's have breakfast!" Bertha pleaded, all the while enjoying stoking his desire.

"Bertha, oh please, we can always order more breakfast," Leo groaned. "And where on earth did you get this scandalous *negligée*?" he grinned. "It can drive men completely wild!"

"Not men," Bertha replied with a wink and mischievous smile. "Just you."

"Well, you succeeded," Leo admitted, "and now you are torturing me!"

Bertha could no longer resist him, and they united in joyful harmony.

Most of that day was spent in glorious togetherness, lazily drifting in and out of sleep, leisurely becoming reacquainted with each other.

"Today we will view Vienna," Leo announced the next morning, "and for this evening, I have tickets to the premiere of 'The Gypsy Princess' by Lehar, a newly written operetta, which I hope we will enjoy."

Over breakfast in the dining room, they laid out their plans for the next few days. A visit to the Prater was a must—Vienna's famous amusement park with the well-known Ferris wheel. A reflective time at an afternoon concert in the Stephansdom, a stroll through the art gallery admiring works by Gustav Klimt and watching a military parade along the Ringstrasse along with the carriage bearing the Austrian emperor Franz-Josef.

A few days later, they ambled along the river Danube in Budapest. Bertha was enraptured with the beauty of the Hungarian capital. She was later completely stunned when Leo ordered their meal in Hungarian.

"After all these years, I did not know you speak Hungarian!" she looked at him with admiration and awe. It was nice that they could still learn new things about each other.

"A Hungarian mother," Leo shrugged. "It just seemed natural."

They took in as many sights they could walk to, up the hill to the castle, the Fisherman's Bastion, and St. Istvan Basilica. They lounged in one of the thermal baths and hung a padlock on Liberty Bridge to signify their eternal love, throwing the key for the lock far into the Danube River, laughing like two children. In between sights, they rested in one of the many coffee houses relaxing by coffee, *Dobos torte*, and violin music.

Both were not eager to return to their lives back home and the routine of on-and-off separation. Leo was not even going all the way to Berlin with Bertha; he got off the train sooner to catch a connecting train back to Stolp and his estate. "I'll come as soon as I can, *mein Schatz*," he promised with a sweet kiss on her forehead.

Bertha picked up Ella so the two of them could spend another week at the summer house before school started again. All the way there, Ella was a little chatterbox, speaking of Karo's children and the time spent with Emil.

"Emil took Martha and I to the zoo!" she exclaimed. "You should see the size of the elephants. I wonder how much they need to eat, and I want to know how giraffes sleep, and then there are…" and on and on she jabbered. Bertha tried to listen, but soon drifted into daydreams about Leo and their times together, wishing with all her heart that they never needed to be separated.

"Mother! Mother—are you even listening?" Ella cried out in a somewhat shrill voice.

"Why certainly, my dear," Bertha replied, coming back to earth. "I was just thinking of your father and how much he would have liked to be at the zoo with you."

Ella eagerly agreed. "He would have liked the monkeys, Mother!" she giggled. "Oh, they were so much fun; one of them stole Martha's hat, she was quite put out over that!" Ella giggled some more.

"Oh my, did she get it back?" Bertha asked half-heartedly.

"No, Emil tried," Ella answered, "but it was so much fun to watch him chasing the monkeys along the cage and them teasing him with Martha's hat, but in the end, the hat was ripped and for sure Martha would never wear it again."

Bertha had to chuckle at that. "It was very nice of Emil to treat you to that. I hope you thanked him and behaved like little ladies?"

"Yes, Mother, of course we did," Ella quickly reassured her. That last week of summer vacation with Ella passed with mother and daughter lazing in the sun, reading, swimming in the Mueggelsee, and playing badminton. Even though she missed Leo terribly, it was wonderful to spend time alone with Ella, and Bertha thoroughly savoured this special mother-daughter bond.

"I missed this with the other children. They came too close together and little Eugen needed most of the attention," she mused. *"And then there was Karl. It was a blessing I had Oma, or I might never have left Karl... Oh, what would have happened? How I miss her."* Now Bertha was missing not only Leopold, but her dear Oma Anna, as well.

CHAPTER SEVEN: 1911

THE FOLLOWING YEAR, KARO, WHO NOW HAD FOUR CHILDREN, CAME TO SEE HER mother by herself.

Even though she and Julius now had a nanny, life was still busy for Karoline. They were a very popular couple, and often favoured guests at many social gatherings and celebrations. Julius was also a highly sought-after paediatrician—in particular with the affluent and upper crust. They were definitely doing well for themselves, and Bertha was somewhat embarrassed by Karo's newly acquired and slightly arrogant attitude.

She recently addressed that with her daughter, only to be rebuked. "My dear daughter, I do not like your behaviour one little bit," Bertha had scolded her. "You are becoming a snob, which is most unbecoming and very unlike you," she had told her, remembering her bright, warm, and sincere child in her younger years. "You are seeing way too much of your in-laws—one can tell their influence on you." At that, Karo had abruptly stormed out and had not been around for a few weeks.

But today, she suddenly came by and wanted to talk, which pleased Bertha immensely.

The two sat down for tea. "So, my dear daughter, what brings you here today? Are the children well?"

"Yes, Mama, everybody is well," Karoline answered. "Julius' father is retiring this year and they want to move, but they can't decide where. Father wants to move to France and mother wants to stay put. Father thinks the political climate in Germany will deteriorate."

"Deteriorate? How so?" Bertha was perplexed "Is this one of your father-in-law's fantasies again?"

"I am not sure," Karo shrugged. "He seems to think this is serious, and even has Julius a little spooked. But that is partly of what I came to see you about," Karo paused, a bit hesitant. "Julius was offered a position as Chief of Staff at the Hartford Children's Hospital."

"But that sounds marvellous, dear!" Bertha exclaimed. "Where then might Hartford be?" Bertha asked while refilling their cups of tea.

Karo laughed, a little louder than necessary, Bertha thought. "Hartford is in America, in a state I cannot properly pronounce, I think it may start with a K." Karo explained.

"America? Why America?" Bertha was shocked. "Can he not find something in Germany?" Bertha was bewildered, trying to process this.

"He could, but as I said, his father has him spooked, and they all think that this is a very good idea before Julius becomes too old for such an opportunity."

"I see," Bertha frowned. "But I still do not understand why you would think that Germany is unsafe." Bertha shook her head. "Your in-laws definitely have fanciful imaginations."

"Well, that may be, Mama," Karo said impatiently. "But I came by to tell you that Julius will accept this offer, and we will likely move to America next year."

"So, that's it? It is decided then?" Bertha's hand flew to her mouth to muffle a sob. "I'll never get to see you or my grandchildren again!" Tears streamed down Bertha's cheeks while Karoline shuffled uncomfortably in her seat.

"Not just yet, Mama. Julius is waiting for the contract and what it will entail," Karo said quietly, trying to soften the blow a little. "We will know more after that."

Bertha's tears continued to flow, and Karo felt uncomfortable. "I will miss you, too, of course, Mama, but you still have Emil and Ella and Leo's boy, and of course Leo—if he is ever around."

"There is no need to say this, Karoline," Bertha rebuked her. "I love all my children and grandchildren—"

"But you love Leo the most!" Karo suddenly blurted out.

"Now stop this nonsense right now!" Bertha insisted. "You know very well the circumstances and how very fortunate I am to have found love later in life. You love Julius, don't you? You follow him to the end of the world, so why would you not allow me to have the same feelings?" she continued to scold her eldest daughter. "Please do not make your and your husband's decision about me. You are making a life-changing decision, and I know you are not doing this because I love Leo—that is totally absurd.

"Perhaps you will be much happier in America, I do not know," Bertha sighed. "I know that my own mother died crossing the ocean to follow a dream, and I could not bear it if this same fate would befall you."

"Oh, Mama!" Now Karo could not suppress her tears. "Nothing will happen to us! We are taking our children along, of course, but Julius is looking at the newest ocean steamers crossing," she explained through sniffles. "In Ireland, the biggest and safest ship is being launched soon, and maybe we will get passages on that one. I think the children will be so excited."

Bertha could tell Karo was trying to get her on board, but it seemed like she was trying to convince herself. Suddenly Bertha felt very tired. "It is fine Karo, I understand," she finally said. "You need to be with your husband and the children with their parents. I truly do understand. I just wish it was not so far away." She rose and hugged her daughter as tightly as she could. "God be with you," she whispered into her ear. Karo kissed her mother and quietly left the apartment.

A few minutes later, Emil came home, shaking his head. "This sister of mine is becoming more and more stuck-up," he frowned. "I just met her in the stairway and she just stormed right by, not even saying a word."

"I know—she has changed a lot, and not necessarily for the better," Bertha sighed. "Anyway, is Ella on her way?" Ella, having recently transferred to a higher level of learning, was now a pupil in the lyceum for girls, the same school where Emil taught music.

"Hmm, yes—I think I saw her, along with a bunch of giggling girls," Emil answered. "In case you have not heard, she is called Elfi now," he grinned. "She sure is a magnet among her peers."

"Sit down for a minute," Bertha motioned to Emil. "I'd like to wait for Ella because I have to tell both of you something."

"I hope it is not something bad. I simply could not cope with that right now!" Emil replied in his melodramatic way. Bertha decided to ignore his comment and waited for Ella.

It did not take long for her to come home, and she carefully hung up her coat, put on her slippers, and took her school bag into the kitchen to tackle her homework after dinner.

"Good afternoon, Mother, and Emil," she greeted them, and dutifully gave her mother a kiss. Bertha gave her daughter a onceover and noticed her dishevelled hair, her rumpled school dress, and rolled-down stockings. Normally she would have reprimanded her wild child, but today, she just said, "Sit down Ella, I have to tell both of you something."

Ella looked over to Emil, not too sure what it could be. She had a chronic bad conscience, always displeasing her mother about one thing or another. She sat at the edge of the chair and waited expectantly.

"Your sister was here this afternoon and there will be a big change in her life as well as ours—"

"Is she having another baby?" Ella interrupted while Emil added that she must be having marital problems judging from the way she stormed down the stairs just then.

"Now, will you both listen for a moment before making silly assumptions!" Bertha chided them. "Their whole family will be moving..." She paused a moment. "They will be moving to America."

The siblings sat in silence before Ella finally asked, "America? But why? That is so far away, and I will never see Martha again!"

Emil shook his head. "Is there a good reason for that? She seems very high-strung lately," he stated. "Are her in-laws putting ideas in Julius' head again?"

"Shh, Emil, we..." Bertha motioned in Ella's direction, "we do not know that. Apparently, Julius received a very good offer from a children's hospital in some city that I have never heard of. It appears they will make the voyage across the ocean in the near future. And no, I am not happy about that either."

"Oh, Mother, I would love to go with them," Ella suddenly exclaimed longingly. "A journey on a large ship, moving to another country? Oh, how exciting that would be!" her eyes shone in anticipation.

"Do you think Karo would take me along?" she asked, wild-eyed. "I can look after the little ones for her!"

"Don't be daft," Emil spoke up. "They have a nanny to look after the children. You are much too young to think about travelling the world, Ella," he had to chuckle.

"Please Mother?" Ella turned to Bertha pleadingly.

"Stop this talk immediately!" Bertha scolded her. "It is foolish talk, and I would have expected you to be more sensible." Bertha felt seriously cross with her young daughter. "We will not continue this line of talk anymore, do you hear? Your place is here, with me and your father. When you are an adult, you can do as you please, for the most part."

Ella started to whine and protest.

"Don't pull that face on me or you will be confined to home for the next week!" Bertha threatened. *This girl is far too impudent and cheeky! I have to nip this in the bud,"* Bertha thought to herself. *"I wish Leo would be around more often to share the discipline."*

"Is this a sure thing now?" Emil wanted to know. "And when are they going?"

"I understand it is decided," Bertha responded. "As to the date, I do not know. Julius is looking into suitable accommodations. I will certainly miss them..."

Emil rose to leave. "I think I'll go and see Anton," he mumbled, ruffling Ella's hair in the process. "See you later, Elfi," he teased her, eliciting an angry scowl. With a laugh, he grabbed his coat and was gone.

Chapter Eight

"Leo, you have to do something about this daughter of ours!" Bertha declared some weeks later.

"Why? What has she done?" Leo raised his eyebrows in concern.

"It's not so much about what she has done," Bertha tried to explain. "It's more about her attitude. She is becoming quarrelsome and argumentative. Everything has to be analysed in detail. Her teachers complain about her combative behaviour, and more than once she has received detentions and even corporal punishment. I am truly worried about your child!"

"Aha, now it is *my* child," Leo teased.

He pictured Ella, his child but no longer a child, tall, her thick hair braided into pigtails, her huge dark eyes and inquisitive face. *"She is a very lovely girl,"* he thought to himself with some pride.

"Is it really all that bad?" he asked. "She seems fine to me, and some punishment in school seems reasonable to me, as well. We all went through that— how else do we learn? Have you spoken to her teachers?" he added.

"Yes, of course I have!" Bertha said indignantly. "But I sure wish that you would do some of that as well. It seems teachers do not take mothers very seriously."

Bertha was frustrated by Leo's laidback attitude.

"You are right, of course, my dearest—I shall go to speak to her teachers," Leo conceded. "Does Emil say anything? After all, he is a teacher there, and he would hear or see some of the issues."

Bertha nodded and could not quite hide a small grin. "Yes, in fact, he tells me she drives the teachers insane with her incessant questions; every explanation has to be re-examined, re-analysed until the teachers lose patience and slap her."

"I shall put an end to the slapping part!" Leo promised. "But it seems to me the teachers are the ones who should be slapped! They lose patience with an inquisitive pupil, they do not know how to ultimately answer her questions, and then mete out punishment," Leo frowned a bit. "Ella is very bright," he continued. "She also has an extremely sensitive nature and any criticism or disapproval goes deep with her, but she will have to learn to control these feelings. Life is not so easy."

"She is certainly a perfectionist and gets very annoyed if she 'only' gets an 'A' in her exams," Bertha added. "But she is no better at home! Everything is 'why this' and 'why that' and there are times I even understand her teachers!" Bertha held a serious face, only to slowly break out in giggles when she saw Leo's feigned stern look, and soon both of them burst into laughter.

"Good afternoon, Papa and Mother," they were soon interrupted by their daughter. "Might I ask what you find so funny?" Ella had just come home from school,

"Oh ho, my daughter, now so formal and well-mannered!" Leo teased her. "Your mother and I were just sharing some amusing conversation. And why are you home so late?" Leo looked at the clock. "You should have been home an hour ago."

Bertha rolled her eyes, curious as to how Ella would answer her father. Ella, darting looks back and forth between her parents and pulling a hair braid to chew on, shrugged. "I had some extra work to do."

"Extra work, I see," her father replied. "Could you be more specific?"

Ella said nothing.

"I asked you a question, Ella!" Leopold said sternly, and by now he understood Bertha's concerns.

"I was...um, I did not...no, I—it's like this..." Ella stuttered, not being used to her father being so stern. "The teachers do not like me, Papa," she finally blurted out. "I never want to go back there again!"

"I see," Leo said again, trying to remain calm. "And where would you like to go then?"

"To America, with Karo and Martha and Peter and—"

"All right, hold it right there!" Leo put up his hand. "So, to America, then. What makes you think life will be any better there?" Bertha was frantically waving her hands, but Leo slightly shook his head at her and continued to speak to Ella, who was dumbfounded. "Please answer me, daughter," he urged. "What makes life better in America? Do you know anything about the country, their schools, and what you may eventually do there?"

Slowly, Ella shook her head, and had to admit that it was frustration that made her say that. "I do want to stay with you, and maybe things aren't so bad here, it's just frustrating at school," she sighed.

Leopold thought for a moment. "You know, my dear daughter, I think I might take you back to my estate next month when you have school vacation. You have never been there, and Fra-Lu will be home for the month, and there is a lot of work to be done with the harvesting and horse grooming," Leo watched as his daughter's eyes lit up. "Fra-Lu can teach you how to ride. I am sure there is a pony available for you and we will give your poor mother a well-deserved rest."

Ella jumped up and down in excitement. "Fra-Lu will be home? I so love Fra-Lu, Papa!" she squealed. "Now I can hardly wait for my vacation to start."

"One condition applies, though" Leo cautioned. "Absolutely no detentions all month, and no complaints from your teachers for the balance of the term. Do you understand and agree?"

A bit vexed, Ella responded that she would try, but could not guarantee her teachers' behaviours. Leo had a hard time stifling a laugh. "You heard me, Ella," he managed to say firmly. "NO detentions, no complaints, no exceptions! And that is final. You may now go to do your homework," he dismissed her.

Cheerfully Ella skipped to the kitchen and her schoolwork.

Leo rose and looked at Bertha, who had been silent. "*Schatz*, let's go to the café across the street," he suggested. "I could use a nice cup of coffee and a piece of cake, and we can discuss my plans a little more."

Bertha immediately agreed and called to Ella that they were going to Café Turm.

As soon as they sat down, Bertha got right into it. "Leo, I don't know what to say," she began. "You are really taking Ella to your place?"

Leo nodded. "I have thought about this for some time now, my dearest, it is time for my daughter—"

"Our daughter," Bertha corrected, a tad irked.

"Yes, my apologies, our daughter," Leo responded. "It is time for her to know my home estate and get used to another lifestyle that she will one day be part of. By the time she is eighteen, she will be introduced at the annual debutante ball," he explained. "She will receive invitations to other estate owners, and she will meet young men of marriageable age. This is also a good time for Ludwiga to meet her and initiate her to the rituals and formality that go with this lifestyle."

Bertha had become very quiet at his talk, stirring her coffee over and over again, refusing to meet his eyes as she felt a schism opening between them. *"He is right, of course—Ella is of a somewhat higher birth rank than me,"* she thought with some slight bitterness, and a sudden sadness took a hold of her.

"I would like to go back home now," she suddenly declared.

Leo reached across to stop her from stirring her coffee, "My dear, you are stirring a hole into the cup!" he gently chided her as he looked at her with great tenderness. "I know what you are thinking my love," he softly began, "but it is not so. Both of us want what is best for Ella. I need to introduce her to my extended family and way of life. It will be up to her to make choices later, as she matures."

"She is not better than you," Leo continued. "She has inherited all your wonderful characteristics, your charisma, your beauty, your zest. I was not even able to give her my name," he added, slightly distressed.

"I feel so inferior next to you, Bertha. You have enriched my life so very much," he said lovingly. "Please, please do not be jealous. Ludwiga is a very loving and kind person. She will not take Ella from you. She will gently teach her and be more like a governess to her."

Bertha was still silent, thinking about what Leo had said. She had not realised she was jealous, but yes, he was right, she felt like an outsider at this moment and wished so much her Oma were still alive. It seemed like everybody was leaving her: Karo and her family to America, Karl-Heinz and his family were long gone, now Ella to the estate; only Emil was a constant—at least for now.

Tears began flowing down her face as Leo watched, panic-stricken and bewildered. "Bertha, my love, tell me, what is it?"

Through tears, Bertha snivelled, "You—you are taking Ella away from me! She might not want to come back here, she…"

"Now I'm becoming a bit cross with you!" Leo interjected. "I am not taking Ella away from you. I am merely expanding her horizons and initiating her to her birthright. One day she will be a very wealthy woman, Bertha."

As soon as he said it, he knew it was the wrong thing to say. Bertha, always having felt slightly inferior and for years having tried to put that "other" side of Leo out of her mind, burst into more tears.

Leo, throwing some money on the table for their coffee, pulled her out of her chair and outside in one swift motion. "We are walking to the park to find a quiet bench and discuss this like two adults," he insisted. "We have always been honest with each other and that will not change." Leo was disturbed at this unexpected outbreak from Bertha.

But Bertha called his bluff as they walked through the park. "You were not honest and open with me when you told Ella you would take her over the holidays!" she protested through tears. "We should have discussed that together, before your big announcement! I felt totally blindsided." Bertha was truly hurt.

Leopold paused in their walk and took a deep breath. "Yes, for that, I deeply apologise," he admitted. "I realise I should have talked to you beforehand, but the situation evolved so rapidly, and I had planned this as a little surprise—and now it has backfired," he sighed, trying to reach for Bertha's hand, but she instead wiped her tears away. "I am so very sorry, Bertha."

The two sat on a bench nestled among some shrubs and well shaded by a linden tree. They sat side by side, not touching, both somewhat dazed at this their first seemingly severe disagreement. Neither one knew what to say or how to ease their pain.

"Is this the end, Leo?" Bertha whispered finally through tears.

"What did you say? The end? The end of what?" Leo looked at her, startled and confused. "You are talking in riddles."

"Us, Leo. Us. Is this the end of us?" Bertha started to cry again. "I wondered when this day might come..."

Leo suddenly grabbed her and pulled her close. "Look at me, look into my eyes," he told his beloved, who complied. "This is not the end of us! I do not know what gave you this silly notion. You know I love you, you know you are the one and only for me, you know you are my wife, and you know I will never, ever leave you." Leo was sincere and adamant.

"I know, Leo, I know all that," Bertha replied. "It's just that, that—I oh, I don't know! I am being silly, I guess. But I often feel like—" she stopped short.

"Yes? Like what? Tell me!" Leo insisted.

Bertha shook her head. "It's nothing," she said quietly.

"If it is nothing, then you don't need to cry," he pointed out. "You would like to be my wife for all the world to see—I know that my love, and I would like nothing better than that as well," he sighed. "I can only keep promising you that one day, it will happen, and one day, Fra-Lu will be secure enough that I can divorce Ludwiga—something she would like, as well. I believe she has found love for herself, but that is another matter.

"Now, the only thing that matters is you and I, our love for each other, and our daughter. If you rather she not go to Hohenstein, I will find a way to leave her here," he promised, though it was clear that was not his first choice.

"No, Leo, you are right," Bertha admitted. "It will be good for her, and I feel like such a goose! Please forgive me, Leo, I love you so much, and—"

Whatever she was going to say next was drowned in Leo's hugs and kisses, and she snuggled into his arms, never wanting to leave this moment.

Leopold finally broke the spell. "In the fall, when everybody is back to school, let's take some time for ourselves again and go away together," he suggested. "What do you think?"

Bertha eagerly agreed, and slowly, hand in hand, they walked back through the park on that beautiful sunny summer afternoon.

Chapter Nine

Bertha paced the platform of the railway station rather impatiently. Ella was to come back from her one-month vacation, and she was eager to meet her daughter again.

This was the longest time she had been away from her, and she missed her. She was also anxious to find out how she had fared with her father, Ludwiga, and Fra-Lu. She did receive two letters from Leo, reassuring her that all was well.

Finally, the train chugged into the station, blowing lots of steam while screeching to a halt. All along the train, the doors opened and passengers disembarked, lugging suitcases and being greeted by eager friends or relatives. Bertha tried to pick out Ella among the throng of people pushing and shoving on their way out as others tried to board the train.

"Over here, Mother!" Ella waved. She was being escorted by the conductor who carried her suitcase.

"Ella, my dear, it's so very good to have you home again!" Bertha hugged her quickly, then thanked the conductor for helping her daughter before taking a closer look at her. "You look so tanned, and I swear you have grown as well."

"I have a letter from Papa for you with me," Ella told her, bouncing full of life. "This was a very long train ride," she complained a bit. "It was so hard to sit still and just look out the window or read in my new book."

Bertha smiled at her lively daughter. "You must tell me all about—"

"I have my own pony now," Ella quickly interrupted, unable to contain herself. "And Fra-Lu taught me how to ride, and Papa took me out to help with harvesting, and Ludwiga—"

"Hold on, hold on, you need to take a breath!" Bertha laughed. "Quick, let's get the carriage that's still available and get us home. Emil baked a cake for you," Bertha happily reported.

"Oh, dear Emil, he is such a good brother!" Ella helped her mother into the carriage while the driver stowed her suitcase. Bertha listened to Ella eagerly recount her adventures while secretly running her hands over Leo's letter in her pocket. She was elated to have her bubbly daughter back, dispelling her fears she might come back haughty or snobbish. In fact, she appeared to be in high spirits, yet more balanced with some maturity.

Leo's letter confirmed her observation, explaining how much Ella had fit in, how well behaved she was, and how she charmed Ludwiga and especially Fra-Lu. But most of all, the letter stated how much he loved Bertha and how much he missed her. He would see her as soon as harvesting was done.

It was early October by the time Leo finally came back to Berlin. "Phew, that was a lot of work, but an excellent harvest year" he told Bertha excitedly. "The sugar beets and turnip crops can be looked after by the estate manager and helpers. Now, I have a little surprise for you," he grinned.

"You do?" Bertha was all ears. "What is it? Do tell me, please!"

"I will be in Berlin until the new year, and over Christmas as well!" he proclaimed triumphantly.

"You will?" Bertha gasped. "Oh Leo, that is so wonderful—how did you manage that?"

"It gets even better," Leo continued. "Fra-Lu will be with us over the holidays, as well." He paused for Bertha's joyous reaction.

"I can't believe that! Ella will be so happy!"

"And how about you?" Leo teased.

"How can you even ask? This is the best Christmas present of all!" Bertha declared while flinging her arms around his neck in jubilant excitement. "Now, do tell me how this happened."

"As I perhaps mentioned before, Ludwiga is in a relationship with a Polish officer, and they have decided to spend the holidays together with their families in Poland," Leo explained. "Fra-Lu did not want to go with his mother, as he is eager to see *Elfi* instead."

Leo grinned some more. "Those two have really hit it off this summer."

"Yes, so I hear from our daughter," Bertha nodded. "According to her, she would move in with you any day."

Now Leo laughed. "I would like that as well! Actually, I would like it if it were both of you. But for Ella, it would be a little too lonely since Fra-Lu is away at school during the year."

"She will be so excited to hear your news. Can we celebrate the holidays in the summer house?"

"I was hoping you would say that!" Leo replied. "It is such a cosy place and with the fireplace, it will be nice and warm. Fra-Lu and I can chop wood. There is enough around to cut."

"And Ella and I can bake Christmas *stollen* and cookies," Bertha chimed in with a dreamy look in her eyes. "Oh, what a wonderful time this will be... What about Emil?"

"What about him?" asked Leo. "He will join us, of course. He is part of our family. It may be a little tight, but then he and Fra-Lu can share the one bedroom, Ella gets the little room, and you and I—well, you know where we will sleep," Leo added with a suggestive smile and wink.

"Oh Leo, even after all these years, you can make me blush," Bertha chuckled while stroking his thick, curly hair.

"Now that this is settled, have you decided where we will go for a couple of weeks, just us?"

Bertha, suddenly serious, replied that she had thought about Switzerland and perhaps combine it with a visit to her son, Karl-Heinz, and meet his family.

"That sounds like a good plan," Leo answered, but noticing Bertha's concerned expression, he waited for her to continue.

"I wrote him a letter to explore where and when it might be possible. His response came a few days ago, and it was rather ugly."

"Oh?" Leo raised his eyebrows. "Would you like to share?"

"*Ach*, Leo, this is pretty sad, and I am still quite upset. He writes that he was—and still is—very angry that neither I nor his siblings came to Karl's funeral. He will not accept any explanations, even that Karoline was so close to her delivery date."

She paused for a moment, uncomfortable. "He also told me as long as I am still living in sin, I am not welcome. His wife's parents are very religious, and they refuse to have their grandchildren exposed to such a 'godless' way of life. I admit that Karl-Heinz was not my favourite child, as he is so much like his father was—brutish, self-righteous, and unforgiving. I do pity his wife and children. At the same time, though, I cried when I read this. I do not feel as if I live a godless life. I believe that God gave us love so that we can give love!"

Bertha stopped to catch her breath before continuing. "I burned the letter before anyone could see it. So, you see, Switzerland is no longer a choice destination either."

Leo had listened quietly to her while a slow anger rose in him. "He has no right to sit in judgment of his mother!" he seethed. "I sure feel like giving him a piece of my mind!"

"Let it go, Leo, please," begged Bertha. "He is not worth your anger." Bertha wiped her tears and tried to calm him down. "I don't want Emil or Karo to hear of this, they have long given up on him and do not need any more reminding. Ella does not know him anyway."

"I just feel like such an imposter sometimes!" Leo replied. "I want so much to legally marry you and take away this veil of deception from you. You have no idea how much I think about this situation and how often I have inquired about a change in the heritage law. If Fra-Lu were not involved—"

"Please, Leo, do not blame the boy!" Bertha admonished him. "He is as much a victim of short-sighted laws as we are. One day..." she trailed off.

"Yes, my dearest, one day it will happen," Leo finished her sentence.

Rather than going away at this time, they decided to spend one week alone at the summer house while Emil stayed with Ella. They cherished their time together, going for long walks through the park, enjoying the last of the warm late fall days.

As they sat in front of the fireplace one evening, Leo reading and Bertha knitting, Bertha quipped, "We're just like an old married couple!" as Leo grunted with contentment. Life was very good in their little house.

Soon enough, it was Christmas and Fra-Lu arrived, loaded with luggage and presents. Ella skipped from one leg to the other in happy anticipation of spending time with her "other brother." On their way, they had stopped to see Karo and Julius to see the children.

"Martha is so jealous of my big brothers!" Ella gushed with pride. "Hers are just babies."

"That is hardly Martha's fault—now go on and be nice!" Bertha chided her with a little smile, all the while holding the youngest child in her arms. "He has grown so much in the past couple of months," she noted as she smothered his little face with kisses.

"Me too, Oma, me too!" little Anna and young Peter begged for attention while Martha snuggled next to her.

"And who wants to come to see me?" Leo boomed in a deep voice and Peter giggled and jumped on his knees. "I will!"

"Mama, we have some news about America," Karo finally found enough courage to speak up.

"Oh, Karo—now?" Bertha was not keen to think about this being their last Christmas together.

"Julius says one day you will be happy for us!" Karo said defiantly.

"Yes, yes, always one day..." Bertha muttered. "Life always comes down to one day."

"Honestly, Mama, I don't know what you are talking about, but here it is—we are leaving in April, and I believe the ship we are booked on is called—just a minute, let me find the flyer, it's a strange kind of name—oh yes, here it is!" Triumphantly, Karoline pulled a flyer out of a batch of papers on the table. "The ship is called 'Titanic' and it leaves early April."

Bertha, choking back tears upon accepting that her daughter was really leaving, mumbled, "It is indeed a strange name," and tried to put it all out of her mind as it was so close to Christmas.

"We are all so excited and—"

"Karoline, please, stop talking about it at this time," Bertha interrupted sternly. "This is not the time to talk about leaving. This is still Advent and we will be celebrating Christmas next week—a time of joy and family and togetherness, so please, I do not want to hear another word of this ship or your departure or—" Bertha's sternness quickly turned to tears.

Leo put his arms around her and shot Karo a warning look. "How about we all sing some Christmas carols for the little ones?" he quickly suggested, earning him a grateful look from Emil, who had been standing rather helplessly next to the kitchen door.

"Yes, let's do that!" Emil agreed, as he walked over to the piano and began to play "Oh Tannenbaum," to which everybody joined in song, first haltingly and then becoming more and more joyful with each carol.

Finally, Bertha, Leo, and their children left to take the streetcar to their summer house, with Bertha giving Emil a quick hug on the way there.

It was cold and snowy, looking and feeling a lot like Christmas. The house smelled warm and of baking. The lake was frozen solid, and the boys took Ella in between them as they skated over the ice, avoiding ruts and cracks. They built a snowman, had snowball fights, went sledding in the nearby park, and came home half-frozen to hot cider and fresh cookies.

Christmas Eve morning, Leo went out to cut a fir tree, as was the custom. All day they decorated it with real candles, stars made from straw, glass bulbs from

Bertha's grandfather, bulbs she had painted herself many, many years ago, and her beloved collection of nutcrackers. She would tell Ella and Fra-Lu how she had made them and managed to save some of these decorations from the big fire before all was destroyed.

Later, when it was dark, they lit the candles, sang carols, recited poems, read the story from Luke in the Bible, and exchanged gifts. Fra-Lu had brought Ella her own riding cap and Ella had knitted him a pair of mittens and a long, colourful scarf. Emil sat immersed in a new book and Leo and Bertha sat close together, enjoying this precious time with each other.

All too soon, this holiday time came to an end, and Fra-Lu, declaring this was the best Christmas ever, was escorted to the railway station to return to school, promising to write often.

Chapter Ten: 1912

APRIL 15, 1912
EXTRA, EXTRA, READ ALL ABOUT IT!
OCEAN LINER 'TITANIC' SINKS AFTER HITTING AN
ICEBERG!
FEW SURVIVORS FOUND

The newspaper boys screamed as loud as they could. Bertha's heart nearly stopped as she rushed out to purchase a paper, still damp from printing. Her knees felt weak and she began to tremble all over.

"My babies, oh my darling babies, this cannot be happening again to me!" her panicked thoughts raced. *"First my mother, and now my daughter and grandchildren?"*

"Oh Lord, how can you be so cruel?" she wailed out loud. Pedestrians stopped to stare at her, not understanding her poured-out grief. Stumbling back to the entrance of the apartment house, she felt faint. Clutching the railing, she barely pulled herself up the stairs before letting herself back into the flat.

Smoothing out the paper, she tried to make some sense of what she was reading, but understood nothing. All she could think of was her grandbabies, the ice-cold water, the last time she had seen them. She just stared at the wall, feeling numb.

About an hour later Emil, tugging Ella along, came running up the stairs, only to stare at the paper on the table and their mother, curled up in a ball of pain, rocking back and forth on her chair.

"Ella, quickly, put on some water for tea!" Emil instructed. "I will run to the post office to send a telegram to Leo!" Emil suddenly took charge.

But Ella was on her knees, her head in her mother's lap, bawling her eyes out. Mechanically, Bertha stroked Ella's hair and half-noticed Emil running out of the apartment. It took him over an hour to return.

"The post office is chaos!" he reported. "They can't get messages in or out fast enough." He looked frantic. "I did manage to send a telegram to Leo. I sure hope he can get away and come here soon."

Bertha just nodded, looking worn and exhausted. No water had been heated yet, so Emil quietly got out the teapot, filled it with water, and lit the stove. There was really not much more he could do, and he sat down as the news of this disaster began to hit him.

He recalled the last few days that Karo and family spent together with them, with Karo excitedly poring over the brochure of this massive and "unsinkable" ship, and how she could hardly wait to get on it.

"How can such a large ship sink, just like that?" he asked himself. Sure, he had heard of the death of his grandmother while crossing the ocean, but the ship did not sink; she simply had died onboard and was buried at sea. But a big ship? With over 2,000 people onboard? He shook his head in disbelief.

The three of them must have sat like that, in stunned silence, until darkness had fallen. Once Emil had run downstairs to get another newsprint, but no names had been disclosed yet—only some of the most well-known people, like the Astors—but nobody knew yet who, or if any, had survived.

The sudden ring of the doorbell made them jump, and Ella ran to open it. "Telegram, young miss," the postman said curtly, and was gone. It was from Leo. "Will be there tomorrow," it read. Bertha folded her arms around her two children, reciting the Lord's Prayer, and clung to the hope of a miracle.

None of them got much sleep that night. Bertha tossed and turned, dozing off only to wake up to some nightmare about drowning, and long-forgotten images of her dead mother whom she never knew. She could only hope Karoline's and her children's deaths were fast and painless. Sitting up, she suddenly felt an eerie calm. *"No, I do not believe they are dead,"* she told herself. *"I would know it; I would feel it. I knew it when Eugen died, I must cling to that hope."*

All next day, bleary-eyed and sullen, Bertha, Emil, and Ella sat and waited, not knowing exactly what they were waiting for. Every two hours, a new edition of the newspaper was printed, and a few more details trickled forth, but none that would tell them anything about their Karoline and family. It was late in the evening when Leo arrived, looking tired and pale. Wordlessly, he collected his little family in his arms, and no words needed to be spoken.

Each one of them recalled the last day they had seen them off at the train station where they were bound for England and ultimately the Titanic. Their many overseas crates had been sent ahead already, so all they carried was their personal luggage. The kids were cranky with excitement, the baby crying from teething pains, Martha running back several times "for a last hug" from Ella, Julius' parents saying their goodbyes in their formal manner, shaking the children's hands, patting their son's back and a final peck on Karo's cheek.

"Have a safe voyage," Bertha recalled him telling them, and she almost laughed out hysterically at those words now. Leo stroked her back methodically, almost in a trance from fatigue. Once again, Emil took charge, and went to the kitchen to scramble some eggs and butter slices of dark, rich pumpernickel bread, and to boil water for tea. Silently, they ate and drank, immersed in thoughts and grief.

"Leo, please lie down, you look drained," Bertha finally urged him.

"Indeed, my dearest," he nodded. "I am bone weary, the train ride was incredibly long and slow today, not to mention packed and loud. Come to bed as well—there is nothing to be gained by sitting up all night."

They shooed Ella to bed and retired themselves. Emil sat up for a while longer, which was why he was the only one who heard the banging on the door.

He glanced at the clock on his way to answer. *"Three o'clock in the morning,"* he noticed in sleepy surprise. When he opened, he saw Dr. Feldmann, Julius's father, standing at the door, white-faced but smiling, waving a lengthy telegram in his hand.

"Come in, please," Emil motioned to him. "I will wake my mother"

"No need, please let her sleep," Dr. Feldmann shook his head. "But I came as soon as I could—I have a taxi waiting downstairs, so I will tell you quickly! Julius, Karoline, and the children are all well and alive, thank God!"

Emil let out a whoop before Dr. Feldmann continued, "Julius just sent the telegram once he realised what had happened. They had all been ill with measles and were refused passage. They were in isolation for a number of days. Karo is the only one who is still not quite recovered, but she is much improved." He checked back on his lengthy telegram to get the facts correct. "According to them, they are booked on the next steamer in two weeks, but all their crates are lost. But then, who cares right? They are alive!"

Emil thanked him profusely for making this trip in the middle of the night, wishing him a good night before locking the door again.

Wide awake, he was unsure whether to wake everybody up, and finally decided he would. Bertha, clad in her housecoat and her hair hanging down to her shoulders, came out of the bedroom in a daze. "I thought I heard voices, Emil, and I wondered—"

He would not let her finish before grabbing her and yelling, "They are alive, they are alive! Mama—Karo, Julius, and the children are alive. They are still in Southampton because they never boarded! Did you hear me? They are all alive!" Emil slightly shook his mother, who seemed to be frozen in a sort of stupor.

By that time, Leo and Ella came sleepily in the sitting room to find out what all the commotion was about. Slowly the unbelievable news sank in and dazed looks turned into smiles, hugs, and shouts of joy.

"It feels like Easter," Bertha murmured. "My babies, they are alive, all of them!" she exclaimed, and silently retracted any harsh feelings she ever had about Dr. Feldmann; how extraordinary of him to come in the middle of the night with this news. She would be forever grateful to him.

Several days later, they received a lengthy letter from Karo, explaining in detail what had transpired and why they were held back. Young Peter had contracted measles just before they left Berlin and promptly infected the whole family, as well as a number of other fortunate people who, at the time, did not feel that fortunate at all. They would have boarded another steamer by the time her letter arrived, and she was to send a telegram just as soon as they landed in New York. She did lament the loss of all their crates and personal possessions, but overall, she sounded well and extremely blessed to have been spared this disaster.

Bertha nearly kissed the letter.

CHAPTER ELEVEN

THE YEAR 1912 SPELLED THE LAST CAREFREE SUMMER FOR FRA-LU AND ELLA TO enjoy their vacations together. He would turn eighteen in the fall and become a full-fledged lieutenant-cadet in the Kaiser's Army. This meant extended times away from home, transferring to different posts, as well as participating in the seemingly never-ending manoeuvres and deployments.

Ella would start confirmation classes, as well as enter her second-to-last grade in school. Emil turned thirty that year and was promoted to head of the music department. He was also heartbroken. Anton was leaving for Denmark to take the position of principal dancer at the Royal Danish Ballet, a huge breakthrough for him.

"I don't think he will come back to Berlin," Emil told his mother sullenly. "He will stay on as a teacher once his performing days are over, and I am sure he will meet somebody else there."

Bertha was unsure how to answer him. On the one hand, she welcomed Anton's departure, as he had played Emil like a puppet for a long time now; on the other hand, she hated her son to have to grieve this loss with such intensity.

"Perhaps you need a change of scenery, as well," she suggested. "Did Karo not invite you to come to America for a visit? They seem well settled now, living in Boston, having moved there from Hartford recently, and all are speaking English."

Emil shook his head. "No Mama, that is not possible. The ocean crossing back and forth is two weeks, it would take most of my vacation. Anyway, a ship voyage does not appeal to me at all." he was clearly glum.

"Today is our last day together..." he stopped for a few minutes to collect himself. "You know, Mama, I almost think he is glad to leave. He never even asked if I would like to come, as well."

"He is a flighty fellow, that Anton, and most likely Emil is right," Bertha thought silently. "Well, son," she reasoned, "I do not know what to say to you, except life always goes on. No matter what happens, there is often a reason behind it. Maybe he is not the right person for you. What I have seen over the years is that you have always been more giving, while Anton is taking, selfish and self-absorbed. He does not deserve you."

Emil said nothing, just turned around and left the apartment. *"He looks defeated, like a whipped dog."* Bertha was concerned about him.

In October, Leo returned to Berlin, once again to stay until spring. But this time, he was quite worried about his son, Fra-Lu, as a war in the Balkans had just broken out and he hoped that Germany would not be pulled into it.

"Why would you think that, Leo?" Bertha asked.

"Austria-Hungary, along with a number of other countries, is heavily involved in this, and these royal families stick together. I'm not so sure how bright our Kaiser is, all show, parades, receptions, and all that."

Bertha burst out laughing. "Surely his advisors would not let him do something foolish."

"You have more confidence than I have," Leo countered. "Still I worry for Fra-Lu."

"And so, we both worry about our sons," Bertha said, giving Leo a hug. "Come, let's pick Ella up from school; she will be delighted to see you."

Fortunately, the Balkan Wars were over by the following July, and everyone breathed a sigh of relief. In the meantime, Emil had tried to "cure" himself of his natural attractions in a rather dramatic fashion. Just past the new year that moved them into 1913, he introduced a young lady to his mother and Leo.

"This is Gerda," he introduced, and before anyone could say anything else, he added, "and we just got married!" Emil just let the bombshell drop.

Bertha's jaw dropped, and Leo took a deep breath before greeting the young woman in his formal manner with a hand kiss. This made her giggle uncontrollably while looking nervously from Leo to Bertha.

"Emil!" Bertha gasped. "You sure know to surprise your mother!" Bertha finally recovered enough to say something.

"Please sit down," Leo invited them, "and tell us a little about yourself. Where did you two meet?"

Emil, shifting somewhat uncomfortably from one foot to another, chose to stay standing. "We met at the Club where I play sometimes; Gerda sings there."

"Oh dear! What on earth was that boy thinking? A singer in a nightclub?" Bertha swallowed hard while trying to stay poised.

"I see! Do you have family in Berlin, Gerda?" she asked pleasantly.

"No, Frau Hoffmann," she shook her head. "I have nobody here; my family is somewhere in the Black Forest area."

"Somewhere? Surely, she should know where her family is," Bertha thought, shooting her son a puzzled look.

Just at that moment, Ella came home from school.

"Papa!" she shouted. "You are here...and Emil! Who is that? Who did you bring?"

"Ella, you are being impolite!" Bertha scolded. "Where are your manners?"

"Yes, Mother, please excuse me," Ella apologised. "Emil, dear brother, would you please introduce me to our visitor?" she asked in an exaggerated polite gesture.

Poor flustered Emil presented Gerda to Ella. "This is Gerda, Ella," he started slowly. "And she...she is my wife—"

"Your wife?!" Ella screeched, her loud shriek echoing throughout the room.

"That is enough, Ella!" Leo thundered sternly. "You will sit with us like the young lady you are or go to the kitchen and start your homework."

Ella hung her head. "Yes Papa," she whispered, but decided to stay and listen to the conversation; she was far too curious.

"So, then, what are your plans for the future?" Leo asked the couple.

"We will have to look for a place to set up house," Gerda piped up. "I think we should start looking soon?" she motioned to Emil.

"Ah, yes," Emil coughed. "I guess it's time we go—"

"Yes, it is, indeed!" Gerda quickly jumped in, obviously glad to leave this tense environment. "It was a pleasure to meet you," she turned to Bertha and Leo and was out the door in a flash.

Emil, trying to follow her, was held back by his sleeve. "You are coming back this evening!" Bertha demanded. "We need to discuss this further."

"But Mama—"

"No, no 'buts'! You are coming home this evening!"

Emil nodded in defeat.

"Where does Gerda live now?"

"She shares a room with two other ladies," Emil mumbled before quickly following his wife.

Shaking her head, Bertha returned to the sitting room. "What is going on in that man's head?" she wondered out loud.

"Let's wait and see what he has to say later." Leo suggested. "Maybe it's the best for him."

It was late evening when Emil came back, looking somewhat defiant. Ella had begged to stay up until he came home but was ordered to bed by her father. Bertha was relieved to have Leo with her to bestow some authority.

"Emil, I believe you owe your mother some explanation for this rather objectionable behaviour on your part," Leo began, "as well as putting the young lady in an absolute embarrassing position. What on earth were you thinking, son?"

"Yes, I know," Emil admitted. "I know I did not handle this very well."

"Please tell me what is going on, Emil," Bertha implored after Emil said nothing else. "You had told me that you are not interested in girls and how heartbroken you were when Anton left. So now, are you going to make some poor girl unhappy? How can you even... What I mean is...become..." Bertha was at a loss for words.

Emil was beet-red. "I don't know yet, Mama," he said quietly. "We have not...well, you know."

Both Leo and Bertha stared at him. "You have not consummated your marriage? Is that what you are trying to say?" Leo asked.

"Yes," Emil nodded. "I have not felt like it, as well we have no private place to be together."

Leo frowned. "Surely you can afford a hotel, and if not, I'll pay for one," he offered.

But Emil shook his head. "She does not want to either," he said. "You see, she is expecting a child, and—"

"Expecting a child?!" Bertha was incredulous, shaking her head.

"Mama, you of all people should understand that a woman needs to have a husband when she is expecting!" Emil protested. "And this is what I am doing— the honourable thing the man who violated her is not doing."

Bertha gasped.

Now Emil sat up and looked his mother in her eyes. "I like Gerda," he said simply. "She is a talented singer, and we get along quite well. And even though I—well, you know—I have always wanted a family, and this was the right opportunity for me. We decided quickly before anybody notices her condition, and I can claim this little one when it is born."

Exhausted, Emil sat back and exhaled in relief.

Leo rose and patted him on the shoulder. "That is indeed an honourable gesture on your part," he said sincerely. "I really wish you all the best and

I hope that it will work out in the long run—and you are not being taken advantage of."

Bertha also rose and gave her son a hearty hug, "Emil, son, whatever happens in your relationship, do not ever take it out on the child," she gently instructed. "He or she did not ask to be conceived. Now that you have taken on the responsibility, you have to carry it all the way. That child is yours, just as much as any others you and your—wife—may have," she looked down apologetically. "I'm sorry, I still have to get used to saying your wife."

"Yes, I understand," nodded Emil. "And I have you as my model. I will always thank you for your love and support—" he started to sniffle and could not continue.

"All right," Leo quickly interjected. "Let us have a toast to your future, Emil." He brought out his cognac and three glasses.

"To a new life," they saluted.

"I think I'll go to bed now; I am dead tired," Emil yawned. "Soon I will be living in my own place. Actually, I am looking forward to married life and being a father," he smiled a little uncertainly before going to his room.

Bertha and Leo sat up for a little while longer to talk about the day's events, both hoping the best for Emil and Gerda. Leo finally pulled Bertha close to him and whispered in her ear that at least the two of them could consummate their union. He winked, got up, and held out his hand. A relaxed and smiling Bertha allowed Leo to pull her to bed.

Chapter Twelve: 1913

Predictably, Ella was beside herself at the prospect of becoming an aunt again. Emil and Gerda had found a flat nearby and Ella could hardly wait for the new little one to arrive.

But when Gerda was ready to deliver, Ella was at the Gut Hohenstein estate for her summer vacation. Much to her dismay, Fra-Lu was not there, and Ludwiga had never returned from her Christmas vacation in Poland. However, Ella had still enjoyed every minute with her father, riding her own horse alongside him, across the fields, inspecting the growth of the wheat and rye, marking trees to be chopped for firewood, and listening to all of Leo's explanations and commentaries. She simply loved being on the estate and the freedom, and altogether it was a wonderful bonding time between father and daughter.

"Papa, I don't want to go back to Berlin and back to school," she told him several times.

Leo chuckled good-naturedly. "You would not like the winters here," he explained. "It is bitterly cold and there is much more snow than in Berlin. We take horse sleighs to get around and it becomes quite lonely at times. Remember, I am not here then, either—only the estate manager, his family, and some farmhands."

"But maybe Mother can move here, now that Ludwiga is not here anymore!" she eagerly suggested.

"Hmm," Leo considered. "Maybe. We will see."

Ella already knew when her parents said, "We will see," they really meant it wouldn't happen, so she just nodded.

"Race you home!" she shouted and was off on her horse, Leo chasing after her, spurning his steed to a faster pace, but not fast enough to catch her.

Laughing, she jumped off. "I am faster than you!" she whooped. Leo applauded her efforts. He cherished this child of his, not a child much longer. He watched as she jumped off her horse with ease and started to unbuckle the saddle. Almost fourteen already, she was tall, slim, almost too slim, with thick dark blonde hair, and an inquisitive look in her gray eyes. He thought her lovely. *"Just like her mother,"* he mused, suddenly missing Bertha with an almost painful yearning.

A telegram awaited him when he entered the house.

"Ella, where are you?" Leo called.

"What is it, Papa?"

"It's a boy! Gerda and Emil are parents of a little boy."

"Hurray!" Ella yelled. "What's his name?"

"It doesn't say," Leo called back. "Only that it is a boy."

In the meantime, Bertha, after sending the telegram, went to see her new daughter-in-law in the hospital. She still had some difficulty becoming close to Gerda, but she seemed loving towards Emil and that was all that mattered. She decided to take some flowers and make a special effort to admire the newborn.

When she entered the room, Emil was standing at the window, looking out while Gerda sat up in bed, holding the baby and sobbing.

"Oh no, what did I walk into now?" Bertha was worried.

"Good afternoon, Mama!" Emil turned around, with a scowl on his face. "Let me introduce you to your new grandchild!" and with an almost angry motion he pulled the newborn from Gerda and handed him to Bertha.

With a puzzled expression, she looked at the couple before taking a close look at the baby. First, she noticed a mass of black curls, and then, aghast, realised that the child was lightly coloured. His skin had the look of golden honey and his big black eyes seemed to stare right at her.

Before she could react, Emil said angrily, "it was the jazz musician!"

Gerda's sobs grew louder while snivelling, "I am so sorry Emil, I did not expect this!"

"What do you mean?" Emil retorted, even more enraged. "How many others were there before the jazz singer? Answer me!"

Bertha couldn't remember the last time she had seen her son so angry. *"Think quick!"* she told herself, still staring at the small bundle in her arms. "That is quite enough, Emil," she reprimanded him. "You knew that Gerda was with child when you were married. It really is not for you to know what transpired before your time together." This earned her a grateful look from Gerda.

"As far as I recall, you promised to take care of her child," she continued. "Now come here and look at him; he is a stunningly beautiful child." She placed him in Emil's arms before he could say or do anything. "He is your son now, so care for him and love him."

Bertha sat next to Gerda and put her arms around the hysterical young woman. "Now Gerda, I want to say the same to you," she said gently. "He is beautiful. Raise him well, as children need the love of their parents."

Gerda's sobs began to subside, and Bertha watched Emil sit in a chair, holding the child. He began to gently stroke his little face.

"What will you name him?" Bertha asked after a while.

Emil, not taking his eyes off the child, answered. "I think he looks like a Felix. Shall we call him Felix?" he turned to Gerda.

"Yes Emil," Gerda nodded. "We shall name him Felix; that is a nice name."

Bertha agreed and sighed with relief.

"Now to let Leo and Ella know," she thought. *"Maybe I'll wait until Ella gets back and write to Leo."*

"Mother, over here!" Ella hopped off the train some weeks later. "Can we go and see the baby now?"

"Good afternoon, dear daughter," Bertha smiled. "How about a civilised greeting from you to start with?"

"Ah yes, pardon me, Mother," she apologised quickly. "I am just too excited to see the baby!" Ella was jumping like a rubber ball. "So, good afternoon, dear Mother, thank you for picking me up," she greeted Bertha politely, but Bertha could see Ella was bursting inside. "*Now* can we see the baby?"

"Yes, yes, we will see the baby," Bertha almost laughed, "but first we bring your luggage home and then we go."

"Mother, what did they name him?"

Bertha was confused. "Did your father not tell you?"

"He didn't know."

"Then he must not have received my last letter yet," Bertha thought out loud. "I did mail it a few days ago..."

"Mother—the name, please!" Ella became impatient.

"Felix, his name is Felix."

"Felix? That's it? No second name?"

Bertha shook her head. "No, just Felix, I believe."

"I like it," she grinned. "It sounds quite exotic."

Bertha gave her daughter a quick look. *"You don't know how exotic,"* she thought to herself. "Yes, it is a little different," she admitted out loud, "but then both your brother and Gerda are a little—well, not exotic as such, just a little different."

"Different? How different, Mother?" Ella wanted to know.

But Bertha just kept nudging her along. "Can you please stop hitting me with your suitcase and move on? We'll get a taxi to take us home, freshen up a little, and then go over to Emil."

"Pardon, Mother," Ella mumbled as they rushed along the train platform.

Two hours later, they rang Emil and Gerda's doorbell, with Ella as jumpy as a grasshopper. She had brought a little outfit along that she had knitted for Felix. Gerda opened the door, looking tired and slightly bedraggled, trying to button the front of her frock. They heard the baby fuss in the background.

"I was just nursing him," Gerda excused her appearance. Ella rushed by her like a flash, saw the child lying on the bed, and gave off a shriek.

Bertha and Gerda looked at each other. "What is it, Ella?" Bertha asked. "Why are you screaming? You are scaring the poor child."

"Oh Mother, he is just so incredibly adorable," Ella gushed. "Look at this perfect little body, those eyes, that hair, and oh, he is so tanned already! Did you put him out in the sun on the balcony without any clothes on?"

Gerda looked somewhat helplessly at Bertha before answering. "Um, no Ella, he came out that way"

"But that's wonderful," Ella smiled. "He will never be so pale like Emil, and his dark hair—that must be from you, Mother."

"Perhaps Ella, perhaps," Bertha said, trying to slow her down. "But Gerda has a Spanish family background, and sometimes these traits are passed on," Bertha tried to explain with Gerda quickly jumping in,

"Yes, my grandparents on my mother's side were indeed Spanish and had darker complexion."

"No matter," Ella shrugged. "He is simply the cutest little nephew I ever had!" Ella was enchanted, picking him up and kissing his honey-coloured velvety skin and breathing in his baby scent.

"Emil did well," she crooned, evoking a coughing spell from Gerda and an awkward silence from Bertha. Ella noticed nothing of that, as she was totally absorbed in little Felix.

Finally, Bertha asked where Emil was. "He's playing at the Club tonight," Gerda informed her, "so he will be home late. But he has been wonderful with Felix—I think he has fallen in love with him," Gerda was quick to add.

Bertha was reassured to hear that while claiming the baby for herself for a little snuggle. *"He is indeed a beautiful child,"* she agreed. *"If he does not get much darker, it may be hard to tell that he has Negro blood in him and make his life difficult."* Returning him to Gerda to finish nursing, she herded Ella out the door to go home.

All the way home, Ella chatted away about her nephew and how she looked forward to playing with him. After a while, Bertha tuned her out, lost in her own thoughts and concerns for this young couple.

Chapter Thirteen: 1914

January 1, 1914 dawned to a totally snowed-in Berlin. It had snowed for days already and most New Year's Eve festivities had been cancelled or severely reduced. Berlin was paralyzed. Mountains of snow had buried the city and yet it was still snowing.

The Army was mobilised to try to dig out main streets and Berliners themselves were out in force with whatever was useful to shovel, push, or scoop snow aside. Hardly anybody owned a shovel; Berlin, a city of mostly apartment buildings, had no need for individuals to own shovels. Pots, pans, cups and even hands had to do.

Because of the holidays, many shops had been closed for several days and with all the snow, they had been unable to resupply their stock and simply remained shut. But Berliners, stoic as was their nature, took it in stride and made do with what they had, sharing food, supplies, and coal. Apartment janitors had shovels and worked around the clock to create paths between the buildings. The only means of communications were daily newspapers, and those had stopped printing because nobody showed up for work.

And so, they kept on shovelling; the snow fell for over a week before it finally stopped. It took many weeks to return the city to normal.

Bertha, with Leo and family, were holding out at their country home. The snow had almost reached the roof and with the windows covered by snow, an eerie light infused the rooms throughout. Leo, along with Emil, dug themselves through the front door and a pathway. The chimney had to be kept free from snow or they could not keep the place warm. There was enough firewood for cooking and warmth piled next to the house, but it also had to be dug out.

Ella, armed with a broom, tried in vain to clear at least one window from the snow. But whenever she had a small hole cleared, the heavy snow from above slipped down and quickly filled the gap once again. Somewhat frustrated, she joined her father and brother in their cleaning attempts. *"I surely wish Fra-Lu were here,"* she thought. *"I miss him, and Christmas is just not the same without him."* She felt a little lost without him, now that Emil was preoccupied with little Felix and Gerda.

Once again, the little house had been filled to the brim with family and Christmas was a bustling and joy-filled occasion. Emil and his family had planned to return to Berlin midweek and celebrate New Year's Eve at the Club but were now stuck. Bertha, with a small frown on her face, took stock of the food supplies on hand. The most worrisome situation was milk for Felix. Gerda had stopped nursing him, as she simply had no more flow and her nipples were painfully raw. Felix was a good eater and his milk now had to be thinned down. Bertha was even more concerned than Gerda, who simply lay back and bemoaned her painful breasts.

"Ella, put on your skis and canvass the neighbours for some milk, please," Bertha said, and sent Ella off with an empty pitcher. Securing the pitcher on a belt borrowed from her father and tied around her middle, she set off, hoping to manage with a filled pitcher.

Leo and Emil came back inside. "The chimney is clear for now," Leo announced, rubbing his hands together for some warmth.

Emil picked up the squawking baby. "I think he is hungry," he motioned to Gerda.

"I have no milk," she wailed. "What can we do?"

Bertha had already filled the bottle with some sugar water and a few drops of milk. "Here, give this to him for now," she offered. "That will at least calm him down a little. Hopefully Ella will bring back some milk and hopefully this snow will stop soon. Fortunately, we have enough food stock in the larder to keep us going for a few days."

A while later, a beaming Ella burst into the house, prying off the pitcher from the belt. "There are three eggs in there! Frau Kersten from a few houses down was just being picked up by her son with a horse-drawn sleigh—the poor horse could hardly get through the deep snow."

"Thankfully, they don't have far to go," Bertha added. "Three eggs, well, with some flour, we can make scrambled eggs!" she laughed.

"Wait, Mother, that is not all," Ella continued, almost out of breath. "At the end of our long driveway, there is a potato sack filled with whatever she had left, including one full bottle of milk. The son dropped it off on their way home, so Papa or Emil, can you please drag it into the house?"

"Ah, what a resourceful daughter we have," Leo said, winking at Bertha. "Up and away Emil, let's get the goods then."

"How very thoughtful of Frau Kersten," smiled Bertha in relief. "We must make sure to write her a thank you note as soon as we get back," she reminded Ella, who had already begun to crack the eggs for their midday meal.

It took the family over a week to make it back to Berlin, which was still encased in masses of snow. However, the streetcars were running again, the shops were open, and by and large life had returned to normal.

With a huge sigh of relief, Bertha and Leo embraced each other and spent the few hours blissfully alone while Ella was at school.

"In a few short months, Ella will be confirmed and finished with school," Bertha noted with concern to Leo. "I don't know what she will do from then on. I know she wants to live with you and work on the estate, or so she says, but I think she needs to learn some kind of trade or continue a path of higher education. I think you need to have a talk with her Leo."

"I have given this some thought, as well," Leo said. "She is quite stubborn with her ideas. Needless to say, I would love to have her live and work with me, but we need to talk about this some more," Leo paused before looking at his wife lovingly. "It also goes without saying that I wish for you to come with me as well..." he let the sentence hang in the air.

Bertha, hearing the mail slot in the door flap, sidestepped any comment and rose to see what had arrived by post. "We have a letter from Karo," she happily announced, "a letter from Fra-Lu, and an official-looking one for you."

Leo tore it open, and several sheets of official documents fell out. He frowned. "It's all in Polish!" he exclaimed, a bit exasperated. "I don't know what it says. Too bad Fra-Lu is not here; he could translate it for me. I can only pick out the odd word, but it makes no sense to me."

"I am sure you can get it translated at the Polish Embassy here," Bertha suggested, "and if needed, it can be answered to straight away."

"What a smart woman you are!" Leo grinned. "I'll tackle that tomorrow. Now, let's see what our children have written."

Bertha, already reading Karo's letter, summarised it for Leo. "They wish us a blessed Christmas season and an even better 1914. Karo is expecting their fifth child, a little American, she writes. They are well settled, have no yearning to come back to Berlin, and Karo now writes her name with a 'C' instead of a 'K' and they dropped the last 'N' from Feldmann. Must be American—Caroline Feldman..." Bertha deliberated.

"I fear I will never see my daughter and grandchildren ever again," she worried. "And they might not even speak German anymore." Bertha was dejected at that thought. "Oh yes, she also writes that Julius' parents have moved to France and perhaps may join them some time in the future."

After a long pause, she asked what Fra-Lu had to write. "He sends us holiday greetings as well," Leo answered. "He is sorry he could not be with us but felt he needed to spend some time with his mother. He hopes to have leave over Easter and come for a few days' visit. He sends special greetings to *Elfi*—"

They both chuckled. "She will be happy to hear that," Bertha smiled. "She was a little sad he was not around for Christmas. Now with Emil busy with Felix, she felt lonely for her other brother."

"Perhaps he will be here for her confirmation" Leo thought out loud "that would be a very special surprise for her. I shall write to him and see if that can be possible."

The following day, Leo had gone to the Polish Embassy for translation of the mailed documents. It took him a long time to come back home and Bertha began to worry what might have happened. Little was she prepared for what was to come!

She saw Leo come home at last and stood almost frozen at the sight of him. He held a bottle of champagne in one hand and a huge bouquet of roses in the other, with a wide smile lighting up his face. He placed the roses and bottle on the table and picked her up with both arms, swinging her around and around until she was dizzy and pleading for mercy. "Leo, my god, what is going on?" she cried out, confused and giddy at the same time. "Please explain yourself!"

"I will, my love, I will," he was breathless from his exertion, fumbling in his coat pocket. He slowly pulled out a small box, opened it before her, and proudly showed off two wedding bands.

A speechless and puzzled Bertha stared at the rings, then back at him. Before she could say another word, Leo suddenly became serious.

"Bertha, the time has come to ask you again," he said fervently. "Will you marry me?"

Bertha gasped, then quickly nodded.

"In three days, we have an appointment at the Justice of Peace," he explained, his seriousness melting into happiness. "We are getting legally married, my dearest! It is finally happening!"

Bertha's knees gave out and she quickly had to sit down. "Leo, oh, Leo, what are you saying? I am overwhelmed with joy and confusion."

Leo explained that the documents were divorce papers from Ludwiga. As of November 1913, they were divorced, but it had just become final and legal. Included was a letter from Ludwiga's Legal Counsel, advising that she is taking the whole blame, she is not asking for any support or settlement, and she will forever be grateful for Leo's care, duty, and love towards her Fra-Lu. She also wished him and Bertha many more years.

Leo was still grinning from ear to ear.

"And what happens to Fra-Lu's inheritance? His entitlement to estate and title?" Bertha was troubled.

"He is safe," Leo assured her. "He is over eighteen and, if necessary, I will give up all my entitlement in favour of his. But the way it was explained to me, that since the divorce is not my fault, everything remains as is. I believe Ludwiga knows that as well, and that is why she waited until now."

Bertha let out a big sigh of relief before allowing the feelings of utter bliss overtake her.

Three days later, Leo and Bertha were legally wed and with deep tenderness and affection, they placed the wedding bands on each other's finger. Emil and Gerda were their official witnesses, with Ella holding Felix and crying her eyes out from happiness. Leo gently tilted Bertha's chin up to gaze into her eyes and placed a kiss on her lips, whispering, "I love you, Frau Hohenstein," which sent shivers up and down Bertha's spine. "I love you too—my husband," she replied, letting the word "husband" roll deliciously off her tongue.

Telegrams went out to Karo and Fra-Lu, and the couple embarked on a short trip, back to Budapest, for a romantic week together.

Fra-Lu, true to his promise, came for Ella's confirmation, and he came in style—on a new, motorised bicycle with a passenger sidecar. "It's called a motorcycle," he proudly announced, "and the sidecar is for my little sister for a spin around town."

Ella could hardly contain her excitement. Of course, Bertha and Leo would not allow her to ride to church in it on her special day. They walked together, dignified, like all the other young people being confirmed that day. Ella was surrounded by her loving family, and she could not have asked for a better day.

In the evening, Bertha took off her first ring she had received from Leo and placed it on Ella's finger. "My dearest daughter, this is a true love ring," she explained. "May it protect you and bring you the same blessings that it did for me. And one day, you may pass it on to your own daughter. Your father and I wish you a wonderful life. We both love you." She gave her daughter a big hug.

Chapter Fourteen

In early June, plans were made for both Ella and Bertha to spend the summer at Gut Hohenstein, a prospect that filled Bertha with some unease. She had never been to the estate before but was now the proud (and legal) wife of Leopold.

She asked Ella question after question regarding the size of the manor, how many domestic servants there were, and how formal she was expected to be.

"It's quite informal in the summer, Mother," Ella assured her. "There is so much work to be done outside that everybody is just glad to be coming home, enjoy some food, and relax for a little bit."

"As to servants," she continued, "let me see, I'm not really sure... There is the cook, the maid, and cleaning staff. Oh yes, there is Papa's personal valet, who takes care of all the things you do for him here!" Ella had a big grin on her face. "He also looks after Fra-Lu when he is home. I am so excited to see him again." Then her smile turned into a bit of a frown. "I will miss Felix, though... Could we not take him with us?"

With a firm "no," Bertha shook her head. "He belongs to his parents, and they need to tend to him and spend the summer devoted to him—all of them need that together time."

Reluctantly, Ella agreed. "You know, Mother, Gerda does not really seem fond of the little fellow," Ella said with a furrowed brow. "Whenever I go over there, she is lying on the couch, reading some love story. It seems Emil is doing a lot of the work."

Bertha was a bit surprised. "I hope you are mistaken Ella," she said, "but sometimes it takes a little while for some women to bond with their child, and—" she glanced quickly at her daughter— "their marriage is rather one of convenience."

Ella brushed that comment aside. "Well, not everybody can be so crazily in love as you and Papa," she remarked, making them both laugh.

It had also been decided that Ella would attend a finishing school in Switzerland for the next two years. Since the only kind of work Ella wanted to do was on the estate, Leo had begun to look into various options for her. As it was expected that she would eventually marry into an estate setting, it seemed the most sensible thing for her to do. Enthusiastically, Ella had agreed, and a school near Geneva was picked as the most suitable. She was to start there right after summer vacation and leave directly from Hohenstein, not returning to Berlin until Christmas vacation.

But then all plans came into question on June 28, 1914, when the newspaper headlines screamed:

"ARCHDUKE FRANZ FERDINAND OF AUSTRIA AND HIS WIFE SOPHIE ASSASSINATED IN SARAJEVO. BOTH SUCCUMBED TO THEIR INJURIES."

"How utterly awful!" Bertha lamented. "Why would anybody do such a dastardly act? Now the poor Kaiser has no more successor to the throne. With Crown Prince Rudolf dead for some time now, the Archduke was to take over once the Kaiser died. He is so old already."

"That might be the least of his problems," Leo suggested. "This is enough to declare war on Serbia," he frowned. "I hope cooler heads prevail."

"War?" Bertha was aghast. "A war? Oh, Leo, you are too gloomy. In any event, what does Germany have to do with the quarrels of Austria and Serbia?"

"I do not wish to frighten you, dearest, but Germany can easily be pulled into some situation," Leo explained. "They are allied with Austria, and Serbia with Russia, and so on. As well, all these royal leaders are somewhat related and feel responsible to come to the emperor's aid. Our Kaiser Wilhelm, Russia's Tsar Nicholas, King George of England—just to name a few."

Indeed, after several weeks of failed negotiations, war was officially declared on July 28, 1914.

Nobody had expected how long and gruesome this war would become and how many countries would be involved. It was devastating.

The military was mobilised, along with Fra-Lu, who came home for three days' leave before heading off to battle. Ella and Bertha were inconsolable, while Leo walked around, stone-faced. Only Fra-Lu himself, with the eternal optimism of youth, consoled them. "This will be a quick war, you will see," he tried to assure them. "By Christmas, it will be all over and I will come back, hopefully with some medals for bravery!" he boasted a little.

And so, they watched their brave young men march to war, singing and full of bravado. Smiling, hugging relatives and sweethearts, they filed into trains and were gone, most of them forever.

The war was not over at Christmas, or the next or even the next. By 1915, the losses of lives began to mount, with black mourning clothes for women— mothers, wives, sisters, daughters—were almost the only clothes one could still get. Women began to work in jobs previously held for men only. A general doom and gloom seemed to grip everybody.

By late 1915, even Emil had to report for military duty. Emil, who had been exempt from conscription, was now considered fit for duty. Leo had tried to interfere by having him classified as an essential farmworker, but the application was rejected.

"We will send you Polish prisoners of war to help with the harvesting," he was told. "A music teacher is not a capable farm help."

Emil, dressed in field grays of a private, came to see his mother, looking sad and dejected. Bertha took his hands and looked at them for a long time—soft hands, long fingers, perfect for playing the piano, but not for holding a rifle. She picked them up, kissed each finger, and tried to suppress the awful feeling inside her gut that she would never see her firstborn again.

For a long time, they stood and looked at each other. "Goodbye, Mama," he finally said. "I guess I should have gone to Switzerland like Karl-Heinz," he tried to joke with a feigned grin.

"I am so happy Ella is there; she is safe there," Bertha could only nod, choking back her tears. "We'll take care of Gerda and little Felix," she promised, kissing his cheeks once more before he ran down the stairs.

Unfortunately, Bertha's premonitions were correct; she would never see her dear son again. Emil fell in Verdun, France, in 1916.

Ella had returned from Switzerland, as the school had sent all non-Swiss citizens back to their own countries.

By now, Bertha had become the main caregiver for Felix, and he spent most of his time with Bertha and Ella. And then one day, Gerda was gone. Nobody knew where she had gone to, nor did anybody ever hear from her again. Felix had become a permanent resident in the Turmstrasse.

"At least we have him to remember Emil by," Ella cried, holding the little body next to her.

"Well, yes and no." Bertha decided to tell Ella about Felix and his biological father.

Ella seemed rather unfazed by this revelation. "Now I understand why he is so dark," she simply mused. "But what are we to do, Mother? He is still ours, isn't he? We will not send him away?" Ella anxiously looked at her mother.

"Of course not, Ella, why would you even think that?" Bertha asked her. "Felix belongs to us, that's all there is to it. Someday, when he is old enough, we will tell him, but that is a long time away."

Leo managed to come to Berlin for Emil's memorial service, and he was shocked at the conditions of the city. Everybody was cold and hungry, ration cards had been issued, but there was no food to be had. The winter of 1916–1917 became known as the Turnip Winter, as these were nearly the only food available.

"You need to move to the country house," he told Bertha. "In the spring, you can plant vegetables. There are also apple trees on the lot, and berries are plentiful, and I'll try to get a few chickens and a few rabbits—at least you can slaughter them and have some meat."

"Me?!" Bertha was appalled. "Slaughter rabbits? What are you thinking, Leo, my love? I can't do that!"

"If you are hungry enough, then yes, you can do that," Leo told her simply. "There is also enough wood to keep the stove going; it will be better than here in the city. I would take you back to Hohenstein, but I do not know how much longer I can stay there. The Russian front is moving forward, occupying all territories as they cross into town after town. I think you, Ella, and Felix will be much safer in the country."

Bertha began to protest. "No, do not object!" He held up his hands. "At least I will know where you are, and that you are safe."

"Then why don't you come with us? Don't go back there, please, Leo, I worry so much about you," Bertha pleaded.

"*Schatz*, I need to be in my home, my ancestral home, Fra-Lu's home," he explained gently. "I cannot simply abandon it. I have workers to consider, livestock to care for, at least what is left. All the horses have been confiscated already, and most of the larders are empty now, but there will be seeding in the spring, and people and soldiers must be fed. I have to defend my home," he declared with resolve.

"I know, I must be brave, I know," she said, once again facing a sad farewell to somebody she loved dearly.

"I just hope Fra-Lu will come home in one piece," Leo tried some grim humour, "and I hope I will not be called to duty at my age."

"Surely not, Leo, you are fifty-five!" Bertha protested. "Way too old to be a soldier." Bertha was surprised he would even consider that.

"I'm an officer in reserve, so I could be called up," he sighed. "What may save me is the farm. Like I said before, somebody has to feed the people." He hugged and kissed Bertha once more before he, too, was gone, swallowed by the never-ending trains filled with men going off to serve their country.

Bertha was devastated at the loss of Emil—such an unnecessary loss. A boy who was never supposed to be born, but who brought her endless happiness, comfort, and support, even with his distaste for women that she could not understand. She had loved him unconditionally. Sometimes, she caught herself standing by a sleeping Felix, seeking to see some of Emil in the little boy, knowing, of course, that this was quite foolish of her. Felix had dark, curly hair and eyes, Emil had been blond and blue-eyed. And yet, he, too, brought her comfort and she began to love him as much as Emil.

During 1917, while the war continued, they received a parcel from Karo. Bertha was actually surprised to receive it at all, fully expecting it to have been pilfered somewhere along the line, but it had come intact with some much-needed foodstuff, sugar, flour, tea, as well as powdered milk for Felix. The toddler was way too thin, and Ella was more than elated to bake a cake with the flour, some sugar, and the watery milk.

Ella, now a pretty young woman of seventeen, had taken over most of the care for the little one. Along with the parcel came the news that their fifth child was another boy, already almost two, and named Henry, in honour of Karo's great-grandfather, Heinrich. Bertha wrote her a long letter, telling of Emil's death as well how they fared in these war-torn years. She was now truly thankful that Karo and her family had chosen America. Karo continued to send parcels every so often; some arrived, and some did not.

By now, Leo and Bertha had been separated for over one year—the longest they had ever been apart in their years together. Bertha and Ella had indeed moved to the country house, and slaved to grow vegetables, chop wood, and feed the rabbits and the chickens. The eggs they bartered with for other food, and Bertha learned to slaughter rabbits. As disgusting as this practice was to her, Leo was right in his prediction that hunger does not care, and one does what one must to survive.

By late 1917, they received word that Fra-Lu had been wounded and was recovering in a field hospital somewhere in Belgium.

Ella nearly went mad trying to find out what happened to him. "I won't survive if I lose another brother!" she wailed.

"Don't talk nonsense," Bertha rebuked her. "One can survive all sorts of horrors. Life goes on, and day by day, you have to be strong and stare it down. With God's help we survive," she added. "I am sure if things were bad with Fra-Lu, Papa would have sent us notice.

"I want to visit him!" Ella declared.

"Are you mad?" Bertha was horrified. "He is in Belgium, in enemy territory, and you a young woman travelling alone? I think you have taken leave of your senses. Here," Bertha said as she pulled out a chair, "sit down and write him a letter. He will get it by military mail. It's enough I have to worry about him, as well as your father. Truly, I do not need to worry about you, as well." Bertha shook her head at such absurdity.

Chapter Fifteen: 1917–1919

In 1917, the political scene unravelled with almost breathtaking speed. Internal unrests and revolutions began among the common populace. In Russia, an unknown Communist revolutionist named Vladimir Ilyich Ulyanov came to power and the Tsar and his entire family with entourage was deposed, banned to Siberia and ultimately executed. Ulyanov became Lenin and the birth of Bolshevism began.

By early 1918, it was obvious that this bloody war would and could not last much longer. Monarchies fell, fascists rose to power, in Italy, a man name Benito Mussolini took over the reins, and an Austrian private began to emerge. The German Kaiser Wilhelm abdicated and went into exile in Holland. The never-ending bad news came fast and furious.

Once the active fighting, and essentially the war, officially ended on November 11, 1918, Europe as well as many other countries mourned their hundreds of thousands of dead and maimed young men, sons, fathers, brothers, husbands. Bertha would eventually learn that all five of August's sons had been killed— *"six actually,"* she silently thought of poor Emil.

Fra-Lu had survived the war but was stuck in a prisoner of war camp in France; he was expected to be returned home soon in a prisoner exchange.

However, peace was far from over. Street battles were fought almost daily in Berlin, and various factions were vying for power, particularly the Communists. Criminal gangs roamed the streets, and police presence was slim to nonexistent. Germany was prohibited to build up any armed forces. In short, life was even more precarious than during the war itself.

Since things were almost as bad outside of Berlin, Bertha decided to move back to Turmstrasse to the relative security of an apartment building. The last of the chicken and rabbits were slaughtered and eaten. Pickled and canned vegetables and fruit were stowed in a baby buggy with Felix sitting on top of the precious goods. Slowly, Bertha and Ella made their way on foot. It took them hours to reach the apartment building. Felix, alternating between babbling, crying, and sleeping, was the only sound they heard for the longest time. People remained behind closed doors and windows. As they got nearer to their destination, Bertha wondered about her decision. Gangs of young men loitered at street corners, whistling at them and making lewd remarks. "Ignore them," Bertha hissed to Ella. "Just keep on walking."

And so, they walked, pushing the buggy with the toddler, and trying to avoid any confrontation. Closer to home, they met up with a few residents from Turmstrasse and together, they walked home, unharmed.

The apartment smelled stale and musty from years of being unused. Both women began the task of cleaning; windows were opened, beds stripped, the stove cleaned, and the old ashes carried outside. Some old and mouldy bread was disposed of and water was heated to make some tea as well as bathe Felix. Every so often, the women would hear shots being fired, and Ella peeked out from the balcony to take in the chaotic scenes below.

"If this is peace, I'd rather have war," she muttered. "I wonder how Papa and Fra-Lu are doing and when we can see them again."

Amid all that, the world was struck with an additional tragedy—a particularly lethal strain of influenza. It was later dubbed the "Spanish Flu" because King Alfonso of Spain had become gravely ill and it was erroneously believed the influenza originated in Spain. King Alfonso eventually recovered; however, hundreds of thousands of people around the world died. It had become the most lethal pandemic in history. War-weary, emaciated, malnourished people dropped like flies. In a cold winter with little fuel for heat, people huddled together in small, damp, and cold quarters, and this highly infectious flu spread like wildfire.

Bertha and Ella managed relatively well, but poor young Felix did not. Only four years old, he, too, succumbed to the flu. It was a devastating blow, particularly to Ella. Despite all their care, the long and sleepless nights carrying the cough-wracked little boy in their arms, wrapping his legs in cold compresses to relieve his fever, in the end, nothing helped. One late afternoon, he simply stopped breathing during a particularly terrible coughing bout and gasping for air. Ella felt him go limp in her arms and tried to shake him awake, but little Felix was gone. Once again, Bertha and Ella mourned the loss of a loved one.

The cemeteries were clogged with crying, wailing, and bereaved relatives of flu victims. Gravediggers worked day and night, coffins were long depleted, and people were wrapped in blankets and laid into the cold graves.

Bertha was more stoic and silent in her grief while Ella, always the more emotional, cried out in sorrow as she stood by Felix's tiny grave. Priests and ministers walked from grave to grave to give last rites before rushing on to the next. By the time they came back home, Ella collapsed in a heap of tears and became severely ill with a fever and chills.

Bertha was beside herself with worry and yearned for Leo to be by her side. When she started to say a prayer next to Ella's bedside one night, Ella opened her eyes, gave a weak smile, and whispered, "Mother, I am not dead yet," before falling into a deep sleep.

Several days later, she was up and about, weak, but fully recovered. Bertha never fell ill, nor did she ever become ill for the rest of her life. An estimated 500 million people became ill with the Spanish Flu, which killed about one-third of its victims.

And then one day, the following year, in 1919, Leo finally made it to Berlin. Bertha couldn't believe it was him—partly because of how he looked, and partly because of how long it had been.

"You look so skinny!" she gasped in shock.

"You don't look much fatter, either," Leo teased. It was so good to see him smile. They embraced and hugged as if they would never let go of each other ever again.

"It has been so terribly long, Leo," Bertha finally spoke, in between tears. "I cannot tell you how much I have missed you. Can you stay now?"

Leo sighed heavily. "Not very long, I'm afraid," he replied. "Things are not in good shape back home. As you might know, as part of the agreement of Versailles, Germany had to give most of East Prussia to Poland, in effect making us homeless."

Bertha's hand flew to her mouth in shock. "Now what, Leo?"

"Actually, *Hohenstein* fared rather well in comparison. Most of the neighbourhood estates were pillaged, plundered, ravaged, and burned. Thanks to Ludwiga's Polish officer husband, Hohenstein was made the headquarters of the Polish and Russian armed forces, and they behaved themselves rather well."

"A new agreement between Poland and Russia is being hammered out to return these estates to us," he continued. "However, Poland wants a seaport to the Baltic Sea. The proposal is for a so-called Polish Corridor cutting through the vast lands of private properties, with the provision of safe passage guarantees for people living on both sides of this Corridor to freely travel from one side to the other. Hohenstein is somewhat affected, as we are on the eastern part of this division. Once this agreement is put in place, we can safely transit through this Corridor by rail only, for the time being. We'll see how that will work."

"Leo, that sounds really complicated," Bertha sighed heavily. "Do you think it will ever go back to normal?"

Leo shrugged. "I do not know, my dearest, for now we will have to work with what we have."

"How did you get out now?" Bertha wanted to know.

"I received a safe pass from the Poles," he answered, "but I need to go back, by the latest when Fra-Lu returns. He needs to be established as the rightful owner and after that, I think I can move to Berlin."

CHAPTER SIXTEEN: 1920

TWO YEARS AFTER THE OFFICIAL END OF THE WAR, THINGS WERE LESS THAN peaceful in Germany. People wanted the lawlessness, poverty, and unemployment to end. The Treaty of Versailles handcuffed any type of progress for the country. The government seemed helpless, security forces were banned from carrying arms, and crime rose to once-unknown levels.

Anti-government marches and protests became an almost daily occurrence. Amidst this anger and insecurity, a new political party was formed in Munich, the National-Socialist German Workers' Party, or Nazis. The speaker was Adolf Hitler, only at around thirty years old, whose rousing speech and promise to scuttle the Versailles pact enthused and inspired people. The vision and promise to create full employment, full healthcare, law and order, and prosperity resonated with the unemployed and poor. By 1921, Hitler became the leader of the Nazi Party.

In the early summer of 1920, when Leo and Bertha were almost sixty, Leo asked her and Ella to come to Hohenstein and spend the balance of the year there.

Somewhat apprehensive, two women, with Ella now nineteen years old, boarded the train to eventually drive through the Polish Corridor. It was exactly as Leo had written. At the last stop in Germany, the German crew left the train, and the Polish crew boarded. All doors were locked and sealed, all curtains were pulled to block all glimpses by the passengers, identity cards were checked, and the train accelerated through the Polish territory. As soon as the Corridor had been passed, the train stopped, the doors were unlocked, the curtains pulled away from the windows, and the crew was exchanged.

Bertha felt a little uneasy with all these strange courses of actions, as were most other travellers.

"I'll be so happy to see Papa and Fra-Lu again!" Ella interrupted her mother's thoughts. "I can hardly wait!" Ella took things in stride, simply focusing on the family reunion.

Fra-Lu waited for them at the rail station, with a big bouquet of flowers in his hand and an even bigger grin on his face. Ella barely waited for the train to stop before hopping off and running towards Far-Lu, hugging him as hard as she could.

"I am so glad to see you, alive and well!" she gushed. "I was so, so worried about you!"

He just laughed and, walking over to help Bertha with the luggage, announced that he has a surprise waiting for Ella.

"Did you come with your motorcycle?" Ella wanted to know immediately.

"What are you thinking? How can we all fit into the sidecar as well as stow the luggage?" he replied, laughing again. "No, I took the horse-drawn carriage and inside is your surprise."

Ella ran out of the station towards the buggy and saw the small bundle of fur rolled up on the seat. "A puppy!" she gasped. "Oh, Fra-Lu, you got a little dog for me, how sweet and thoughtful of you!" She picked up the little mewling dog and buried her face into the soft fur. She was completely happy. "I will call him Max," she announced.

Everybody settled into their seats and off towards Hohenstein they went.

On the way, Bertha wanted to know how Leo was, how things were at the estate, and most of all, how well her stepson recovered from his wounds. A somewhat-embarrassed Fra-Lu admitted that he was not wounded at all, but instead had suffered an appendicitis attack and required surgery.

"Not very valiant," he said, "but then, it likely saved my life. My whole unit was wiped out while I was recovering, so I suppose it was not my time to go yet."

"Well, thank goodness for that!" both women agreed wholeheartedly.

Coming closer to Hohenstein, they saw Leo walking down the dirt road towards them, waving and smiling, the smile that Bertha loved so very much. She jumped off the carriage and ran towards him, straight into his waiting arms.

"You go on," she waved to the young people, "your father and I will walk together."

It was a beautiful summer evening, the air mild and sweet. The wheat fields swayed slightly in the warm breeze, and red poppies and blue bachelor buttons lined the country lane. "It is so peaceful here," Bertha sighed. "It's hard to imagine after all the noises and unrest in Berlin. I hope we are not heading towards another war."

Leo put his arm around her. "Let's not think about that now," he said softly. "You are here and we are together. What can be more important at the moment?" He nuzzled his face into her hair and covered her face with kisses.

"Leo," Bertha feigned indignation, "what if someone sees us?"

"And who might that be?" Leo laughed out loud, "perhaps the birds?"

"Or the bees?" she continued with a mischievous little smile.

"My dear wife, you are putting ideas in my head," Leo teased.

"I am sure they were there already!" Bertha teased back.

Slowly and leisurely, they walked towards the house, stopping every so often for a kiss or to admire a butterfly on a flower or watch a red fox slink down the lane.

By the time they reached the house, Ella and Fra-Lu were already lounging on the front porch with a glass of wine. "You sure took a long time to walk home! I was ready to send out a search party," Fra-Lu kidded.

"My son, you cannot rush old people!" Leo replied, laughing, which earned him a little poke from Bertha.

"Old? Who is old? Not us!" she declared.

Their good-natured bantering and laughter carried well into the night, all of them relieved and delighted to be together again. Ella retired with Max in her arms.

"She always needs someone to cuddle," Bertha remarked. "She was so good with little Felix, poor boy."

Once they retired for the night, Bertha and Leo spent most of the night rediscovering one another, whispering endearments during tender embraces. They felt like newlyweds. Even though they were well into their latter fifties, with sixty right around the corner, their love for each other never diminished, and neither did their desires. It was already dawn by the time they finally fell into a deep, contented sleep, rolled up into each other's arms.

Rising quite late the next morning and looking a little sheepish, they made their way to the breakfast room, only to find that the children had already eaten and left for an early morning ride. Ella's puppy was curled under the table, happily chewing on a dry crust of bread.

The atmosphere was one of blissful normality. Bertha poured a cup of the now-standard chicory coffee into Leo's cup. "I sure miss the smell and taste of real coffee," Bertha noted, "but at least here we have decent bread, milk, and jam—things that one can hardly get in Berlin, even with ration cards."

"Well then, eat up, and put a little meat on you," Leo quipped. "I am so happy both of you are here to ease our bachelor existence. It is always so lonely without you."

"I know," Bertha agreed. "I have missed you so much, as well. We have a lot to talk about. It has been a terrible time the past few months."

Enjoying their breakfast, their time together, and the sunny and peaceful morning, Bertha recounted the horrible events, including Felix's illness and death, and her fear that Ella would die, as well. She also shared news from America, the general unrest and protests in Berlin, and the overall political climate. The morning passed by like a flash, and soon Fra-Lu and Ella returned, full of life and exuberance.

"The wheat is looking good, Father," Fra-Lu told Leo. "I think if we have a good harvest, we can invest in a couple of more horses. We need to build up our stables again."

Ella, playing with her puppy, added that they needed more chickens, as well as to restock the pond with fish. The conversation became very animated, and Bertha marvelled at her daughter's knowledge in agriculture.

In the afternoon, Bertha decided to laze in one of the deckchairs in the garden and read a book she picked out from Leo's large library, but soon dozed off and was surprised when Leo woke her with a kiss.

"Time for dinner, my dear," he smiled. "Ella made a fine stew for us—rabbit meat and vegetables and freshly baked bread."

"Oh, that sounds delicious!" Bertha jumped up. "I feel very hungry now."

Another wonderful day came to an end.

Summer passed quickly, and fall, even faster. The harvest was indeed a good one, and Leo managed to find two young horses for a decent price. Everyone looked towards a better future.

CHAPTER SEVENTEEN

FALL PASSED INTO WINTER, AND IT WAS THE FIRST WINTER AT HOHENSTEIN FOR Bertha.

As Leo had predicted, the winters were tough, being so far northeast. Far more snow than she had ever seen piled up quickly, and icy cold winds blew across the empty fields, heaping mountains of snow everywhere. The roadway disappeared, and the only mode of transportation was by horse-drawn sleighs. The men were kept busy shovelling snow away from entrance ways to house and stables, with Ella joining in, enjoying the physical work and even the frigid temperatures.

Bertha, for the first time in her life, had nothing much to do. The estate employed several people, including a cook and a maid, who did the cleaning and the laundry. Somewhat lost, Bertha wandered from room to room, but often settled into her favourite armchair near the fireplace, where a crackling wood fire heated the room. She would spend her time reading or knitting, as well as sewing a wardrobe for Ella and herself.

Christmas had been festive and formal, and the New Year rung in quietly, with memories of the war years, the terrible flu, and the many losses of life, as well as prayer for happier and peaceful times.

Leo, looking at Ella, announced that during the winter months, neighbouring estate owners would visit regularly, often staying for several days because of the long travels. This was meant to introduce young women to prospective future husbands from the pool of likely matches.

"It's time we show you off, my good-looking daughter," he said proudly. "You will make some well-bred young man a wonderful wife! And you, Fra-Lu," he turned to his son, "it is time for you to find a partner. This place needs a young family."

"I am in no rush, Father," Far-Lu replied quickly. "I know most of the young ladies in the area, and no one appeals to me."

"Well, no matter," Leo shrugged. "We still do what we do best around here in the winter—socialising!"

"Do you think there are any young men left?" Bertha wanted to know, thinking of the war and the flu.

"We will find out," Leo grinned.

"Mother, Papa," Ella protested. "This sounds like a market. Do you really want to marry me off to the highest bidder?" Ella was annoyed.

"Not at all," Leo said, "but you must admit, it is rather desolate around here, and you two need more young people around you. And your mother and I—"

"Don't say it, Leo!" Bertha wagged her finger at him.

"I was not going to say *old*—just more, *staid*," he replied with a smile. "We need friends, as well. Hardly anybody has met my wife, and that needs to change." Leo was firm.

And so, a round of social gatherings began, with invitations sent back and forth, dinners arranged, musicians hired, and the latest magazines examined closely for the most current fashions.

Even though nearly all things were still rationed, conditions were far better in the country than the city. The estates existed for generations and held a trove of items stowed in chests in attics or cellars. Old dresses were cleaned, altered, and refitted. Fra-Lu and Ella practiced new dance steps to music from a gramophone. They burst into gales of laughter when this strange machine slowed down and messed up their dance steps.

Leo had sent out invitations for the first of such post-war gatherings to be held at Hohenstein. Virtually all the neighbouring estate owners had accepted— everybody was yearning for the return of normal life and fun after such hard and difficult years. Mid-January, they all came by sleighs, wrapped in warm, furry blankets, with luggage secured at the back of the sleighs, and coachmen safely guiding the heavy draught horses along the snow-covered paths.

Maids had readied the rooms for those guests staying for a few days. In the meantime, stable hands were commissioned to unhitch the horses, rub them down, feed and water them, and house them in the warm horse barns.

The house was lit up with hundreds of candles and gas lights. Dozens of guests began to mingle and were introduced to Bertha, who had a hard time remembering all the different names. After the tenth or so introduction, she did not even try anymore, but just smiled and made small talk.

Dinner was served, but Bertha was too nervous to eat much. Leo and Fra-Lu looked smashing in their tuxedos and Ella wore a deep red dress with a rather daring cleavage, eliciting many appreciative glances from the young men present. Bertha could see her excitement in her flushed face and realised that up to now, she had not had much lighthearted fun in her life.

"Poor child! She deserves to laugh and dance and be courted," she thought. *"She has only known sadness, hunger, cold, and fear in her young life."* With that thought in mind, she gently pushed her way towards Leo, lightly touched his arm, and mouthed "Thank you" to her somewhat startled husband.

"Our children are entitled to have some fun," she told him.

"I agree, but so are we!" Leo laughed and pulled her to the dance floor. As they held each other close, they officially opened the dancing part of the evening. Eventually, the older folks made way to the younger people, with the men retreating with cigars and port and the women keeping an eye on their children, contemplating potential matches.

It certainly was an evening to remember. Several days later, everybody departed in good spirits and invitations for return visits were passed out. Bertha collapsed in her chair. "Leo, this was absolutely wonderful, but now I am beat. How often do these socials occur?"

"Quite often, my dearest; you have to build up your stamina," Leo kidded, and Bertha groaned.

"Did you see any young man who showed interest in Ella?" Leo wanted to know.

"There were so many, and I don't know them all. I just noticed Fra-Lu keeping a close eye on them and her, big brother being watchful," Bertha laughingly replied.

Leo gazed out the window, lost in thought.

CHAPTER EIGHTEEN

SEVERAL WEEKS AND MANY FESTIVITIES LATER, BERTHA SECRETLY YEARNED FOR time alone with Leo in her little country house. She was more of an introverted person, and truly enjoyed those times alone.

Leo, having recognised her slight reluctance, had already returned a few invitations with apologies. Even Ella and Fra-Lu enjoyed more time at home. But Leo was not surprised at receiving requests from various neighbours with marriage-eligible sons and daughters to have Ella and Fra-Lu attend several balls, dinners, music recitals—the list was endless.

Settled down for breakfast, Leo opened a few such invitations, elegantly embossed with family crests. "The Grigoleits request your attendance to their daughter's piano recital," he faced his son. Fra-Lu pulled a face while Ella snickered.

"Ha, there is one for you Ella," Leo turned to his daughter. "The young Schuricke asks for my permission to court you, and Captain and Frau Wischnewski would like the honour of you escorting their son—let me see which son they are talking about...oh yes, it is Paul—to their other son's wedding."

Before Ella could reply, Leo had opened the other envelope. "And here we have the Tharaus. Hmm, they are one of the largest estate owners in the country," he remarked. "Their son would like to be your escort to the same wedding! Actually, he would be a great catch for some lucky lady, good-looking boy, very old and established family, extremely wealthy." Leo looked up from the heap of notes and letters in front of him.

"Papa, please stop," Ella begged. "I don't even recall what that young man looks like!" Ella's look of helpless confusion made Leo smile.

"You will, once you meet him again."

While Ella shook her head, Fra-Lu, looking grim, announced, "Papa, he is no good for Ella! He has a bad temper and Paul Wischnewski, well, he is an oaf."

"Fra-Lu, that is enough!" Leo thundered. "It is up to Ella to decide—you are not her guardian."

"But Papa, he can give his opinion," Ella protested, coming to her brother's rescue. "He knows these boys better than I.

"In any event," she declared, "I do not really want to be married off. I might never want to marry!" She declared vehemently.

Bertha, following this conversation closely, turned to Leo. "Can we not let things develop naturally, Leo? There will be more get-togethers and dances where all will become more familiar with each other, and who knows what may evolve?"

"Of course, my dear," Leo nodded, "but for the time being, I have to reply to these invitations and need to know Ella's and Fra-Lu's reactions and answers."

Both countered with a resounding, "Please Papa, turn them down."

Leo looked intently at both of them. "I will not do that," he insisted. "That would be rude and unbecoming."

Turning in particular to his son, Leo said rather sternly, "Franz-Ludwig—" Leo only called him by his full name when he was serious— "you are of the age to earnestly look for a good wife, a mother for your children, and suitable heirs to Hohenstein. You are well aware that your title and the estate are inherited throughout generations. It is your obligation to fulfil your part in securing this for future generations. Unfortunately, you are the only heir, and therefore this duty befalls you. Have I made myself clear?"

Bertha had never known Leo to be so indignant before, and she watched Fra-Lu's reaction. "I understand my duties Papa," he said, defeated. "And I will not disappoint you, now may I be excused?"

Once Leo gave his nod of consent, he rose, as well as Ella, who quickly rose in a rush to catch up with Fra-Lu. "Ella, I did not excuse you!" Leo shouted, but she was already gone.

"Bertha, my dearest, what to do with these children?" Leo groaned. "Young people have no discipline anymore. I will not allow Fra-Lu to fritter away his inheritance after I essentially gave up my own life to ensure his rightful place."

"I understand, Leo," Bertha nodded, "and I am sure Fra-Lu will do the right thing, but we also want him to be happy, to find love and to share his life with a wonderful woman—not just a—a birthright producer."

Leo stared at her and then burst out laughing. "Birthright producer? Where on earth did you come up with that description? You are too funny. But of course, we want him to be happy, but some things are just as important—like respect, honour, and admiration. Those are also love."

Bertha nodded again. "I agree, but Leo, attraction is the beginning of all of these, and without the physical attraction, the deep affection, the total abandonment of one's self, it remains a pleasant, quiet union at best and an heir-producing one at worst. I want our children to experience what we have."

Leo looked at his wife tenderly. "I know, *Schatz*, I truly understand. But we have a very special, once-in-a-lifetime relationship. For that, I am eternally grateful. However, we must give our children the opportunity to meet and experience other appropriate young people. They will have to make informed decisions about potential life partners.

"And yes, love will play a big part. Both of them are quite emotionally charged, therefore I am confident they will eventually come to a decision that is right and good."

"Time will tell, Leo," Bertha quietly replied, "but please do not push them, they are still young."

"Fra-Lu is twenty-seven and Ella twenty-two; they are not *too* young, Bertha," Leo said. "But you are right, I will give them some more time to grow into adulthood, which was so sadly interrupted by this impossible war. The whole order of family and relationships have come under question since then!" Leo fumed.

"*Ach*, my love," Bertha soothed him with a kiss, "it will all work out, you will see. Now let's leave it be for now. Accept whatever invitations you need to accept, and we will take it from there."

Leo, regaining some of his good humour, rose and hugged his wife. "Bertha, what would I do without you? You always know the right thing to say. I love you so much."

Bertha put her finger on his mouth. "You will never be without me; I will love you into eternity."

When the maid came in to clean off the breakfast dishes, she was startled to see the master of the house and his wife standing by the window in a close embrace. They did not even appear to hear her, so preoccupied they were with each other.

Chapter Nineteen

By spring, Bertha felt the strong urge to go to Berlin and check on her apartment and country house.

"Oh, my dear, does it have to be now?" Leo groaned. "It is seeding time, and we all have our hands full right now!"

"I'll be back very soon, Leo," she promised. "I just need to see that all is still in order. And Ella will come with me, right Ella?" Bertha briefly looked at her daughter.

"No, Mother," she shook her head. "I apologise, but I will not come with you. As a matter of fact, I will never go back to Berlin! I am staying here for the rest of my life, even if I have to marry boring Paul." Ella stood her ground to a surprised Bertha.

"You won't have to marry Paul," Leo reassured her. "You can stay here for as long as you like, or until Fra-Lu throws you out."

"I will never do that Papa," Fra-Lu reacted furiously. "How can you even suggest that?"

"I did not suggest anything," Leo returned. "You are quite touchy these days, son." Leo frowned at him. "Are you feeling well? Do we need to talk about something?"

Fra-Lu shook his head, "No, Papa, I overreacted, and I apologise."

Leo nodded but gave him a curious look anyway.

"I think it may be of benefit if I leave you alone for a little bit," Leo suggested. "I do have some business in Berlin to attend to, so I might as well go along with my wife and you can work some of your surliness out of your system." Leo was cross at his son, as well as his daughter.

"Perhaps they have each found a love interest," Bertha wondered later when she and Leo were alone. "They both seem a little moody these days."

"Hmm," Leo pondered. "Perhaps. Might that be good news?" he smiled. "All right, my dearest, we will go to Berlin next week and spend a few weeks together. Hopefully things will have calmed down somewhat there, and we can finally put this war business behind us."

Things had not calmed down much, however. There were fewer uprisings and no more curfews. People had no time for protests; they were too busy struggling with money and food issues. However, politically motivated street riots were ongoing.

One day, Leo took Bertha along to the Dresdner Bank in Berlin. He was concerned about the beginning of hyperinflation of the existing currency in Germany; the daily increases distressed him. He discussed this with the bank manager, voicing his unease, in particular as to financial security for Bertha. A Swiss bank account was arranged, and Leo deposited a substantial amount into that account. At his insistence, the account was put in Bertha's name.

"It is my absolute heartfelt wish to see your future secured, my love" he reasoned to her.

The bank manager applauded his foresight. It was this money that sustained Bertha for the balance of her life, and a permanent reminder of Leo's love for her.

It also proved to be the best financial decision Leo had made, as the Reichsmark became of little value and lost more value practically by the hour, one kilo of bread already cost 223 billion Reichsmark and money was printed like mad. Bundles of still-damp money was carted to the nearest grocery store to be rapidly turned into food before its value was already lost. Workers were paid every hour and wives waited at factory doors for the wages passed on to them, put into wheelbarrows, and quickly carted off to be exchanged into food. Grocers hardly had enough time to rush to the banks to deposit these substantial packages of billions of Reichsmark.

In all that turmoil, Leo and Bertha still found time to take care of the apartment and country house. Much to their surprise, the country house was completely intact—not vandalised or even destroyed.

"Sitting that far back from the road and hidden behind the big park trees must have protected it," Leo concluded.

But they decided to stay at the apartment, simply because of the proximity to the grocery store. "I should have taken up weightlifting," Leo joked as he trotted off with his huge bundle of almost-worthless money to buy some bread and milk.

"At least we can tell our grandchildren one day that we once were billionaires," Bertha teased back.

They did, however, make time to enjoy the spring in Berlin, and delighted in attending different concerts and operettas. The big attraction was the invention of "moving pictures" on a screen and they laughed their way through a Charlie Chaplin spoof. A piano player accompanied the pictures on the screen while another person used a pointer for effect.

A relaxing and romantic visit to restaurant Nussbaum cost them an absolute fortune and a whole month's worth of both their ration cards. Leo told Bertha it was worth it while Bertha was worried how they would survive the balance of the month. But somehow, they managed, most likely thanks to bribes from Leo.

In the summer, they received mail from Karo telling them that her daughter, Anna, had become engaged to a Naval officer, and they were planning a wedding the following year.

"When did my grandchildren get so old?" Bertha exclaimed, looking surprised. "She asks us to come to America for the wedding."

"A rather interesting thought," Leo noted, "but at this time in my life, I really cannot see crossing the Atlantic for a wedding."

Bertha was still trying to digest the news of these little grandchildren having all grown up. "That means that my Karo is now a middle-aged woman," Bertha commented, still bewildered at that thought. "I would not even recognise them anymore; I still think of her as my young girl, but then, Ella is already in her twenties," she shook her head in wonder.

"But when I look at you, Leo, I still feel like a young woman myself and you are my dashing, handsome prince."

"You mean, I am no longer dashing or handsome?" Leo pretended to be in a huff.

Bertha examined him, squinting her eyes in the process. "I still see my dashing, handsome prince," she said solemnly. "To me, you have not changed at all."

"And I still see you as you were the first time that I laid eyes on you," Leo smiled at her. "You were looking so serious, so focused on your work, and such beautiful eyes when you looked up..."

Silently, they recalled all the years they had already spent together, and both hoped for many more.

"I will answer Karo and decline her invitation with our sincerest regrets and congratulations," Bertha decided after a while.

Leo nodded. "And I also think it is time to return to Hohenstein, see how our other two children are faring."

CHAPTER TWENTY: 1920-1927

LEO NOTED WITH SOME IRRITATION THAT IT WAS NOT HIS SON PICKING THEM UP at the station, but rather the coachman. "Good evening, Gustav," Leo greeted him, with concern in his voice. "I trust all is well at Hohenstein?"

"Er...I believe so, sir," Gustav answered with hesitation while loading their luggage.

"Well then, let's go home," Leo gave Bertha a curious look but decided not to pursue any further dialogue with Gustav.

"I hope there is no problem," Bertha whispered to Leo, snuggling close to him on the hard coach seat. Enjoying the ride through the summer-drenched countryside, they both were preoccupied in their own thoughts.

When they finally arrived home, neither Fra-Lu nor Ella were present to greet them. This was not like either of them. Leo and Bertha exchanged puzzled looks but opted to freshen up first.

"Do you think they have gone to some social event?" Bertha casually asked Leo, sensing his displeasure. "Perhaps they did not get our message early enough to rearrange their plans?"

"Perhaps," Leo's reply was clipped, and Bertha knew he was truly upset.

"It is truly rude not to be present. I hope they are not in any kind of trouble." Bertha thought to herself, and then said, "I'll go to the kitchen and ask for a light meal."

Several minutes later, she rushed back upstairs into the bedroom, looking ashen and shaking all over. She needed to sit down before passing out.

"What in heaven's name is going on?" Leo demanded.

"Leo, most of the staff has quit!" Bertha exclaimed.

"Quit?" Leo repeated, both upset and confused. "Why?"

"The cook said they cannot work in such a 'sinful' household," Bertha answered quickly.

"Bertha, what do you mean?"

"Oh Leo, I can hardly bring myself to tell you what is being said, but..." Bertha paused, upset. "... One maid had said—they—were found..." Bertha paused again, trying to catch her breath. "Oh, dear, I can't say it!"

Leo grabbing her by her shoulder and shook her lightly. "What have they found?" he demanded. "Tell me now!"

"They found them in Ella's bedroom, sleeping together," Bertha finally managed to say quietly.

"Sleeping with whom?" Leo was still confused.

"With her brother!" Bertha cried. "My God, is history repeating itself? I could not bear this."

Leo sat down without saying a word as he went through many emotions. Finally, he rose. "We need to find them before they do something stupid," Leo said, grabbing Bertha's hand as they both hurried to Ella's room.

Without first knocking, they threw the door open and were relieved to find Ella sitting by the window with Fra-Lu standing behind her. The two young adults turned around slowly.

Both looked hollow-eyed, white-faced, and shaken. All four just stood and stared at each other, no one wanting to say a word.

Eventually, Leo waved them all out the room. "We will meet in the den and have a strong drink," he instructed. "I believe we all need one right now."

Bertha was surprised at Leo's calmness, but followed him, along with their children, who staggered as if in a stupor. So far, they did not say one word. Ella was crying silently, and Fra-Lu was clenching his teeth so tight his face was almost square.

Downstairs in the den, Leo took out the decanter filled with brandy and handed everyone a glass. "Now talk," he directed at his son, who was looking down.

Fra-Lu stammered, "Father, Mother Bertha, I—that is, we—we have to... I have to—"

"Stop stuttering—out with it!" Leo raised his voice. "Being a man is more than bedding a woman!"

Ella began to sob loudly. "Papa, please," she begged. "We... we..."

"Ella, we will talk after," Leo told her quietly. "First, I need to hear from my son, who, as an officer, hopefully has some honour and responsibility left in him."

Bertha flinched at that. *"Oh, Leo, please don't push him too far,"* she pleaded silently.

Those words obviously stung, because Fra-Lu immediately straightened up and stared at his father. "Papa, I will do the honourable thing," he said seriously. "As an officer, I must bear the consequences, and shoot myself for what I have done."

Bertha and Ella screamed out loud and Ella rushed to his side. "No, no, Fra-Lu, it is not your fault!" she howled like a wounded animal.

Leo jumped up and slapped his son in the face. "That is not honourable—that is cowardly!" he thundered. "As a man of honour, you face your actions and deal with the consequences. You will not leave this room until you tell me what you have done!"

"Father, I have violated my sister," Fra-Lu said in a flat voice.

"Papa, wait!" Ella cried before Leo could speak, jumping to Fra-Lu's defence. "I love him! I always have—"

Leo held up his hand. "We will talk about this in a moment, daughter"

"But that is not all Papa," Fra-Lu interrupted. "Ella is expecting our child!"

Bertha gasped while Leo frowned.

"Now you know the whole story and we no longer know what to do," Fra-Lu continued hurriedly. "All I know is that I have loved Ella since I was a child, and when she told me of her feelings for me...well, it was just too overwhelming, and I—we both—we just lost all our restraints. After that, we dreamt only of being together, even if for just a few weeks. We thought of going away together, but to where?" Breathlessly, Fra-Lu stopped and hung his head in shame, with Ella hanging on to his hand as tightly as she could.

There was an uneasy silence for a while, until Leo spoke up, now quietly. "I have felt your—attraction—to each other for some time already," he admitted. "And I was trying to nip it in the bud. But now let us work out a solution to this."

"A solution, Father?" A little flame of hope flickered in Fra-Lu's eyes.

"What solution?" Bertha let out a little sigh of relief. *"Of course,"* she thought. *"Leo will know how to handle this."*

"Yes, a solution—it is actually not that complicated," Leo continued. He looked at both his children. "You are not brother and sister. Not biologically, not legally."

Leo let the news sink in to an astonished Fra-Lu and Ella.

Bertha remembered registering Ella under her own name and breathed another sigh of relief.

"We are not?" Ella exclaimed, most confused.

"No, you are not," Leo answered. "We never told you, because we thought it to be irrelevant, and under normal circumstances, it would have been. Fra-Lu was too young to know it, but son, your biological father was my brother, and your mother, his wife before mine."

Leo went on to explain the whole situation to his children, who hung on to his every word, a ray of hope on their faces.

"We are cousins?" Fra-Lu was thunderstruck.

"So, Papa, what does that mean for us? For our child?" Ella nervously asked.

"It means that you can now do the honourable thing, my son, and propose to the mother of your child," Leo said to Fra-Lu.

"You mean, we can get married? We can love each other openly?" Fra-Lu was aghast, trying to process this. "Is this even legal?"

"Yes, it is, son," Leo reassured him. "It has been legal for generations, in order to keep properties within families."

Ella reacted much more quickly, jumping up and alternately hugging her father and her mother and Fra-Lu.

At last, Fra-Lu came about and, hugging Ella, whispered to her, "Will you marry me, Elfi?"

"Yes!" Ella exclaimed without missing a beat, and two embraced.

Much later on, Leo remarked to Bertha, "You are a very smart woman, my wife," he smiled. "It was a good thing that Ella kept your name Hoffmann—that will make bureaucracy much simpler for them to get married, and there's no need to explain that both might have had the same last name."

"*Ach*, Leo," Bertha threw up her hands and sat next to her husband. "what a day this was! And both of us completely understand love, don't we?"

"Yes, my dearest, we do." Leo put his arms around her, and they sat together like that for a long time, every so often hearing the happy chatter and laughter from the kitchen where their children had retreated.

One month later, Fra-Lu and Ella were quietly married at City Hall in Stolp, being the closest city to Hohenstein.

In early 1924, Ella gave birth to a daughter, whom they named Johanna. Three years later she was joined by a sister, Charlotte. Leo was still hoping for a grandson to continue the title and estate inheritance, but in the end, it never mattered.

BOOK FIVE
THE GOLDEN YEARS

CHAPTER ONE

THE NEXT TEN YEARS WERE CONSIDERED THE BEST YEARS OF BERTHA'S AND LEO'S lives.

Shortly after Johanna's birth in 1924, Leo handed the reigns of Hohenstein over to Fra-Lu, and he and Bertha moved permanently to Berlin. Most of the time they spent in their cosy summer home, only moving to the apartment in winters. The 1920s were rather exciting, not only in Berlin but across most of Europe as well as America; they were called the "roaring twenties" or the "golden twenties."

For some, prosperity had returned after the First World War, new technology brought the automobile, and moving pictures and radio were available to a large segment of population. Jazz rose to renewed popularity and many nightclubs offered burlesque shows. A more sexually liberated and vibrant scene developed, in particular in Schoeneberg, Emil's earlier stomping grounds. More than one hundred venues for homosexuals were active, in clubs, bars, and cabarets.

"Oh Leo, how Emil would have loved being alive now," Bertha commented rather sadly, thinking of his untimely death and how she missed him. "You did know that he was more interested in men than women, did you not?"

"Oh, I knew," Leo replied, clearly ill at ease.

"Well, it is all history now," Bertha shrugged. *"I think men are more uncomfortable with this than women are,"* she mused, and decided to no longer speak about it.

Leo bought himself an automobile, a 1926 Mercedes-Benz, and learned to drive it. Now they were completely independent to drive wherever they wanted to go—back to Hohenstein to visit family, or a vacation in the Black Forest, and even as far as Vienna. It was also significantly easier to transport goods back and forth from the apartment to their country retreat. Bertha loved sitting next to Leo as he drove and watch the scenery go by, exploring areas they had never been to before. On the surface, life appeared to be as good as it gets.

Politically, however, the unrest remained. Violent clashes between communist and fascists continued and at times Bertha persuaded Leo not to go out for the evening.

"When in heaven's name can we enjoy some measure of law and order once again?" Leo ranted. "This situation is becoming intolerable. The government seems powerless and the population feels insecure. It is no wonder people are seeking comfort in frenzied, unbridled, indecent behaviour. One day it will all come crashing down," he predicted.

"Leo, you are sometimes far too pessimistic!" Bertha scolded him a bit.

Leo gave her a quick smile. "I do hope I am wrong."

But he was right. By 1929, Wall Street crashed, launching what became to be known as The Great Depression. Just as Leo had said, the recent prosperity was artificial and short-lived. Almost overnight, the better standard of living that had been enjoyed by so many was ruined by events outside of Germany. The people were once again cast into poverty and deep misery just ten years after the war and began looking for solutions—any solution.

Adolf Hitler and his Nazi Party knew their opportunity had arrived. Promising a return to prosperity, full employment, decent housing, healthcare for all, and respect for the country, he was elected in 1934 to lead Germany towards a promising future.

The change for the positive was felt almost immediately. Law and order were established, street riots and demonstrations were beaten down, and it was safe once more to go out at night.

People were fully employed, and the youth were channelled into activities from cradle to maturity. For the first time in history, working class folks enjoyed an annual vacation. Ten days at a Baltic Sea resort or the North Sea, Bavaria, or Austria; it was all attainable for a very low cost. The people were ecstatic. The military became all-powerful and if there was unease among the populace, it was quickly appeased.

Once more, life was good.

CHAPTER TWO

IN 1927, AFTER ELLA HAD HER SECOND CHILD, CHARLOTTE, LEO AND BERTHA drove northeast towards Hohenstein for the baptism. Fra-Lu and Ella looked wonderful, tanned, and healthy, and now with two beautiful children—they obviously enjoyed their life.

Leo held little Charlotte in his arms and whispered into her ear teasingly, "If only you were a boy—"

"I heard that, Papa!" Ella admonished him, indignant but with a little smile. "But we can't exchange her now."

"There is always next time," Leo grumbled a little. He clearly wanted an heir to continue with the estate.

Ella rolled her eyes. "Oh, Papa, things will change!" she scolded him a little. "Women have the vote now, and I am sure the inheritance act will be amended one day. So please don't fret, and please enjoy your granddaughters."

"Oh, I do love them," Leo assured her. "I am just waiting for a male heir."

"At least they will never have to go to war," Bertha added.

"Oh please—no war talk!" Fra-Lu exclaimed. "They may not be actively in war, but one day, they will have husbands or sons, so no more war please. The last one has basically just come to an end."

"How are things agriculturally?" Leo asked his son, changing the subject. After the ladies' objections to be part of "business talk," he and Fra-Lu retreated to the den for conversation, while enjoying a cigar and a brandy.

In 1930, it was Bertha's and Leo's seventieth birthday. Neither one felt their age, as both were quite healthy. Bertha still had a full and dark—not even gray—head of hair, as well as all her own teeth. Never in her life did she have to see a dentist. Her figure remained slim, and her eyes bright. Ever since her twenties, she could have passed for at least ten years younger. Leo's hair was now a silvery gray, and with his erect walk, he was still a very handsome man. Even though the passions of youth had lessened and quieted, they remained physically attracted to each other and very much in love. They were quite the charming couple.

They were aggrieved to learn of Julius' sudden death. By the time they received Karo's letter, he had already been gone for more than three months.

"My poor little girl! All alone in a strange country," Bertha was near tears.

"You forget that she has been in America for longer than she has lived here," Leo reminded here. "Also, she has five children, all married, as well as grandchildren. I think she must also have a number of friends by now—she is hardly a poor little girl."

"I forget that she has become older, as well," Bertha replied. "I still remember her as she was the day they left, all those years ago. I wished they were still here."

Suddenly, Leo became serious. "I am not so sure," he said slowly. "Perhaps it's best they left when they did. With their last name Feldmann, it might have become rather uncomfortable for them."

Irritated, Bertha questioned Leo. "What do you mean by uncomfortable?"

"I cannot tell you much, my dear, as I am not exactly sure what is going on either," Leo admitted, "but here and there, I have heard that some Jewish businesses have been vandalised and a number of Jewish people are beginning to leave Germany."

"But why, Leo?" Bertha persisted. "Surely your sources of information are not well founded! I can think of no reason why people would leave. Things are so much better now."

"Let us hope this is just a temporary flash in the pan, but in any event, Karo is better off where she is."

Shaking her head, Bertha decided not to pursue this. *"Sometimes Leo has peculiar ideas,"* she thought to herself.

But as time went on, she began to notice herself implausible events. Her longtime Jewish family doctor suddenly disappeared, and his practise closed. Her lifelong neighbours in Turmstrasse, Herr and Frau Morgenstern, never returned after leaving their apartment one morning.

The green grocer across the street had closed, and the bakery abruptly changed ownership. One day, Bertha went to the bakery for buns and complained to the new owner that the buns were not as good as the Bergmanns' buns, only to be hissed at as a "Jew lover." Most perturbed, Bertha asked Leo where all these people had gone to and why.

"I don't know my dear," he said. "I heard rumours that they were either in workcamps or being interned. I believe they are being processed to leave the country—at least that is what I was told."

Bertha frowned. "I will never go to that bakery again," she swore.

Chapter Three: 1935

For most people, life improved dramatically for the better. The working class found a type of prosperity never before enjoyed.

Satisfied and contented people do not pose a challenge for dictatorial governments, and by the time everyone realised the depth of deceit, it was already too late.

Bertha and Leo had enjoyed their waning time together, particularly their visits to Hohenstein, and especially their granddaughters. Often Leo would hint at hearing happy news of another child, certain it would be a boy.

Ella just laughed. "It's not for lack of trying Papa," she would chuckle. "Believe me, you will be the first to know."

Many times, Leo and Bertha brought the girls back with them to Berlin and took them to the cinema. There they would sit, totally mesmerised at the moving pictures. In particular, Charlotte was very attached to her Oma Bertha and often, she begged to come without her big sister.

They were quite different in both looks and character. Johanna was a robust girl, tall and obsessed with sewing. Her most prized possession was a sewing machine, and she would eventually sew most of the family's clothes. In comparison, Charlotte was small and dainty, a little dreamer, always having her head buried in a book or magazine. She also loved jewellery, which Johanna did not. It was Charlotte who eventually received Bertha's precious promise ring, once passed on to Ella and now given to her on her confirmation date. Charlotte wore that ring until her own daughter received it on her confirmation.

Bertha enjoyed taking one or both girls to her favourite café for cake and hot chocolate. They would skip alongside her, asking and commenting about something or other. Leo took them swimming in the summer and sledding in the winter. Those were precious times.

One November day, in 1935, Leo complained of not feeling well and remained in bed.

"I'll make you some tea and you rest," Bertha assured him, not too concerned. "It has been nasty weather and a lot of folks have had colds."

Two days later, he was still not improved but had developed a nagging cough.

"I will call the doctor and ask him to drop by," Bertha decided.

"Not necessary, my dear," Leo said with a raspy voice. "It will get better soon; I just need some sleep."

Unconvinced, Bertha wrapped herself in a warm coat and walked two blocks to request a visit from the doctor. *"If my dear Dr. Goldberg would still be here, he would be along immediately. I simply cannot take to that youngster who took over his surgery."*

Sure enough, the doctor did not feel it necessary to come for a visit, but suggested Bertha rub Leo's chest with camphor oil and keep him in bed. Bertha raised herself to her full height of five feet.

"You will come to the apartment now and take care of my husband, even if I have to carry you on my back!" she demanded. "I have been doing these things for the past few days, but I feel he should not be in bed for that length of time. Something is just not right. His cough is worse, and his fever will not go down. I will wait until you come with me."

With a resigned sigh, the doctor promised to come by within the next couple of hours. "If you don't, I will be back tomorrow!" Bertha warned.

By evening, Leo took a turn for the worse, and when the doctor came, he diagnosed him with pneumonia.

"Hmm, this is not very good," the doctor said, shaking his head. "I will give him some *sulfonamide*—that has shown very good success in pneumonia treatment. But I must caution you," he turned to Bertha, "given his age, he may not survive this. I will look in on him again in the morning." He left a stunned, shocked, and silenced Bertha behind. *"Surely Leo would survive this?"* she asked herself, unable to handle the thought of him being gone, too.

Sitting by his bedside, she put cool clothes on his head and chest, suddenly recognizing how thin he had become. The same feeling that she had when Emil went off to war suddenly gripped her, and Bertha almost let out a gasp. She didn't want to alarm Leo, but deep in her gut, she knew that her beloved, her true love, would not be with her much longer.

She silently lay beside him, listening to his laboured breathing and wrenching coughs, stroking his hair, and letting her gaze fixate on him throughout the night. Every so often, she heard him mumble, "Bertha, my dear, are you here?" and she would reply, "Yes, Leo, my love, I am," and just hold his hand.

She must have fallen asleep, because when she woke up, Leo had passed away. Even though Bertha knew it was coming, she could not bear it. The doctor came by early and could only confirm his death. He promised to contact the undertaker from his office. Silently and in shock, Bertha got dressed and walked to the post office to send a telegram to Ella and Fra-Lu. "Papa suddenly died - stop - please come quickly - stop."

On a drizzly, cold November day, Leopold Friederich Graf von Ullmannshausen-Hohenstein was buried in the Hohenstein family crypt. He was seventy-five years old and had shared more than thirty-five years with his beloved Bertha. Ella and the young girls wailed loudly, Fra-Lu looked sullen and grim, and standing close together, holding hands, were Ludwiga and Bertha. Nothing needed to be said between them. They each loved Leo in a different way and for different reasons.

Standing close together in the freezing drizzle and gray skies, the two older women were the last to leave the cemetery, Bertha to join her children and Ludwiga to go back home to her family in Poland.

CHAPTER FOUR: 1936

BERTHA STAYED AT HOHENSTEIN THAT WINTER, RELUCTANT TO RETURN TO A cold, empty apartment, never mind the precious summer house where she and Leo had relished so much time together.

Ella's little girls really bonded with Bertha during those few months after Leo's death, much to Bertha's relief and joy. Even after all the deaths of so many loved ones in her lifetime, none hit her like Leo's. It was like she had lost a part of herself.

From all her children, young Johanna and Charlotte were all that were left to her, and she delighted in their presence. Nighttime stories, all cuddled up together under a blanket, was the highlight of every day.

Ella was very glad to see her mother relieve some of her deep sorrow through her girls. She was particularly glad to have her mother around, as she struggled with her grief over the loss of her precious father, as well the loss of an unborn baby. The long-yearned-for son was stillborn, and the two girls were to remain Ella's and Fra-Lu's only children.

After Easter, Bertha decided to return home. "Why do you have to go to Berlin, Oma?" asked Johanna. "Grandpa is not there. He is here in the cemetery and we will visit him and bring him flowers."

"You do that. Grandpa will like that," Bertha assured her. "But I must go and see to the apartment, and some of my friends are waiting to see me. But don't worry, I will come back. You and Charlotte will come for a visit when you have your holidays."

Both girls came to the railway station with Bertha, waving with both arms and a handkerchief until the train had turned around the bend. Bertha sank into her seat and began her lone trip back to Berlin, wondering how she would ever cope without Leo by her side. The raw pain had given way to an unremitting deep ache in her heart. She felt as though her soul was always crying, and she would just have to endure it. *"There is hardly a reason for me to go on,"* she mused, but then remembered her two granddaughters and scolded herself. *"Leo would be very upset with me now. I must be very thankful for all those wonderful and magical years we spent together. He will always and forever live within me."*

Armed with resolve, Bertha arrived at her home and the chores of cleaning and sorting out Leo's clothing. Then there was the summer house. She needed to take care of that, as well, although she was unsure if she ever would spend another summer there. "Maybe this summer with the girls," she said out loud to no one, as she was used to having someone to talk to. So, she began the habit to talk to herself. Some of her closest neighbours regularly called on her, and a new understanding and appreciation developed among them.

The following years passed with ups and downs. She heard from her daughter, Karo, that she had contemplated visiting after hearing of Leo's death, but changed her mind. "In view of what is going on in Germany with the Jewish population, I have decided to stay here. I simply do not feel safe being in Berlin," she wrote. Bertha accepted this but thought her daughter to be a bit overdramatic. Then, in discussing this with her neighbours, she got different opinions.

"I am not so sure, Frau Hoffmann," Herr Krieger spoke softly, eyes darting anxiously from side to side. "I have heard there are indeed some sinister things going on..." He left his sentence hanging because Herr Kulicke challenged him immediately.

"What do you mean—sinister? Certain people have no business being here and must be removed."

"Removed? Removed how?" Bertha asked, worried. "Surely you don't mean harming anybody, do you?"

"Well, there are rumours—" she began.

"But best not to talk about it. The Secret Police seem to know everything!" Herr Krieger added.

"Oh yes!" Frau Baum excitedly turned to Bertha. "The Secret Police were here a few weeks ago, asking about you."

"Me?" Bertha was shocked. "But whatever for?"

"How would I know? They did not tell me!" Frau Baum was indignant. "I don't make it my business to know everything about everybody."

"Since when would that be, Frau Baum?" Herr Guenther wanted to know, teasing her. A few offered meek laughter.

"Please," Frau Nowack interrupted. "Let's get back to our original discussion and why Frau Hoffmann's daughter Karo is correct to stay where she is."

"Because she married a Jew!" Herr Kulicke yelped.

"But Karoline is Lutheran." Bertha objected.

"Guilty by association," Herr Kulicke explained.

Bertha still did not understand what being Jewish had to do with anything. "Association to what?" she asked. "I want to know what she or Julius did that was so horrible!" Bertha was near tears.

"Please Frau Hoffmann," Herr Krieger comforted her, with an angry glance towards Herr Kulicke, "don't listen to Kulicke. He is bitter and very cruel to upset you so shortly after your dear husband's death."

"Hear, hear!" the others chimed in.

"There are a lot of things being said," Herr Krieger continued. "Most likely none of them have much substance. If your daughter feels more comfortable at home, so be it, and there's no need to discuss it further."

Deep in thought, Bertha went back to her apartment. *"I wonder what the police wanted from me."*

One day, the Gestapo did in fact come to her door—two men, young, dressed in the black leather coats they had become known for, demanded to be let in.

"There is nothing to see inside my home!" Bertha denied them entrance, staring them down.

"We need to ask you some questions," one of them finally spoke in a stern voice.

"Yes?"

"Where is Dr. Goldberg?"

"Now that you ask, I would like to know that as well!" Bertha exclaimed, surprising the two young men. "He was my doctor and I miss him. If you find him, please tell me."

They stared at her, confused, as they were expecting a trembling old woman. One of them referred to some notes in his hand. "We are also looking for Dr. Feldmann."

Bertha couldn't understand why they were looking for her doctor and her deceased son-in-law (and his father). "Which one? The younger or the older?"

The two men exchanged curious glances. "Both, then," said one.

"The older Dr. Feldmann died in France a number of years ago, and the younger one died in America a couple of years ago, but really, you should already know that!" Bertha was frustrated and becoming angry.

"We must insist to search the apartment!" they demanded.

Bertha stood tall and shook her head. "You have no right to come here at my bedtime and ask me silly questions!" she yelled. "If you don't leave immediately, I will beat you with my umbrella!" she threatened, while pulling her black umbrella out of the coat rack and holding it up. "Now go home, boys! I could be your grandmother. You should be ashamed of yourselves!"

The two just stood there in stunned disbelief.

"We could arrest you," one finally said, hoping to scare her.

"Yes, you could, but what do you want with an old woman?" she frowned. "Now I really must urge you to leave. I am tired and need to lie down." She closed the door in their faces.

A few moments later, she heard their heavy footsteps going down the stairs and she exhaled in relief.

"Bravo, Frau Hoffmann!" Herr Krieger yelled across the hallway, and Frau Nowack banged the doorframe with a broomstick in solidarity.

CHAPTER FIVE:
THE FINAL YEARS

By late 1938, it was apparent Germany was heading for another war. Nobody wanted to believe that this might happen, as it was only a few short years since the First World War—the war that was to end all wars.

Bertha was very concerned for her family. She had replied to Karo, agreeing that she was better off in America. She would have loved so much to have seen her again— after all, her life was winding down—but she would not want her to be in danger.

During that year, Austria, Hitler's home country, was annexed by Germany with an Austrian ninety-nine percent popular vote. It also was the year of the infamous *Kristallnacht*—a *pogrom* against Jewish businesses, schools, synagogues, homes, and people. One whole night of systematic destruction. Bertha was appalled. *"What kind of people do that? I don't understand this world anymore. I wish I could join my beloved Leo,"* she cried to herself.

Ella and Fra-Lu, horrified to hear what has been going on, and somewhat isolated in the northeast, sent Bertha a telegram and requested her immediate return to Hohenstein. Bertha was more than happy to oblige; it was nearing the first anniversary of Leo's death, which she knew would be difficult, and she wanted to be close to her family—especially over Christmas.

So, once again locking her apartment up, as well as the country home she rarely had visited, she boarded the train and left for Hohenstein. Delighted, she embraced her granddaughters, no longer little but almost young ladies by now. Johanna had been confirmed that year and had begun an apprenticeship as a seamstress. She simply was not a scholar and both Ella and Fra-Lu insisted that the girls learn a marketable skill. Charlotte was eleven and short for her age, but she was a very clever girl, with excellent marks in mathematics and languages.

Already she had begun doing simple bookkeeping at Hohenstein. Bertha was very proud to see that, recalling her own young years in her grandparents' factory.

With grave concerns, the family followed the news from events around the world. They now had a radio and heard with distaste the shrill voices of Hitler and Goebbels whipping people into a frenzy.

"The whole world has gone mad!" Fra-Lu commented while shaking his head. "From Stalin in Russia, to Franco in Spain, Mussolini in Italy, as well as the Asian countries. Not to mention what is happening here.

"Everybody wants to go to war," he continued solemnly. "I had enough of war the last time."

"Like boys in a sandbox, they gang up and kick sand at each other," Ella added, looking frightened.

"But these are not boys—these are people who will have hundreds of thousands of innocent people's lives on their consciences. If only it were sand," Bertha lamented.

"Let us try not to think about it right now and go along with Gustav and the sled to pick up Charlotte from school," Ella tried to change the sombre mood that had suddenly descended on them.

"Good idea!" Bertha grabbed her coat and an extra blanket. It was a bright and snowy winter afternoon, the setting sun glistening across the snow, bouncing off icicle-covered trees and bathing their little world into a wintery fairyland.

"How beautiful it is," Bertha murmured, soaking up the countryside and putting all thoughts of war aside. "If only Leo were sitting here with me," she sighed, with a deep ache inside her. "I miss him more—not less—with each passing day."

"I know, Mother, I know," Ella agreed sadly. "Whenever I walk into the house, I expect to hear his booming voice greeting me with, *'And how is my little girl today?'*

Silently, they snuggled closer together, taking in the peaceful landscape around them, interrupted only by the snorting of the horse, and the rhythmic sound of the sleigh's runners in the snow. Another war seemed impossible at that moment.

Yet by 1939, the rhetoric increased to a fever pitch, diplomatic attempts seemingly futile, and the world spinning out of control.

Bertha, her little family, and their friends could only wait and see, holding their breath in dread and worry about the future. That summer, the girls came to visit their grandmother during their summer vacation. Bertha decided to spend those weeks in her summer house with them. Shrieking with joy and brimming with zest for life, the girls spent what would be their last carefree summer with Bertha, swimming, picking berries, lying lazily in the sun with a book, or riding an old bicycle through the neighbourhood.

Johanna, already eying the boys in the area, became "too boring" for Charlotte, who preferred to spend her time with Bertha. Those were precious times, with Bertha fondly recounting to her granddaughters her blessed years with Leo and of all the places where they had travelled.

"When I grow up, Oma, I will go to all those places and I will have my own Leo to go along," Charlotte sighed dreamily.

"You do that, my dear," Bertha smiled. "I pray it all works out, just as you wish it to be." Bertha stroked over her hair, hoping that their family would be spared the horrors of a war.

Unfortunately, that was not meant to be. By September, war was declared, and all military troops were mobilised. Once again young, tanned, and healthy boys, smiling and singing, crowded into trains, waving flags, hugging their mothers and sweethearts, and promising to be back by Christmas because the war would be over by then.

"When have I heard all that before?" Bertha thought wryly as she watched the military parades from her balcony.

CHAPTER SIX

BERTHA TURNED EIGHTY IN 1940, AND THIS MILESTONE WAS CELEBRATED IN Hohenstein. She decided to spend the next few months with her family, having the unshakeable feeling that this would be the last summer they were all going to be together.

Even though the news from the war fronts had been full of bravado and of battles won, there were many young men who already had died or returned maimed. Ella was frantic about Fra-Lu having to report. He tried to ease her fears and pointed out that he was already forty-five—an "old man" in military terms, and certainly capable people were needed to run the farms and feed the soldiers and civilians.

However, as the war years progressed and began to spin out of control with no end in sight, Fra-Lu's optimism was crushed. He was called to duty in 1941.

Ella was beside herself with worry about him, the estate, her girls, and her mother.

"My dear, you will have to do the best you can," Fra-Lu tried to assuage her worries. "We will get Polish, French, and Russian prisoners of war to work the harvest. All the horses have gone again, confiscated."

"Prisoners of war? To work here? With me and the girls by ourselves? Are they mad?" Ella was upset. "I will not have that, Fra-Lu. The girls are in their teens, and I need them to help. What do you think these guys will do to us?

"The Poles are no longer friendly towards us since the invasion," she continued, panicked. "Your mother has passed away, and her officer husband can no longer be helpful. What are we to do?"

A tormented Fra-Lu stared at his wife, also unable to believe this was happening. "Ella, what do you want me to do?"

Bertha, who was spending another summer at Hohenstein, pleaded with Ella to come to her senses.

"Please calm down, my dear," she said. "Fra-Lu is right—what can he do about this? If he does not go, he is of no help to you here, either—he would have to go into hiding.

"If he is found—and they surely will find him—he will be shot as a deserter," Bertha continued with the cold truth. "So, grit your teeth, be brave, and do not make it any harder on him than it is already. With God's help, he will come back home."

Ella hung her head in distress. "Will you at least stay, Mother?" Bertha nodded. "I will for a while."

"No need to upset her further," Bertha thought, *"but I will have to go back to Berlin soon. Who knows what will happen to my places?"*

Ella managed with the help of Gustav, the coachman, and the elderly estate manager who had only one arm. His other one had been lost in the first war, and he had joked that this saved from being called up for duty once again—one can't shoot with just one arm.

In 1944, Fra-Lu came home for what was to be his final leave. The Russian front was moving closer towards Germany, with Hohenstein too close for comfort. Fra-Lu suggested they flee to her mother in Berlin, even though it was being bombarded daily by the American and English air forces.

"Do you realise that your nephews, and your nieces' husbands, are at war with us?" Fra-Lu remarked to Ella, referring to Karo's adult children in America. They shared a sad smile. "Families are pitted against families," he continued. "I am so sick of this war!" Fra-Lu and Ella held each other in a long embrace before he left again.

A few weeks later, Ella received the dreaded news that her husband was missing in action and presumed dead. She and her daughters were devastated. Ella would never know if and where he had fallen. Fra-Lu never returned, and all subsequent searches for him over many years proved fruitless. He, along with so many others, had simply vanished.

As soon as Bertha heard the news, she wanted to hurry to her daughter, but it was no longer possible. All civilian travel had ceased. The Russian front had broken down, Russian soldiers marched into Germany, and once again, terror and destruction began. Ella and her daughters had to flee as fast as possible, which they did. The long trek of refugees towards the West had begun.

In the meantime, Bertha and her neighbours rushed almost nightly to their fortified coal and root cellar of their apartment building as soon as the air raid sirens began. There they huddled, a collection of nearly twenty elderly people who had lived in the same building for most of their lives, Bertha for sixty-five years. They'd lived through the turn of the century, the sinking of the Titanic, the First World War, the Spanish Flu, The Great Depression, and now this. All around them was destruction, chaos, and anarchy. They scrounged for food wherever they could find anything and shared it faithfully with each other. All of them had family scattered throughout the country, but no one had any news of those who weren't already dead.

And so, they sat, night after night, listening to the high-pitched whistle of falling bombs, waiting for the thud and bracing for the shaking of the building. Coughing and breathing heavy from the dust and plaster pieces that had fallen, they tried to move their old, aching bodies into a somewhat comfortable position and getting a few minutes of sleep.

"Just like rats," Bertha commented one night in defeat.

"Oh, I think rats live much better right now than we do!" Herr Guenther said sarcastically. "Just think of all the bodies under all the rubble around us." They shuddered in sadness and disgust.

CHAPTER SEVEN
APRIL 25, 1945

THE PLANES KEPT COMING, DUMPING THEIR PAYLOAD OF BOMBS OVER BERLIN, over and over again. Turmstrasse had become a street of rubble, piled several meters high. Not one building had been untouched, and whatever people had remained huddled in various cellars reinforced with wooden beams.

Bertha looked at the people she had known for many, many years. All were old, sick, and the only "younger" man was fifty-seven and had his left arm and right leg amputated from the first war.

"Have you heard anything from your daughters, Frau Hoffmann?" Herr Krieger wondered one day. "No," Bertha sadly shook her head, thinking of poor Ella and Karo and their children. Her sons Emil and especially Eugen had long been gone, and she had not heard from Karl-Heinz for decades. "Not a word. One can only hope that they and their children somehow survived this inferno. My youngest daughter lost her husband early in this war; I don't know how she will make out."

A long pause followed. Everyone was thinking of their families somewhere and hoping that somehow, they pulled through and they would see each other again.

The silence did not last long as another barrage of bombing was let loose over Turmstrasse.

"What on earth are they still finding to bomb?" Herr Kulicke grumbled. "There are no more buildings—just us old people and the rats."

Frau Baum sighed. "I would like a nice soft bed to sleep in again, to sleep all night without interruption."

"I need some fresh air!" one of them suddenly screamed and then started to sob.

"Soon," Bertha tried to soothe her. "Surely they must be running out of bombs by now!" She thought for a moment. "You know, I was able to get some peppermint tea the other day, and if the water is still running, I can quickly go to my kitchen, or what is left of it, try to heat it, and bring it down here for us."

"You still have some coal in your stove?" Frau Baum asked.

"A little bit," Bertha nodded. "I have to see if I can find some more soon. It is very cold, with no windows, and half the walls gone."

"You better stay here," Herr Krieger warned her. "They have not sounded the 'all clear' yet."

"*Ach*," Bertha waved her hand, slowly standing up. "They are always late with that. I'll be back quickly!" and she rushed out the door, but carefully made her way up the rickety stairway into her apartment.

"It sure is a horrible mess in here!" she said out loud, almost as if to Leo, who had been gone ten years. She often found herself in "conversation" with him during these chaotic and lonely times, and it brought her comfort.

She found two cups and threw in the few peppermint leaves, filling them with cold water she had saved in some jugs. She carefully balanced them down the stairs and outside the door to cross the walkway into the cellar.

Suddenly, she heard a plane above her and looked up. The last sound she ever heard was the loud whine of the bomb before it exploded in the courtyard.

There were no survivors in Turmstrasse.

Two weeks later, the war in Berlin was over.

It took many weeks to collect the dead from Turmstrasse. They were identified as best as possible, tagged, stuffed into potato sacks, rolled into blankets or cardboard, and quickly buried in makeshift cemeteries.

Many years later, they were exhumed and re-interred in the Ploetzensee War Cemetery in Berlin for the war's deceased—civilians, soldiers, and victims of Nazi crimes. There remain thousands of such mass graves.

Bertha was buried in such a grave, along with her neighbours, in section N, row six, grave number thirty-two. About fifty years later, her last resting place had finally been located by her great-granddaughter.

Not even in death was she reunited with her beloved Leo. His family tomb was in present-day Poland but was never found after the war. Hohenstein was destroyed. Ella and her daughters eventually made it to safety to southern Germany. Ella died at age sixty, generally believed of a broken heart. Her daughters moved on to productive lives, married, and had children.

Nobody ever heard from Karo and her family in America.

May Bertha rest in peace.

EPILOGUE

MY GREAT-GRANDMOTHER, BERTHA, WAS DESCRIBED AS BEING BRAVE, courageous, progressive, ahead of her time, accepting, thoughtful, passionate, and loving. She was stubborn, determined, and feisty.

Since I did not know her, except as a baby, I had little to go on regarding her relationship with Leopold. What I do know is based on descriptions my mother, Charlotte, gave me and some letters my grandmother, Ella, had sent to Bertha. In order to picture the deep love Bertha and Leo shared, and since I am said to "have a lot of Bertha" in me, I took my own marriage as a model in the dialogues and interactions.

In the early 1960s, my mother and I ventured to Berlin in an effort to locate Bertha's grave. Since the city was still divided, it was impossible to find any facts. Only after the Berlin Wall fell in 1991 and I began my search again was I successful. Sadly, my mother, Charlotte, had passed away by then. She had always remembered her beloved Oma and regretted not being able to put flowers on her grave.

Finally, in 2012, I travelled to Berlin to fulfill my mother's wishes.

It was a sombre moment to stand in this massive cemetery, surrounded by countless mass graves of civilians declared "war dead" and sensing their silent laments—innocent people mowed down senselessly. Elderly people who deserved to die with dignity in their own beds were instead killed like rats in a gutter. It was particularly heart-wrenching to read so many inscriptions, such as:

"Male, approximate eighty years old" and "Unknown female, found on Turmstrasse"— there were far too many of those. My heart broke when I thought of all those relatives who never found their loved ones or their last places of rest.

But I was relieved to finally have found my great-grandmother's grave, displaying her name, date of birth, and date of death.

Gently, I placed my bouquet at the foot of the long row of graves that she shared with many, many others.

Her death certificate reads: "Found dead in front of Turmstrasse 82."

Eventually, Turmstrasse was built up again and is now a thriving part of Berlin. The little summer house was never found, likely to have been bombed into oblivion. Even its location was difficult to pinpoint, as that area was located in East Berlin and was not accessible for decades.

The Swiss bank account Leo had put in Bertha's name was "not found."

In Hartford, Connecticut, there are relatives with whom my mother had some contact—in particular, a second cousin called Emil. When he died, there was no more correspondence, and I never searched for them.

About the Author

Lisa Hutchison is a Canadian author, living with her husband in Stratford, Ontario. She has penned two very successful books, *Pieces of Us* and the award winning book, *Iron Annie and a Long Journey*.

Both are books based on first-person experiences and both are compelling accounts of her own life. Her latest book, *Bertha*, retraces the life of her great-grandmother.

Lisa was born in Germany, immigrated with her parents as a child to Canada, and grew up mainly in Toronto. She has a degree in Commerce and has worked mostly in the financial field. Since retirement, she has, together with her husband, Robert, travelled the world. She is also an active volunteer at the local hospital, church, and retirement homes.

Lisa has always loved to write essays, short stories, poetry, music lyrics, and journals, and was instrumental in setting up and administrating her church's monthly newsletter for many years.

While conducting research into her family's history, she found enough material to write *Iron Annie and a Long Journey*, a biography on her parents' life.

Lisa and Robert have three adult children and six grown grandchildren. When they're not in Stratford, they can be found in Portugal, their favourite winter retreat.